WITHDRAWN

Essays and Studies 1998

Series Editor: Gordon Campbell

The English Association

The objects of the English Association are to promote the knowledge and appreciation of the English language and its literature, and to foster good practice in its teaching and learning at all levels.

The Association pursues these aims by creating opportunities of cooperation among all those interested in English; by furthering the recognition of English as essential in education; by discussing methods of English teaching; by holding lectures, conferences, and other meetings; by publishing journals, books, and leaflets; and by forming local branches.

Publications

The Year's Work in English Studies. An annual bibliography. Published by Blackwell.

The Year's Work in Critical and Cultural Theory. An annual bibliography. Published by Blackwell.

Essays and Studies. An annual volume of essays by various scholars assembled by the collector covering usually a wide range of subjects and authors from the medieval to the modern. Published by D.S. Brewer.

English. A journal of the Association, *English* is published three times a year by the Association.

The Use of English. A journal of the Association, *The Use of English* is published three times a year by the Association.

Newsletter. A *Newsletter* is published three times a year giving information about forthcoming publications, conferences, and other matters of interest.

Benefits of Membership

Institutional Membership

Full members receive copies of *The Year's Work in English Studies*, *Essays and Studies*, *English* (3 issues) and three *Newsletters*

Ordinary Membership covers *English* (3 issues) and three *Newsletters*.

Schools Membership includes copies of each issue of *English* and *The Use of English*, one copy of *Essays and Studies*, three *Newsletters*, and preferential booking and rates for various conferences held by the Association.

Individual Membership

Individuals take out Basic Membership, which entitles them to buy all regular publications of the English Association at a discounted price, and attend Association gatherings.

For further details write to The Secretary, The English Association, The University of Leicester, University Road, Leicester, LE1 7RH.

Essays and Studies 1998

Romanticism and Gender

Edited by
Anne Janowitz

for the English Association

D. S. BREWER

PR
13
.E4
v.51
1998

ESSAYS AND STUDIES 1998
IS VOLUME FIFTY-ONE IN THE NEW SERIES
OF ESSAYS AND STUDIES COLLECTED ON BEHALF OF
THE ENGLISH ASSOCIATION
ISSN 0071–1357

First published 1998
D. S. Brewer, Cambridge

D. S. Brewer is an imprint of Boydell & Brewer Ltd
PO Box 9, Woodbridge, Suffolk IP12 3DF, UK
and of Boydell & Brewer Inc.
PO Box 41026, Rochester NY 14604–4126, USA

ISBN 0 85991 526 3

A catalogue record for this book is available
from the British Library

The Library of Congress has cataloged this serial publication:
Catalog card number 36–8431

This book is printed on acid-free paper

Printed in Great Britain by
St Edmundsbury Press Ltd, Bury St Edmunds, Suffolk

Contents

Preface

Over the last fifteen years the study of Romantic period literature has been remarkably altered by the growth of feminist literary criticism. The first stage in the feminist consideration of Romanticism was a sustained critique of the ways in which women were represented in the poetry of the male Romantic poets, in tandem with a consideration of why it was that there were so few women in the canon itself. Critics and literary historians, including Marilyn Butler, Stuart Curran, Margaret Homans, Mary Jacobus, Cora Kaplan, Gary Kelly, Anne Mellor, and Marlon Ross, reshaped our sense of the central questions we wish to ask of Romantic period texts. The result of that grounding work has been a more complex sense of what the image of woman meant within the received Romantic poetic, and as well a fuller sense of who those women were who wrote poetry in the late eighteenth and early nineteenth centuries. An intense period of archival work has been recovering to us the poetry and poetic intentions of, amongst others, Helen Maria Williams, Charlotte Smith, Anna Letitia Barbauld, and Mary Robinson. At the same time, feminist criticism helped to demonstrate that Romantic period literature includes a striking and valuable range of texts beyond lyric poetry. Epics in poetry and prose, novels, prophecies, polemics, philosophical tracts – all these were the stuff of literary culture, and their value becomes clearer as we make sense of these texts in the context of women's history.

Feminist literary criticism has been a crucial force in the development of what we now more broadly call 'gender studies', and the essays in this volume of *Essays and Studies* build upon and extend the collaborative work of feminist and gender study. These essays, written by both established and newer critics, take up a range of issues and question assumptions about what Romantic literature is, as well as what its periodic boundaries might be. The essays address problems of the relation between class and gender, imperialism and gender identity, and gender and genre within the period understood as stretching from the 1770s to the late 1820s. And the reassessment of Romanticism as guided by feminist criticism has also made it important to think about the period constraints of Romanticism as well. Is Romanticism a mode or an historical period? Does it include American poets? This collection includes essays which think about women poets who bring Romantic poetics into the mid-century; and as well, about the meaning of gendered Romanticism to fin-de-siècle writers. Taken as a group, this collection of papers gives a good indication of roads that students of Romanticism may follow well into the next century.

Feminine Romanticism, Masculine History, and the Founding of the Modern Liberal State

GARY KELLY

IN *NORTHANGER ABBEY*, Jane Austen has her heroine, Catherine Morland, admit that ' "history, real solemn history" ', she cannot be interested in:

> 'I read it a little as a duty, but it tells me nothing that does not either vex or weary me. The quarrels of popes and kings, with wars or pestilences, in every page; the men all so good for nothing, and hardly any women at all – it is very tiresome: and yet I often think it odd that it should be so dull, for a great deal of it must be invention.'
>
> (vol. 1, ch. 14)

Readers of *Northanger Abbey*, whether in 1805 when it was completed and sold or in 1818 when it was eventually published, would recognize that the comment applied to the majority of historiography written before that time, to the received idea of what constituted history, and to much of the history being made or recently made just across the English Channel. Readers would also know that women had begun to appear in history, to the consternation of many of Austen's compatriots, and probably of Austen herself, in the French Revolution and the Revolution debate in Britain. Such events and the British debate on the French Revolution radically recontextualized the meaning of history and the uses of historiography. Those engaged in the Revolution debate referred repeatedly to history for an analogy to the French Revolution and as a guide or a warning to Britain. Paradoxically, what was widely acknowledged as the unprecedented nature of the French Revolution was seen by many to challenge the meanings customarily derived from history, and to indicate the limits of historiography written up to that point, as a guide to the present and immediate future or, in Bolingbroke's classic formulation, history as 'philosophy teaching by examples'.

The passage of time has not changed the relevance of Catherine Morland's complaint. For example, the first volume of Elie Halévy's classic early twentieth-century account of Britain's formation as a – or *the* – modern liberal state is a survey of *England in 1815* (1913, in English 1924) that mentions Austen and a few other women (Frances Burney, Princess Caroline, Princess Charlotte, Maria Edgeworth, and 'Women, emancipation of'). Halévy's next volume, *The Liberal Awakening* (*1815–1830*), gets down to 'real solemn history', however, and women and women writers, as Catherine Morland would have expected, disappear. The same pattern may be found in literary historiography, and even recent claims for the distinctiveness, quality, and quantity of women's writing during 'the liberal awakening' in Britain tend to ignore its role in the processes of 'real solemn history'. Here I claim that post-Revolutionary women's writing, or women's writing of the Romantic period, did play a role, though as yet difficult to estimate, in the process Halévy celebrated – the founding of the modern liberal state in Britain. At the same time, Halévy's work shows that modernized, liberal Britain also marginalized women.

What later came to be called Romanticism was one of several post-Revolutionary movements. There was, for example, the plebeian religiosity of Primitive Methodism or the sect following Joanna Southcott and the bourgeois religiosity in Church of England Evangelicalism. Established philanthropic movements such as the anti-slavery campaign developed new tactics to meet post-Revolutionary fear of reform that might go 'too far'. Utilitarianism, political economy, and programmes for administrative, managerial, financial, and monetary reform reconstructed various elements of Enlightenment philosophy, science, and research. Plebeian political movements, such as the Spenceans, continued to form and re-form in a desultory and disrupted way, occasionally planning actual political violence, and forming a loose but broad national coalition with middle-class movements at certain crises, such as the 'trial' of Queen Caroline. Professionalization accelerated from the late 1790s and was implicated in many of these movements.

Common to many or all of these movements was the sublation of ideas and programmes of the eighteenth-century Enlightenments and late eighteenth-century revolutions in forms that would sustain continuing demands for change and reform, assuage post-Revolutionary fears of extremism and political violence, and envision repair of Revolutionary social, economic, and cultural disruption. This post-Revolutionary culture developed central aspects of the pre-Revolutionary and Revolutionary critique of a supposedly corrupt and decadent hegemonic order of court government and its supporting systems of patronage, paternalism, and patriarchy. It formulated new models for resolving interconnected conflicts of class, gender, religion, race, region, and nation. It reconstructed models of subjectivity, domesticity, gender, region, and nation from the pre-Revolutionary culture of Sensibility. It addressed post-Revolutionary anxiety about the groundedness, integrity, and reproducibility of discursive orders of all kinds, especially personal identity, sociality, the 'nation' as a spatio-temporal condition and continuity, language, and writing and literature. These issues were central to founding the modern liberal state.

The roles of women in post-Revolutionary movements and culture were various and problematic. This was due to the implication of gender difference in social differences of other kinds, as these varied in importance from one place, group, moment, and movement to another. For example, the plebeian followers of Joanna Southcott could regard their female prophet and leader as an appropriate or even necessary sign of their difference from the male-led and dominated established church. For the same reason, Protestant Dissenters and Anglican Evangelicals could allow important roles to women in their various evangelizing and philanthropic organizations and intellectual, cultural, and literary life, while still excluding women from their clergy and providing their organizations with male officers. In politics, working-class women could parade together in support of Queen Caroline because women were licensed to sympathize, even publicly, with a distressed woman.

In Romantic writing, as in the literature of Sensibility, men took up topics hitherto considered more appropriate to women, especially certain kinds of subjective experience, the 'domestic affections', quotidian common life, local community, and plebeian knowledges later called folklore. Doing so challenged conventional and historic upper-class codes of masculinity seen by many as characteristic of oppressive and outmoded social hierarchies, economic relations, and political regimes. Yet the 'progressive' feminized masculinity of Sensibility was associated before the Revolution with genteel amateur belletrism and during the Revolution with social and cultural transgression and political violence. In the Romantic movement, men reacted with a complex remasculinization of writing that professed to reject but in fact subsumed the literature of Sensibility, appropriated 'feminine' themes, styles, and genres, combined them with conventionally 'masculine' discourses normally barred to women, such as philosophy, scholarship, satire, and the erotic, and as a result restricted women even more to acceptably 'feminine', subaltern and subliterary discourses.

Faced with this remasculinization of writing, women writers adopted several strategies in order to retain a place in Romantic literature and thereby shape Romanticism's role in a transformation of the public and political sphere through cultural revolution. Women Romantic writers develop representations of domesticity, especially in afflicted relation to a vitiated public and political sphere; they extend the domestic sphere into the local, regional and national, thereby domesticating the public political sphere; most importantly, they critique and reconstruct history which the Revolution had radically questioned as discourse, discipline, and knowledge. These strategies were soon appropriated by male writers, however, and given the intellectual, cultural, and literary legitimacy of conventionally 'masculine' discourses. The pioneering work of all but a few women Romantic writers was forgotten or buried in order to protect the predominantly masculine character of the public literary artist and the new national institution of Literature. Nevertheless, women Romantic writers' feminization of history played a major role in the formation of post-Revolutionary culture and thus in founding the modern liberal state.

Women Romantic writers represent history as 'masculine', or characterized by competition, conflict, violence, and destruction in male-dominated societies, and especially in both aristocratic-courtly and revolutionary regimes of recent times. Such 'masculine' history is represented as damaging to discourses and practices becoming central to bourgeois civil society. These discourses and practices included individual subjectivity, domesticity and the domestic affections, localism and communitarianism, and the 'nation' considered as an agglomeration of subjectivities birthed and berthed in domesticity and civil society but marginalized and oppressed by 'masculine' history. As Catherine Morland complains, historiography is the record of 'masculine' history. The Revolution, Napoleonic imperialism, and reactionary monarchic restoration that followed showed that history could not be reformed or revolutionized by masculine means, especially by main force – historically the defining domain of masculinity. Rather, history would be reformed by 'feminine' action, including the pacific and widely acclaimed revolutionizing power of writing and literary discourse. Women writers sought to feminize history and thus change its course in two main ways – by feminizing historiography and by historicizing established literary genres of drama, fiction, and verse narrative.

Feminizing historiography was a delicate task. What Catherine Morland called 'real solemn history' was gendered 'masculine' and the preserve of male writers. Crossing that boundary was dangerous, as criticism of the pre-Revolutionary historiographer Catharine Macaulay Graham had shown. One way to do so was to keep to the acceptably feminine subject of women themselves. Interest in the course of the Revolution and the role of individual character in shaping it had produced an expanding market for biography of all kinds, including women such as Marie Antoinette and Charlotte Corday. Such women were controversial, and in the Revolutionary aftermath women recovered from and for history had to include those who were both intellectually remarkable and properly domestic. Memoirs, letters, and new biographies of past women were published, such as the work of the so-called 'Bluestocking' writers and Lucy Hutchinson's biography of her husband, along with her shorter autobiography, which had previously circulated in manuscript. In 1796 the Revolutionary feminist Mary Hays pointed out that numerous women could be included in a history of human achievement, and she associated their exclusion from historiography with history as a record of despotism and tyranny (*Monthly Magazine*, vol. 2, July 1796, pp. 469–70). Hays compiled a six-volume *Female Biography; or, Memoirs of Illustrious and Celebrated Women, of All Ages and Countries* (1803), and was later commissioned to produce *Memoirs of Queens Illustrious and Celebrated* (1821), exploiting interest in the 'Queen Caroline affair' as an instance of the victimization of women in and by masculine history. Elizabeth Benger published a biography of her near contemporary, Elizabeth Hamilton (1818), then two biographies of queens well known as historical victims of masculine history – Anne Boleyn (1821) and Mary Queen of Scots (1823). Lucy Aikin began by writing a reginal biography, of Elizabeth I (1818), but went on to James I (1822) and Charles I (1833), though she made these acceptably 'feminine' and yet counters to masculine history by treating them as sociocultural histories. She also aimed to make her historiography accessible and to avoid the often dry monumentality of historiography written by men. To be 'popular' in this way was acceptably feminine. Aikin's approach, developed from Enlightenment 'philosophical history' of the progress of civil society and applied by early nineteenth-century women writers of history for children, was made even more popular by successors such as Agnes and Elizabeth Strickland.

Most women writers avoided engagement with historiography as such, however, and sought to feminize history by historicizing forms of the *belles-lettres*, which were regarded as acceptable domains of female literary practice. Women Romantic writers experimented with drama, prose fiction, and poetry in order to influence the reading public, who would in turn, through the institutional reforms of the late 1820s and 1830s, become the political nation who formed the modern liberal state.

In the Revolutionary aftermath, drama was still produced for the licensed theatres, with their historic repertory system. Joanna Baillie revolutionized this major public cultural institution by feminizing the drama with her *Plays on the Passions* (first series 1798, second series

1802, third series 1812) and other plays. These include both comedy and tragedy, or the serious play referred to then as a 'drama', and are set in both contemporary English life and distant times and places. Thus Baillie's project is not thoroughly historicizing, but she critiques and reforms history by rigorously domesticating and localizing (masculine) passions of excessive selfhood, especially ambition and rivalry, that many saw as dominating the public and political sphere, past and present. Within this large project, individual plays employ different tactics. For example, the tragedy *De Monfort* (1798) and the comedy *The Election* (1802) show women engaged in post-Revolutionary social mediation, harmonization, and repair. Other plays represent a feminized male protagonist in contrast to brutal and corrupt excessively masculine men, weakly or corruptly feminine women, and masculinized and tortured self-sacrificing women, as in *Constantine Palæologus* (1804). Settings are not consistently historicized. For example, *De Monfort* has a very lightly historical and Continental setting, *The Election* is set in contemporary provincial England, but *Constantine Palæologus* is purposely set in the last moments of the eastern Roman empire, as the idealized historic character of Constantine Palæologus, a cultivated, benevolent, patriotic, christian, but unwarlike hero, tries to save his people and state from the excessively masculine militarism and imperialism of the Turks. These efforts are undermined by the selfishly treacherous or cowardly among Constantine's own officers, people, and even family – an allusion to Britain's divided state in face of the threat from Napoleonic France.

In a long introductory discourse to *Plays on the Passions* Baillie defends her form of purposely non-theatrical and implicitly anti-theatrical drama as morally, culturally, and socially superior to that of the public stage, which was in any case widely regarded as vitiated by upper-class decadence and plebeian disorder. By domesticating drama, Baillie relocates this powerful channel of ideological communication from a public theatrical space, historically dominated by men and upper and lower classes, to the realm of private, domestic reading dominated by women and the professional middle class to which Baillie herself and most of the reading public belonged. Baillie's discrediting of the public theatre and her feminization of drama influenced women writers to turn from the theatre-play to 'closet' drama and historical subjects, establishing closet drama as artistically and morally superior to the theatre. The public theatres eventually had to recapture this form of drama, and in the process they had to reform themselves from their historic character. By her feminization of the drama, Baillie also contributed to the embourgeoisement of the theatre, thereby making it an instrument for constructing the modern liberal state.

In broad cultural influence, prose fiction and the novel surpassed even the drama, being the most widely read form of print apart from newspapers. The novel, unlike the drama, had long been considered a feminized form in that it was thought to be largely written by women and to appeal mainly to them. Partly because of this association, however, the novel was considered sub-literary and even dangerous, distracting young male readers from the 'solid' and 'useful' reading required in professional life, and encouraging impractical fantasy and desire in young women, resulting in their courtization. Thus the task of women novelists was somewhat different from that of women dramatists. The novel was already a private and domestic form of cultural consumption. Women novelists did, however, effect thematic and formal restructurings similar to those of Baillian drama, including a prominent role for women as reconcilers and mediators, representation of feminized male protagonists, and plots of romantic restoration. More than the drama, however, the novel needed to have its intellectual and artistic status raised; one way to do so was by appropriating elements of historiography to the novel. For several centuries dramatists and courtly prose romancers had used vaguely historicized settings to disguise, distance, and defamiliarize critique of social and political issues of their own day. These works continued to be read through the eighteenth century. Late eighteenth-century Gothic novelists used generalized historical settings for similar purpose.

In the Revolutionary aftermath, however, women novelists made more determined attempts to appropriate history and historiography in order to feminize them. Some of these writers used the novel to write historiography without risking defeminization, producing historical quasi-novels, or novels dominated by a non-novelistic discourse, in this case, historiography. As early as 1792, Ellis Cornelia Knight incorporated classical learning and ancient history, discourses otherwise gendered masculine, in the 'feminine' genre of the novel, in her *Marcus Flaminius; or, A View of the Military, Political, and Social Life of the Romans*. This was in itself a feminist move, though Knight was a counter-Revolutionary. Elizabeth Hamilton risked defeminization by publishing two satirical and political novels, *Letters of a Hindoo Rajah* (1796) and *Memoirs of Modern Philosophers* (1800), and though her work was accepted by reviewers, she was criticized for maintaining a 'paper war' that, by 1800, many wished to leave behind. Hamilton then produced her own historical quasi-novel, *Memoirs of the Life of Agrippina, the Wife*

of Germanicus (1804). The subject focuses on woman in history and offered many parallels to the 'masculine' history that victimized women in
Hamilton's day. The novel is also a comprehensive christian and feminine critique of the classical pagan imperial Roman culture that had furnished the foundation of male humanist education for some centuries,
and which could therefore be indicted as a cause of the 'masculine' character of history.

Knight's and Hamilton's quasi-novels were generally condemned by
critics as hybrids and seem to have been little read. Nevertheless, the
combination of historiography and romance was soon developed by
several women writers and proved to be more acceptable to the reading
public. Maria Edgeworth's experimental *Castle Rackrent* (1800) brings
together her knowledge of Irish 'popular antiquities', or folklore, with
her understanding of plebeian oral narrative, and her knowledge of the
French short fictional form of the *conte*. The novel even has an elaborate and at times parodically learned apparatus of explanatory notes to
validate the facticity of its fiction. The novel is precisely post-
Revolutionary in representing the conditions that led to the French-
assisted Irish rebellion of 1798 and indicating a way past the economic
and social conflicts that converged in that event. Accordingly, the
novel is purposely located in time just before the Anglo-Irish gentry's independence movement of the early 1780s and her father's introduction
of a thorough programme of economic, social, and cultural modernization, according to the ideas of the Midlands Enlightenment, on his own
estate. Edgeworth's professed aim was to suggest by implication the need
for such a programme at the national and indeed imperial level. This
programme was similar in many respects to that eventually shaping and
undertaken by the modern liberal state. Unfortunately, Edgeworth
seems to have felt that her novel encouraged readers in Britain to retain
their stereotypic image of the Irish as quaintly pre-modern and marginal. She did not repeat the experiment in historicizing the novel.

Nevertheless, Edgeworth's experiment in a range of other fictional
forms made her the most respected novelist in Britain in the first two
decades of the century, and even Walter Scott, who appropriated her
method and the work of her women followers for his Tory social vision
and best-selling historical Waverley Novels, acknowledged her influence. Before that, Edgeworth's historicizing work and that of the women
Gothic novelists such as Ann Radcliffe in the 1790s were carried on by
other women writers. In *St. Clair; or, The Heiress of Desmond* (1803),
Sydney Owenson (later Lady Morgan) adapted her knowledge of Irish
history, culture, and society to the lyrical and expressive Sentimental

novels of Bernardin de St Pierre and Charlotte Smith. Morgan's next
novel, *The Novice of St. Dominick* (1805), is a 'historical romance' set in
the time of the French king Henri IV (reigned 1589–1610), a revered
but controversial historical figure often referred to in the Revolution debate. Here, Morgan represents the fate of private individuals affected by
revolutionary events in the public political sphere. Morgan went on, in
a career lasting into the 1830s, to become a major voice for colonized
and subaltern peoples, including the Irish, the Greeks (*Woman; or, Ida
of Athens*, 1809), and the Hindus of India (*The Missionary: An Indian
Tale*, 1811).

Anna and Jane Porter experimented with historical fiction of several
kinds. Anna Porter published an early historical romance entitled *Don
Sebastian; or, The House of Braganza* (1809) while Jane Porter specialized
in novels dealing with the topical subject of national liberation. These
novels allude at once to Revolutionary and Napoleonic claims to be liberating European and colonial peoples from imperial monarchic regimes and to contemporary indigenous liberation movements in Europe
and the New World. Jane Porter's *Thaddeus of Warsaw* (1803) represents
Polish aspirations for nationhood, Poland having been partitioned by
neighbouring absolute monarchic states in the late eighteenth century.
Porter then anticipated Walter Scott in using Scottish history as analogy for the Revolutionary and post-Revolutionary age of emergent Romantic nationalism. Her novel *The Scottish Chiefs* (1810) represents the
historical thirteenth-century figure William Wallace as leader of national resistance to English monarchic expansionism. Significantly,
Wallace is shown to receive his patriotic motivation from treacherous,
English-inspired Scottish violation of his home. The novel was widely
read and reprinted through the nineteenth and early twentieth centuries, although, like many such novels originally written for adults, publishers later marketed it as an adventure story for adolescents.

These women novelists and others constructed what would become,
after appropriation by male writers such as Walter Scott, Alessandro
Manzoni, and Honoré de Balzac, the most influential form of the novel
in nineteenth- and twentieth-century Europe, its empire, and ex-
colonies. For women writers, however, the appropriation of the historical novel by Scott changed the conditions of writing historical fiction.
For many critics and members of the reading public, Scott elevated the
form, and the novel in general, to literary status, any future historical
novelist was seen as his epigone, and the pioneering work of women
novelists was eclipsed. Through the 1810s and 1820s, however, women
Romantic writers continued to write feminized historical novels of

various kinds. Lady Caroline Lamb's *Glenarvon* (1816) is apparently set at the time of the Irish rebellion of 1798 but has a European context that echoes Germaine de Staël's influential Romantic nationalist feminist novel, *Corinne; ou, l'Italie* (1807). Lamb's ambitious novel brings together elements of the novel of manners, the *roman-à-clef*, the Edgeworth regional novel, and the late Sentimental tale of Amelia Opie. *Glenarvon* was notorious as a confessional *roman-à-clef*, but its purpose is larger than that, showing again that the male-dominated public and political sphere and history as male conflict victimize women and are futile.

As the daughter of two prominent 'English Jacobin' writers, Mary Shelley had a personal and familial investment in creating a post-Revolutionary Romanticism. Four of her six novels engage with 'masculine' history, though in different modes. These historical novels resist the ideological import of Scott's and also experiment more widely with the possibilities of the form. As its sub-title suggests, in *Frankenstein; or, The Modern Prometheus* (1818) history ('modern') collides with myth (Prometheus) in two ways. Through the sub-title and a pattern of quotation and allusion within the novel, 'modern' history from the Enlightenment through its products, the Revolution and Napoleon (often called 'Promethean'), is implicitly contrasted with the mythic, or the ideal for which humanity, in its fallen human condition, necessarily yet unsuccessfully strives. The novel retrospectively refigures Revolutionary Napoleonic history in terms of the Enlightenment's belief in the ability of 'philosophy' as (masculine) critique and method to create a 'new man'. The novel's version of this project, the creation of a super-male, repeatedly causes the breakup of domesticity and victimizes women. Both history and myth are implicitly indicted as masculine productions, the former of male action and the latter of male imagining. Both history and myth, as the Revolution and its Napoleonic emanation, excluded and victimized the feminine, and both failed. As in the major novels of Shelley's parents William Godwin and Mary Wollstonecraft, *Frankenstein* offers no precise solution in the text, though it implies that the restoration of the feminine to history and myth, resulting in a feminized society, is the way to break the cycle of masculine history implied in the novel's plot and its historical and literary allusions, including Plutarch's *Lives*, Milton's *Paradise Lost*, and Volney's *Ruins of Empire*.

Shelley's second novel, *Valperga; or, The Life and Adventures of Castruccio, Prince of Lucca* (1823), adopts the Scott form of historical novel, with fictional characters, notably the female philosopher, pacifist, and patriot Euthanasia, arranged around a partly fictionalized historical figure, the military leader Castruccio Castracani. Against Scott's Tory legitimism, however, Shelley poses a liberal view of history derived from the French historian Sismondi. Though Euthanasia fails in her attempt to remake Castruccio into a benefactor of humanity rather than a self-serving individualist, his militarist state-building enterprise, like that of Napoleon, proves futile. The separation of masculine and feminine spheres is represented in the very construction of the text, for the 'life and adventures of Castruccio' come from history and are grounded in historiography, whereas the character and 'adventures' of Euthanasia come from romance and are grounded only in the author's imagination. Thus the partial, public and political, 'masculine' element is supplemented and thereby subverted by the 'feminine', here represented by Euthanasia who, with Valperga, her fictional domain, is characterized as domestic, cultivated, hierarchical yet communitarian and philanthropic, egalitarian, and patriotic. Euthanasia, with what she represents, is rejected by Castruccio and masculine history. She is sent into exile and disappears in a storm at sea. The ending seems pessimistic, but as in the novels just discussed, there is the possibility that the spirit of Euthanasia may reappear, or should be evoked, as the novel does, after the storms of modern history.

In *The Last Man* (1826) Shelley again treats history by analogy, though between present and an imagined future, not present and a particular past moment. Shelley refigures the transition of England from the Commonwealth of the 1650s through the Restoration of court monarchy in 1660 to the constitutional monarchy of the Glorious Revolution of 1688. This period parallels the transition in Shelley's day from Revolutionary republic through Napoleonic imperial era and Restoration of court monarchy to the liberal revolutions of the early 1820s, which called for a British form of constitutional monarchy. Thus three cycles of revolution and restoration are figured in Shelley's novel, all three involve conflict and destruction, and all three prove futile. Like these cycles, Shelley's fictitious future cycle marginalizes the feminine, intrudes on the subjective and domestic spheres, and fails to establish a modern, liberal order. Linked to these parallels is the history of conflict between East and West. The protagonists participate in a future recapture of Constantinople from the Turks, whose conquest of the city in the Middle Ages drove classical learning to Western Europe, initiating the Renaissance as a feminization of masculine feudalism. In Shelley's fictitious future, however, the historic cycle is not closed by restoration of East to West. The reconquest is rendered futile by the plague, which deals mass death indiscriminately to both warring sides. Man-made mass death of earlier cycles of revolution and restoration is outdone by 'natural' mass death. This *deus ex machina* progresses westward, disrupting personal identity, domestic affections, social relations, institutions of church and state, national boundaries, and historical and cultural meanings, revealing the 'merely' human, constructed character of identity, culture, society, nation, and history. This revelation creates a powerfully elegiac sense of what is about to be lost, and the plague finally leaves the feminized male narrator alone, the 'last man', hoping to find a partner in the East to restart the human race and, by implication, human history.

The Fortunes of Perkin Warbeck: A Romance (1830) returns to the form of the 'biographical romance' pioneered by women writers two decades earlier, which fictionalizes a historical character. In this case the figure was already a fiction, regarded by historians such as David Hume as an impostor claiming to be the rightful king of England in place of Henry VII. Shelley's counter-history both supports the pretender's claims on historical evidence and fictionalizes him as a feminized leader more fit than the enthroned king to govern and unite a broken nation. Thus Shelley's novel links legitimacy and legitimation, especially common themes in post-Revolutionary writing. Legitimacy concerns personal and social identity, continuity, and stability, which ground and are grounded by legitimation in the public political sphere, especially during social upheaval, economic dislocation, and the overthrow and restoration of governments, states, and empires. Shelley chooses such a moment of 'masculine' history in the ending of the long baronial wars and the creation of a centralized court monarchy in England, and she suggests that this was but a transition from one masculine regime to another, from near anarchy caused by ambition, conflict, and violence masquerading under the partly feminized code of chivalry, to a government that is apparently stable, benevolent, and 'national' but is in fact autocratic and thus masculinized. A similar pattern could be found in the early modern history of many European states and their empires. Clearly, the novel parallels the transition from Revolution, civil strife, international war, and imperialism to the restoration of masculinized court monarchies in Europe and its empires during the 1810s and 1820s, closely followed by Shelley and her circle. Warbeck was eventually captured and executed; his masculine ambition and aggression, like Castruccio's or Napoleon's, proved futile.

Masculine history could be countered in the novel by other means than overt revision, however. Jane Austen's proleptically post-

Revolutionary burlesque, 'The History of England from the reign of Henry the 4th to the Death of Charles the 1st' (completed November 1791), remained unpublished, and her novels appear to ignore history and historiography, apart from Catherine Morland's complaint in *Northanger Abbey*. As readers would recognize, however, Catherine's complaint about historiography arises from a sexist gendering of discourse in contemporary culture. Female education manuals and social critics recommended historiography as an antidote to novel reading, as properly 'solid' and 'useful' reading, and as a narrative form that could be grasped by the supposedly weaker intellects of young female readers. In *Northanger Abbey*'s well known defence of the novel (chapter 5), too, the narrator sneers at the praise bestowed on, among others, 'the abilities of the nine-hundredth abridger of the History of England' at the expense of those novels 'which have only genius, wit, and taste to recommend them'. History and the novel comically conflict when Catherine and Eleanor Tilney misunderstand each other about 'something very shocking' that will soon come out at London, Eleanor imagining a Jacobin uprising and Catherine meaning a new Gothic romance (ch. 14).

More broadly, Austen assumes readers' awareness that history and historiography were supposed to be opposed to and superior to the novel. Many novels disparaged the novel in authors' prefaces, narrator's remarks, and characters' dialogues. Some novels, such as Edgeworth's *Belinda*, claimed despite all appearances to be something other than a novel. Novelists increasingly tried to dignify their works by including elements of more prestigious discourses, such as poetry, learned disciplines, and of course historiography. Austen's novels exclude these devices and, in one place or another, allude satirically to the fact that they do so. All of Austen's published works have the defiant sub-title 'A Novel', and they achieve textual distinction as 'art' and 'Literature' partly by foregrounding and playing with 'novelness'. Readers at the time might well feel that Austen's novels deliberately exclude and marginalize history and historiography. In this sense, Austen's novels continue the counter-historical project of her 'History of England from the reign of Henry the 4th to the Death of Charles the 1st'.

Though poetry was read by far fewer people than novels, the narrative poem enjoyed considerable popularity in the Romantic period and was regarded as the most prestigious form of verse of the day. Most women Romantic poets kept to acceptably feminine personal, domestic, and local subjects, yet foregrounded these otherwise marginalized domains and endowed them with something of the high cultural status of poetic treatment. Some women Romantic writers did engage in the major poetic forms of the time, however, especially the annotated descriptive or narrative poem of some length, and the verse drama. These forms usually adopted a historical perspective or used historical characters and settings, like historical romances in verse. Most of the prominent practitioners of this form were men, including writers such as Scott and Byron, who became best-sellers. Women writers, again, sought to feminize the form, mainly by focusing on female protagonists and the destructive effects of masculine history on individual subjectivity and domestic affections, by introducing lyrical narrative and descriptive effects, and using poetic discourse to personalize and domesticate the public political sphere, including history. The most prominent women poets in this field were Felicia Hemans and Letitia Landon.

Landon published a large number of personal and occasional lyrics, but achieved fashionable popularity with a number of narrative and frame narrative poems, including *The Fate of Adelaide* (1821), *The Improvisatrice* (1824), *The Troubadour* (1825), *The Golden Violet* (1827), *The Venetian Bracelet* (1829), and *Romance and Reality* (1831). Her success depended on her development of forms that merged the lyrical and the narrative and on marketing her work and herself. Landon developed a type of dramatic monologue based on the monodrama of the literature of Sensibility, in which the protagonist partly narrates and partly enacts her or his (usually her) victimization by some aspect of the Old Order. In Landon's form of dramatic monologue the situation is implied and the narrator-protagonist is the only character, permitting intense focus on subjective experience and identification of reader with narrator. There are moments of distancing, when the narrator momentarily appears unreliable; but Landon uses such irony much less than do later, male appropriators of the form, such as Robert Browning. In this discursive binary, sympathetic identification characterizes the 'feminine', while ironic distance and judgment characterize the 'masculine'. In Landon's larger works, the dramatic monologue frames inset narrative poems which develop themes similar and stories parallel to those of the frame, thereby multiplying and diversifying the effect.

Landon gives generalized medieval and Renaissance settings to her poems, broadly evoking an invented tradition of chivalry that was widely popular in Romantic and Victorian literature. This historicizing evokes nostalgia for a finer world that never was but that, like the modern world, also crushed the beautiful soul. Implicitly, history is rejected as always and inevitably vitiated while intense subjectivity, however afflicted and even extinguished by history, is strongly valorized and even somehow transcends history. This relationship between history and subjectivity is formalized in Landon's style. Like her contemporary John Keats, she returned to the poetry of Sensibility and especially the Della Cruscan group. In their work, lyrical expressive intensity, verging on loss of semantic and formal control, is associated with transgression of supposedly rigid, oppressive, and outmoded social conventions and structures. The discrediting of the Della Cruscans in the 1790s by their association with Revolutionary transgression led to a politicized opposition between stylistic registers in Romantic poetry. A style seen as lush and highly expressive, or 'gushing' (a favourite word in Landon's poems), was associated negatively with the feminine.

Landon's success with this style may have been due partly to the appeal of the fashionably decadent to an increasingly powerful and self-consciously 'respectable' reading public, an appeal also purveyed in scandal magazines, Gothic romances, novels of manners, and 'silver-fork' novels. More important was the way Landon's poems addressed this reading public's conflicted ideology – on the one hand promoting identity as authentic subjectivity against 'merely' social identity of upper- and lower-class cultures, celebrating the 'domestic affections' as authentic sociality against upper-class 'caste' and lower-class communalism, on the other hand profiting from practices that increasingly commodified individuals and social relations. Landon's poems both acknowledge and mask the contradictions in emergently hegemonic bourgeois ideology, contradictions also central to the modern liberal state. Among these contradictions was the illiberal hierarchy of gender that Landon registers and protests.

Felicia Hemans took a different line and had perhaps the greatest influence of any woman Romantic writer in shaping the modern liberal state. For both ideological and commercial reasons, Hemans aimed to make her work accessible to the mainstream reading public, to keep it within the bounds of acceptably 'feminine' discourse, and to endow it with the prestige of poetic literariness. According to an unpublished poem of 1817 ('Reform'), Hemans rejected the Della Cruscan style and politics that Landon developed, though she later did respond to Landon's work. Hemans avoided the appearance of strong originality by which male Romantic poets established poetic and thus public authority. She engaged in respectful pastiche and avoided overt signs of poetic rivalry. She avoided conventionally 'unfeminine' modes such as satire, and her rare excursions into that mode were apparently left unpublished. With few exceptions, as when she responds to Landon ('Arabella Stuart' in *Records of Woman*), she employed established and familiar verse forms and poeticisms, avoided startling imagery or conceits, and developed the resources of syntax combined with verse structure (what Donald Davie calls 'articulate energy') in poetry from Milton through the eighteenth century.

Yet Hemans's successive works track the major political developments of her time, from Revolution debate to Reform Bill in Britain, and from revolutions to Liberal revolts on the Continent and in the New World. The war between Britain and France ruined her father's business, and two brothers and her husband served in the Peninsular War in Spain. Consequently, she had a personal and familial engagement with contemporary masculine history. Apart from her 'juvenile' poems, published through the network of the Midlands Enlightenment, she began her career with apparently patriotic poems such as *War and Peace* (1808), *England and Spain; or, Valour and Patriotism* (1808), and *The Domestic Affections* (1812). In fact, these poems are less exhortations to resist Napoleonic imperialism than celebrations of 'Albion' as world historical power for freedom and consequently peace, commerce, and the arts, placed in the narrative of the rise and fall of civilizations. This thematic complex dominated Hemans's work into the late 1820s.

In the post-war poems *Modern Greece* (1816) and *The Restoration of the Works of Art to Italy* (1817) Hemans extended the acceptably feminine theme of the arts, with the riskier subject of the social, economic, and political conditions needed to foster the arts for the national interest in history. These poems also treat the arts in relation to decidedly 'masculine' topics of the post-Napoleonic European settlement and Britain's imperial destiny in light of the cyclical history of civilizations. In her next important book, a set of historical narrative poems entitled *Tales and Historic Scenes* (1819), Hemans made a decisive claim to be a major public poet. The poems, in third-person omniscient narration, are set in times and places ranging from the second century BC to the late fifteenth century AD and from Palestine to late Moorish Spain, and the history is validated by footnotes referring to works in various learned discourses. The temporal settings are usually turning points in masculine history, such as the final defeat of Carthage by Rome or the fall of Moorish Granada to the forces of Christian Castille. The poems usually represent or anticipate the final moments of a major figure (Antony of Rome or Alaric the Goth), peoples (the Spanish Moors), nations (Carthage or the Hellenistic states), or empires. Most poems show the dangers of internal conflict and dissension to national coherence and survival and most are set in places of continuing post-Revolutionary and post-Napoleonic conflict and repression. Most represent the damage that masculine history inflicts on the individual subject, domestic relations, and communities, and all suggest the futile, merely cyclical and unprogressive nature of such history.

She was stimulated to her best work and to poetic representation of something like the liberal modern state by the Spanish liberal revolution of the early 1820s. This was based on the Spanish constitution of 1814, which was modelled on British constitutional monarchy and which inspired liberal nationalist movements throughout Europe and the New World. Against this implied ideal Hemans sets various examples of masculine history, dramatized or fictionalized in *The Siege of Valencia* (1823), *The Vespers of Palermo* (1823), *The Forest Sanctuary* (1825), and *Records of Woman* (1828). These works represent even more forcefully than before the disastrous effects of excluding women from history, resulting in the victimization and defeminization of women and the destruction of individuals, families, peoples, and civilizations. In *The Forest Sanctuary* and *Records of Woman*, Hemans also represents more positively the benefits of returning woman and the feminine to history.

The Forest Sanctuary is a dramatic monologue by a Spanish conquistador who returned from the work of imperial genocide to find a comrade in arms and his sisters executed for religious heresy. As a result of this shock, the narrator-protagonist converted to protestantism, suffered imprisonment by the Inquisition, fled Spain, lost his wife over their religious differences, and sought retirement and ideological freedom in a virtually uninhabited North American 'forest sanctuary'. The dramatic monologue represents powerfully the progressive feminization of a man raised for and engaged directly in masculine history. The unnamed narrator represents what the history of Spain and Europe and their empires might have been were such feminization spread more broadly; he also represents what the post-Revolutionary subject, and thus the liberal state founded on such subjects, should be. *Records of Woman* follows *Tales and Historic Scenes* in representing positively the heroism exacted from women by masculine history and thus the distinctively feminine power that women can bring to the public and political sphere.

After *Records of Woman*, Hemans concentrated on the personal lyric. She had progressively moved the figure of woman and the feminine into history, and had constructed herself as a public voice without jeopardizing her femininity. She now assumed the identity of feminized history herself, as the idealized subject of the future modern liberal state that would embody the feminine and thus break the cycle of masculine history. This figure, present in her poems from the outset, came to have an enormous appeal to the reading public. Hemans became the most widely read woman poet of the nineteenth-century English-speaking world. Of course, this fact alone would not prove that Hemans, with the other women writers considered here, and still others, founded the modern liberal state through their construction of a post-Revolutionary, feminine Romanticism. It is difficult to prove even a generalized influence of literature or print on the reading public, even in the case of very widely read texts.

Nevertheless two suggestive incidents may be offered here. In December 1824 a young man from a Dissenting mercantile family of Liverpool gave his sister Margaret, a religious young woman, a specially bound copy (now in the Huntington Library) of three poems, all by Felicia Hemans – *The Sceptic* (second edition, 1821), *Modern Greece* (second edition, 1821), and *The Restoration of the Works of Art to Italy* (1821). Margaret Gladstone died a few years later, but her brother, William Ewart Gladstone, credited her with having had a powerful and lasting influence on him. To read Hemans's poems for their major themes and to read his career as principal founder of the modern liberal state is in a way to read parallel texts. In February 1835, a young prime minister, of Lancashire manufacturing background, was struggling to sustain his minority government, but made time to write to Felicia Hemans. He wrote that, though a stranger to her, he was concerned to hear of her illness and poor financial straits, and offered £100 to her and a clerkship in a respectable government department for her 17-year-old son. He did so, he assured her, 'to prevent the reproach which would justly attach to me, if I could permit a Lady so distinguished for literary exertions, which have aided the cause of virtue, and have conferred honour on her Country and her sex, to suffer from privations, which Official Station gives me the opportunity of relieving' (BL MS 40413 f. 291). Hemans accepted Robert Peel's offer, but died three months later. Peel's government was defeated soon after, but he turned to modernizing the Tory party and when he eventually returned to office pursued a programme that also contributed greatly to founding Britain as a modern liberal state.

Flogging: The Anti-Slavery Movement Writes Pornography

MARY A. FAVRET

THIS ESSAY ARISES FROM my fascination with an image, central to anti-slavery propaganda during the Romantic period in England, and it ends with an apology for that fascination. My initial goal is to document a recurring elision between the anti-slavery campaign of the Romantic era and the consumption of violent pornography, an elision accomplished through the trope of flogging. This implied critique of the abolitionist movement, however, quickly whips around and slaps me as well. Why does this particular image, and the correlative image of a 'proper' white audience gazing upon the stripped, exposed and desired truth of the black slave's abjection, strike me (or anyone else) as an appealing topic? So I am led to consider as well our romance with violence, our tendency to turn toward representations of violence – in particular sexualized violence, performed on bodies distanced by history, race, geography, class, publicity – when we need an argument.

Rather than letting my rhetoric or my title tantalize any further, I will hand over the image itself [figure 1]. The illustration before you depicts a black woman being flogged; it is one of many made in the wake of the notorious 'Kimber affair', where a Capt. Kimber ordered a pregnant, teenage slave girl to be flogged on the deck of his ship, for having refused to dance for his pleasure. Nearly naked, surrounded by a collection of phallic weapons and by several white men dressed in military uniform, the woman's body, especially her backside, is sensually displayed to view. Her posture – the arched back, the shielded face – suggests suffering, perhaps shame, while the looks of the men register a range of responses from disaffection to cruel pleasure. Is this not pornography? In the face of this sadistic spectacle of violence, how ought we and how do we look? And how were the imagined audience for this reiterated image – the white, middle-class Christian women and gentlemen of Great Britain – meant to look?

Addressing these questions, I will explore how representations of flogging in the anti-slavery debates vacillate between invitations to the dissolution of an integral self, most frequently depicted by the flayed body of the slave woman, and aggressive reminders of the sovereignty of the individual, variously represented by the slave master and the male

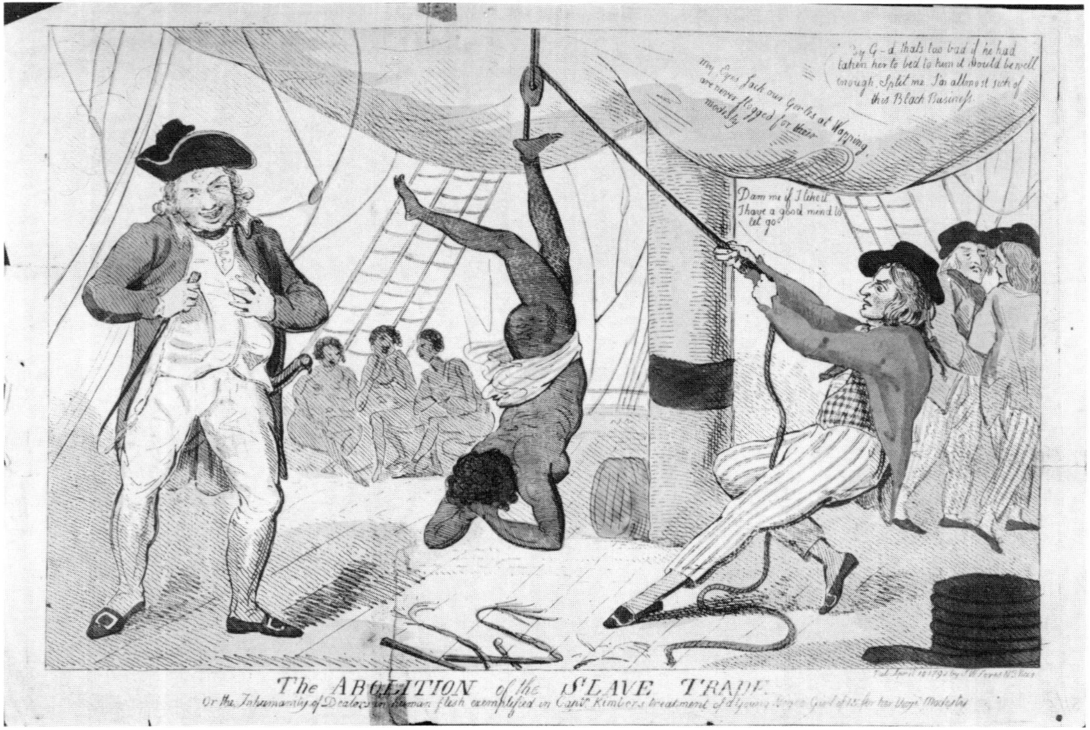
By G—d thats too bad if he had taken her to bed to him it would be well enough. Split me I'm allmost sick of this Black Business
My Eyes Jack our Girls at Wapping are never flogged for their modesty
Dam me if I like it I have a good mind to let go
The ABOLITION of the SLAVE TRADE
Or the Inhumanity of Dealers in human flesh exemplified in Captn. Kimbers treatment of a Young

Figure 1

abolitionist. Like the Marquis de Sade, the abolition movement was struggling to articulate sexuality with freedom, using the violence of slavery in place of the cruelties of Sade's aristocracy.

I will consider first the complicated arousal of passions effected by the rhetoric of abolition in the House of Commons during the years of debate over the slave trade bill. Here, in speeches made before a roomful of men, scenes of flogging were offered up as scenes of instruction: lessons in the meaning of humanity and duty, lessons in the role of English manhood. But just as schoolroom floggings served as both punishment and sexual excitement, so too did these speeches produce a dynamic of erotic pain and pleasure among the members of the House. Through fantastic scenarios of flogging, the production of transporting passions in Parliament produced, in turn, a confusion of slavery with freedom.

I will then consider how those passions were converted to aggressive action in abolitionist literature. Here I will be more concerned with analyzing the difficult, unstable semiology of flogging, an act which threatened to destroy the boundaries of identity. The threat to identity inherent in flogging, and associated with its erotic charge, had to be countered if English manhood were to maintain its difference from women and slaves. In short, abolitionist literature demonstrated, with some anxiety, how to master the passions even as it called them forth. In doing so, it contributes to our understanding – racialized, sexualized, and forged through violence – of the liberal subject and his work.

Flagellation and Pornography

Most histories of obscene and pornographic literature inform us that the term 'pornography' fell out of use in England and France from the late eighteenth until the mid-nineteenth century.[1] The modern sense of pornography, according to William Kendrick's Foucaultian history of the genre, did not take shape until the mid-nineteenth century.[2] Before then, 'the focus . . . the specific realm of the "sexual", had not yet been fully demarcated or assigned a leading role in the conduct of human life' (Kendrick 53). Neither Kendrick nor Foucault, however, directly

---

[1] Walter Kendrick, *The Secret Museum: Pornography in Modern Culture.*
[2] Ian McCalman points to the 1830s in England; pirated editions of Sade appeared in England at that time *Radical Underworld*, 151.

address the sexualization of violence that prepared for that demarcation, anticipating the pornography of the nineteenth century and facili-
tating the formation of an autonomous, self-determining, 'sovereign'
individual. What we call the Romantic period, then, oversaw a silent
realignment of the discourses of sexuality, identity, politics and violence. And, I will argue, representations of slavery and race were instru-
mental in this realignment. A crucial figure in this history would be the
Marquis de Sade. For Foucault, the coincidence of sexuality with violence accompanies a 'retro-version', an attempt (by Sade and others) to
return the 'analytics' of modern sexuality to the *ancien* 'symbolics' of
blood and its corollary, 'a unique and naked sovereignty'.[3] If sovereignty
used to be symbolized by blood (bloodlines as well as the power over life
and death), the power of blood was transfused by Sade into the realm of
sexual pleasure.

Yet, as Foucault maintains, 'the new concept of race' developing at
the very end of the eighteenth century 'tended to obliterate the aristocratic particularities of blood' (Foucault 148). In the place of blood, race
began to inscribe the metaphoric and literal vagaries of skin onto the
domain of pleasure. The discourse of race thus received its erotic charge
less from the flow of blood than from the movement – or transport – of
human flesh. In libertine works of the eighteenth century, flagellant
erotica tended to emphasize the blush of blood below the skin, or the red
blood 'blooming' on the snowy flesh of white boys.[4] But when flagellation entered the realm of slavery, the blush disappeared, blood was no
longer highlighted, and fascination turned to the flayed skin itself. In
scenes of flogging, it is not blood that 'flows through the whole dimension of pleasure', but rather skin (Foucault 148).

Flogging takes even nakedness away from the body: skin itself is ruth-
lessly unveiled, opened, stripped, removed and closed again with scars,
the signs of its disintegration.

---

[3] Michel Foucault, *The History of Sexuality, Volume 1: An Introduction*,
148–50. See also Lora Romero, 'Vanishing Americans: Gender, Empire and the
New Historicism', in Shirley Samuels, ed., *The Culture of Sentiment: Race, Gender and Sentimentality in Nineteenth-Century America*, 115–127. Romero analyzes
the position of race in Foucault's work, concluding that 'even if race remains a
largely undeveloped category of analysis in the history it traces, *The History of
Sexuality* does theorize interracial conflict as an inevitable component of modernity' (118).
[4] See Ian McCalman, Ian Gibson, *The English Vice* (1979), and Adela Pinch,
'Learning What Hurts: "The Schoolmistress", the Rod, and Poetry'.

He has seen a negro woman flogged with ebony brushes, so that the skin of her back was taken off down to her heels; she was then turned around, and flogged from her breast down to her waist.

I read, in the Jamaica Gazette, an account of a female slave of the age of fifteen, flogged by one of these drivers, till she fell senseless on the ground. . . . She was dragged by the legs to a place called a hospital, till her mangled flesh was torn completely from her bones.

> How shall the suff'rer man his fellow doom
>   To ills he mourns or spurns at; tear with stripes
>   His quiv'ring flesh. . . .

The frequency of the sight has rendered her callous to its common influence upon the feelings. . . . Mrs. —— expressed surprise on observing me shudder at his [a slave's] shrieks. . . . 'Aha! it will do him good! a little wholesome flagellation will refresh him. – It will sober him. It will open up his skin, and make him alert. . . .'

My husband . . . , express[ed] a desire to be furnished with some description of the marks of former ill-usage on Mary Prince's person, – I beg in reply to state, that the whole of the back part of her body is distinctly scarred, and, as it were, *chequered*, with the vestiges of severe floggings. Besides this, there are many large scars on other parts of her person, exhibiting an appearance as if the flesh had been deeply cut, or lacerated with gashes, by some instrument wielded by most unmerciful hands.[5]

In these representations, whipping performs a total stripping of the body, which thereby loses not only its integrity as a distinct body ('her mangled flesh was torn completely from her bones') but also the very skin whose visible difference (black, brown, colored) underwrites the lack of bodily self-possession. Deconstructing the logic of racial slavery, these scenes also reproduce slavery as an erotic spectacle. The opening and closing of skin, its quivering and shuddering, all testify to a charged,

---

5 William Cobbett, *The Parliamentary History of England from the earliest period to the year 1803*, 29:291 and 292; hereafter cited as Cobbett. William Roscoe, 'The Wrongs of Africa', quoted in Thomas Clarkson, *The History of the Rise, Progress, and Accomplishment of the Abolition of the Slave-Trade by the British Parliament*, 1:227. *Pinckard's Notes on the West Indies*, 3:192, from James Grahame's *Poems on the Abolition of the Slave Trade*, 99. And 'A letter from Mrs. [Mary] Pringle to Mrs. [Lucy] Townsend . . .', printed in Mary Prince, *The History of Mary Prince, A West Indian Slave, Narrated by Herself*, ed. Moira Ferguson, 119–20.

violent move toward the dissolution of the human body, an overdetermined loss of self-possession that invites erotic transport.[6]

Passions in Parliament

> He could have wished to drop forever all recital of facts which tended to prove the cruelty of those associated with this abominable traffic; but there was an instance he could not omit. . . . The case of a young girl of 15, of extreme modesty, who finding herself in a situation incident to her sex, was extremely anxious to conceal it. The captain of the vessel, instead of encouraging so laudable a disposition, tied her by the wrist, and placed her in a position so as to make a spectacle to the whole crew. In this situation, he beat her, but not thinking the exhibition he had made sufficiently conspicuous, he tied her up by the legs and then also beat her. But his cruel ingenuity was not yet exhausted, for he next tied her up by one leg, after which she lost all sensation, and in the course of three days she expired. This was an indisputable fact. ['Name, name, name!' resounded from all parts of the House.] Captain Kimber was the name. If anything could, in the annals of human depravity, go beyond this, he owned he did not know where to look for it.
> (William Wilberforce, House of Commons, April 1792)

> It is material to the honour of the house, that under the influence of strong passions, they had admitted of the injustice and impolity of this trade.   (Wilberforce, House of Commons, May 1804)[7]

> We have no sympathy but what is propagated by pleasure. . . . wherever we sympathize with pain it will be found that the sympathy is produced and carried on by subtle combinations with pleasure.
> (William Wordsworth, 'Preface to Lyrical Ballads')

In their arguments against the slave trade, the abolitionists aimed to arouse the strong passions of the gentlemen of the House, and scenes of

---

6   For Bataille, for instance, sexuality and death unite in an image-breaking search for 'a more essential truth, a more radical purity, an absolute'. 'To be wounded, exposed, open or flayed, on the one hand, or to wound, expose, open or flay, on the other, means to lose oneself in an abyss that ruptures the body's deceptive [self-] continuum.' Mario Perniola, 'Between Clothing and Nudity', Fragments for a History of the Human Body, Part Two, ed. Michel Feher et al., 245.
7   Cobbett 29:1069–70, T.C. Hansard, The Parliamentary Debates from the year 1803 to the present time (London: Longman, Hurst, et al., 1812), 2:445. Hereafter cited as Hansard's.

flogging served as the crucial means of arousal. Again and again, Wilberforce and his allies would paint a picture of 'wanton cruelty' for their colleagues to contemplate, with the hope that the strong emotions evoked by these representations would, finally, lead the House to submit to their call for abolition. Speaking at the end of a long series of debates on the subject in 1792, Edmund Burke declared that the strategy had finally overpowered him. It was impossible, he said, for the House not to 'surrender up their hearts and judgements to the cause'.[8] Others were less willing to surrender, and protested that Wilberforce's 'impassioned address' was itself wantonly heating up the House. The opponents of abolition frequently requested a delay in proceedings until a time when 'a more cool and temperate discussion' could ward off 'momentary impetuousity and sudden effects' (Cobbett 29:295). Lord Abingdon, a supporter of the trade, complained that the images presented to the legislators were 'too terrible even for the administration of thought'; he requested postponement of debate 'to a period when intermediately mankind may be restored to their senses' (30:653). On the other hand, William Pitt insisted, 'I should detest myself for the exercise of moderation. I cannot, without suffering every feeling and every passion that ought to rise up in me in the cause of humanity to sleep within me, speak cooly upon such a matter' (32:1279). Repeatedly subjected to deliberately 'inflammatory' accounts of violence performed on young women and boys, some members of the House charged that abolitionists were denying them the use of their reason, while others proudly confessed that they had 'give[n] full and free scope to the unsophisticated beatings of [their] heart' (29:1255). In a sense, Wilberforce and friends were simply following David Hume's argument that 'reason is, and always ought to be, slave to the passions'.[9] By the same token, however, the rhetoric of abolition reproduced slavery and the very logic of flogging in the House of Commons, in a form which threatened to dispossess the very men of property who presided there.

Well before Freud studied the etiology of 'beating-phantasies',

---

[8]   Cobbett, 29:358.
[9]   For a helpful discussion of this phrase, see Adela Pinch, *Strange Fits of Passion: Epistemologies of Feeling, Hume to Austen*, 18–44. By contrast, John Locke would begin his first treatise of Government with the word 'slavery,' which he defines as the exercise of power beyond right, 'when the satisfaction of any irregular passion comes before the preservation of the people' (II.199).

whippings and representations of whipping were understood as a mode of sexual excitement linked to the education of reason. At the same time, the experience of being whipped in grammar school by the school mistress or her female assistant, or of watching one's classmates being whipped, was frequently cited as a boy's moment of sexual awakening. At such a moment, sexuality was produced through a discipline both painful and pleasurable. National and gender identities were being produced as well. The link between flogging and learning was written into the creation of English national identity: both educational tracts and pornography disguised as educational tracts claimed that the practice of whipping boys would result in masculine valor and civilized behavior. William Shenstone's 'The School Mistress' (1742), for instance, announced its didactic mission 'to illustrate the secret connexion betwixt *Whipping* and *Rising* in the World'. A popular anthology piece read by countless schoolboys throughout the eighteenth century and into the next, 'The School Mistress' may be said to have successfully established that 'secret' connection.[10] For abolitionists, the 'secret connexion betwixt *Whipping* and *Rising* in the World', however risible in Shenstone's poem, found an urgent, racialized articulation. Inversely, when we read the abolitionists' accounts of slave ship and plantation floggings within the context of Romantic culture's pedagogical and sexual investment in the whip, we uncover difficult questions about the relationship between abolition and education. Who was whipping, who was rising, and what was being learned?

To understand the extraordinary affective force of abolitionist rhetoric in Parliament, one needs to recognize how, in this rhetoric, slavery was given the labile form of passion. The emotional register for the debate, especially in the 1790s, was nearly always the 'passions' – the discourse of sympathy had not yet established itself in the cause.[11] Even

---

[10] I am indebted here to Adela Pinch, 'Learning What Hurts': The School-Mistress, the Rod, and the Poem'. Pinch cites the 1742 edition of *The School-Mistress, A Poem. In Imitation of Spenser* (London: R. Dodsley; reprint Oxford: Clarendon Press, 1974). On flogging in the schools, see W.A.C. Stewart, *Progressives and Radicals in English Education, 1750–1970*, and Gibson, *The English Vice.*

[11] Sympathy would become the major term for the anti-slavery debate in the United States and England in the 1830s and 1840s. But at the turn of the century in England, passion predominated over sympathy and sensational over sentimental depiction. In this more volatile form, individual feelings troubled established models of social and legal order. On the role of sympathy in religious

when, as in Pitt's testimony above, these were passions roused 'in the cause of humanity', they were also roused by erotically charged scenes of violence. Though these accounts of violence were presented as evidence, a survey of collected facts, the very scrutiny given to the slave's body, especially when that body was naked and nubile, involved a sexualized looking that spliced legislative surveillance with the often unconscious desires of voyeurism.[12] In other words, the MPs' entitled distance or enlightened survey, working to disclose the cruel truth of the slave trade, was caught in the bonds of its own desire, its own sexualized practice. A 1794 cartoon by James Gillray features Wilberforce and Clarkson, the period's most prominent abolitionists, cavorting with black mistresses dressed in West Indian costume, while, on the wall of their trysting-room, hangs the engraving of a scene of flogging – the aforementioned Kimber affair – inspired by one of Wilberforce's most sensational speeches. Gillray's cartoon promotes the suspicion that the 'phrenzy' at work in Parliamentary debates was fueled by sexual, and what Robert Young would call colonial, desire.[13]

As Gillray's cartoon acknowledges, the abolitionists carefully created an imaginary theater for their arguments, on which were staged extravagant fantasies. 'A still more dreadful scene was opening to their [the MPs'] view', offers Wilberforce in a prelude to another lurid episode; 'Let them but represent to themselves a vessel, in a sultry climate . . .'. Later, summarizing his previous speeches, he 'conjures the gentlemen . . . to consider well the dreadful pictures of slavery from one end [Africa] to the other [the West Indies]'.[14] According to Wilberforce, 'it [is] impossible for a feeling mind to survey the picture [of slavery] without indignation, sympathy and disgust'. Pitt follows Wilberforce's lead,

and abolitionist thought, see Elizabeth B. Clark, ' "The sacred Rights of the Weak": Pain, Sympathy and the Culture of Individual Rights in Antebellum America', *The Journal of American History* (September 1995), 463–493.

[12] As Griselda Pollack has explained, sexuality, especially in the domain of the visual, 'both collaborates with and disrupts the technologies and discourses of disciplinary surveillance'. 'Feminism\Foucault–Surveillance\Sexuality', in *Visual Culture: Images and Interpretations*, ed. Norman Bryson et al., 38.

[13] Robert Young, *Colonial Desire: Hybridity in theory, culture, and race*. On the abolitionist's, especially Wilberforce's, perceived 'phrenzy' and 'fanaticism', see Cobbett 29:358; 30:513–14; 30:659.

[14] It is worth noting that the speeches are reprinted in a form that insists upon a third person address. In all likelihood, Wilberforce used 'you' and 'yourselves' in addressing his colleagues.

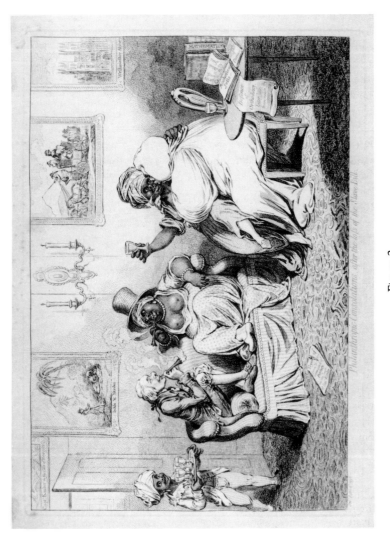

Figure 2

arguing for the value of graphic 'pictures' of slavery's horrors: 'Such a scene as that of the slave ships, . . . if it could be spread before the eyes of the House, would be sufficient of itself' to win the vote.[15] No single emotion, but rather the collective force of contending emotions (indignation, sympathy and digust) guarantees a rousing response. By enlisting his listeners in the creation of a visual scenario – 'let them but represent to themselves. . . .' – Wilberforce's rhetoric shanghais legislative surveillance and puts it to work in the fields of fantasy.

At the same time, fantasy, even as it destroys surveillance's illusion of distance and impassivity, allows the individual to be both the master and the slave of his own desires. If we recognize fantasy in the words of Laplanche and Pontalis as 'an imaginary scenario in which the subject is present and which embodies . . . the fulfillment of a desire', we can begin to see how the abolitionists' rhetoric delivers their listeners into the practice of slavery itself, imagined as a realm where bodies are subjected to vicious men whose own self-possession has been sacrificed to sexualized excitement. In some cases the flogged body of the slave served to unveil the flogger's own brutish enslavement to uncontrollable desires:

> The moment I hear of such power [the whip], uncontrolled, in any hand, I conclude that the depravity is unlimited. . . . It is a horrible truth, that when once the lash is lifted by an angry man, . . . his rage is inflamed by every stroke he gives. . . . *the decrees of passion are executed by passion.* (Cobbett 29:288–89)[16]

Beating unceasingly on a stripped body, passion unveils its own horrible truth. It insists upon the confusion of master and slave.

Emphasizing this theme in their speeches, the abolitionists' play upon passion created a tense identification between the men listening in the House of Commons and the victims of the lash, translating suffering from the body to the invisible realm of the mind and heart. Mr.

---

[15] The first two Wilberforce quotes can be found in Cobbett 29:252. The third comes from Hansard, 2: 457. Pitt's speech can be found in Cobbett 29:343.

[16] Mr Francis, quoted here, was not, strictly speaking, an abolitionist. In the early debates he tended to argue for stricter regulation of the slave trade and less cruelty to slaves on the plantations. At the very least, Francis argued, 'If you cannot have an indifferent judge of the offense . . . at least let there be a cold, indifferent executioner.' He seems to have forgotten his claim that the act of punishment itself would deprave any executioner.

Francis, seeking stricter regulation on the slave trade in 1792, refused to paint again 'the horror of the Middle Passage', since 'the most deter-mined mind, the most obdurate heart, if it be human, could not listen to the evidence . . . without torture' (Cobbett 29:287). Many a speaker for abolition lamented the intrusion of such painful scenes into the cham-ber of gentlemen, but there would always be 'an instance he could not omit . . .' (29:1069). Charles Fox, for instance, consistently reminded his colleagues how difficult it was to 'bear' such horrid tales: the subject 'would not bear to be discussed', he admitted; neither he nor the rest of the House 'could . . . wish to hear recitals of cruelty'; 'they could not lis-ten to it without shrinking'; 'the bare recital . . . was sufficient to make them shudder'. Yet 'it was their duty . . . to open their ears to them, and the House, exclaimed Mr. Fox, *shall hear them*' (29:293, 347–48, 352, 351).

Even if the stories themselves were a punishment that the members could not bear without shrinking or shuddering, bear it they must. Like the victims of flogging, the members of the House of Commons had to 'open up' without complaint. What had been portrayed as physical suf-fering was now translated into a collective education. Fox's conflation of the two words, bear and bare, underscores the price of Parliament's knowledge. John Martin also traded on the pains of bearing\baring to drive the point home:

> Were we to suffer innocent creatures to be whipped, scourged, and tortured without discretion . . .? While we could hardly bear the sight of anything resembling slavery, even as a punishment among our-selves? (29:285)

The exciting confusion of knowledge with punishment, familiar to men who had suffered or witnessed routine floggings in school, was 'replaced and more than replaced', to borrow Freud's language, with these sensa-tional scenarios.[17] In seeking to rouse the members of the House, the

---

[17] See Freud, 'A Child Is Being Beaten'. According to Freud, once past the age when beatings were routine, the child encountered scenes of whipping or beat-ing in his reading – of books such as *Uncle Tom's Cabin*. In terms of emotional in-tensity, these scenes 'replaced or more than replaced' childhood memories. 'The child began to compete with these [fictional representation of beatings] by producing its own phantasies and by reconstructing a wealth of represen-tations, in which children were being beaten. . . . The phantasy of a child be-ing beaten has pleasure where the actual sight of such a beating did not' (173).

abolitionist campaign could be said to have borrowed the wisdom of this
bit of eighteenth-century erotica:

> That Birch was useful, ancient Father held,
> To lay the head-strong Member which rebell'd;
> But now for different Ends our Females praise it,
> And swear, sound Flogging is the way to raise it.[18]

The opposition to the slave trade bill thus found itself, ironically,
both begging for deliverance and rising to the challenge to produce its
own fantasies of flogging. This irony was not lost on the pro-slavery
lobby. 'These long speeches', complained Lord Carhampton,

> reminded him of the old story of a slave on board a ship, commanded
> by a captain who . . . had made many harangues in that House, and
> who now harangued elsewhere. The story was, that when the slave
> was tied up and going to be flogged, he looked over his shoulder, and
> seeing the captain beginning to speak to him, said, 'Captain, if you
> please to flog me, flog me, but if you intend to speech me, speech me,
> but don't flog me and speech me too.'   (Cobbett 32:1282)[19]

Announcing his identification with the slave, Carhampton resituates
the evils of slavery: Wilberforce's harangues, he suggests, make flogging
look good. Not only the content, but the very form of the abolitionist
campaign in Parliament was, as Lord Abingdon charged, 'indecent', fusing punishment with arousal in nearly endless repetition (Cobbett
31:409). Yet even as they ridiculed their opponents, Carhampton and
Abingdon acceded to their basic gambit, locating the realm of slavery
within the House of Commons itself. Slavery, in their constructions, is a
matter of the mind and heart, not the body; and words are both the
weapon of violence and the means of liberation.

The fantasies of flogging produced in Parliament thus made available
to its members a range of positions: they could participate as inflamed
malefactor, abject victim, and tortured witness. At the same time that
the flogging scenario offered up these roles for identification, it also

---

[18] From 'The Lure of Venus, or the Harlot's Progress', by John Durant Breval,
a.k.a. Joseph Gay. Canto II: 57–60.
[19] For another remarkable scene of flogging presented by the proponents of
slavery, see Sir William Young's speech, where he quotes from Umfreville's *The
Present State of Hudson Bay* (Cobbett 29:301).

masked these roles through the differences of place, gender, and most distinctively, race.[20] Thanks to the volatility of desire and the very nature of flogging, however, both identifications and defensive masks were distressingly mobile, as we will see presently. Passion made every man a slave, and fantasy made every man stage-master of his passion; but fixed divisions (mastery/slavery; abolition/pro-slavery; Parliament/slave-ship) seemed impossible to guarantee.

While these scenes of flogging made possible the exploration of sexual roles eliding the differences between freedom and slavery, they also imported the difference of race into sexual fantasy. What abolitionist tactics contributed to the literature of flagellant erotica was an explicitly racialized sexuality, where black women, substituting for the usual blushing white boy, were displayed as erotic objects for the punitive desires of (usually) white men, who in turn substituted for the pornographer's 'Mistress Birchem' or 'Mr. Thwackum'.[21] Though we generally consider that, until recently, the exploration of racialized desire was hidden in the far reaches of white, bourgeois sexuality, here we find it elaborated by the gentlemen of Parliament.

Abdul JanMohammed argues that racialized sexuality, unlike Foucault's version of modern bourgeois sexuality, did not develop into a ' "scientific discursive" knowledge of the sexual violation of the racial border'. Indeed, 'white patriarchy's sexual violation of the racial border – the master's rape of the female slave – was an "open secret" ' that could not be represented 'analytically'.

> . . . On the political-libidinal register, the necessity for this 'open secret' can be traced to the white man's sexual desire for a slave [woman]. Since the desire implicitly admits the slave's humanity, it undermines the foundations of the border – the supposed inhumanity of the black other, her putative ontological alterity. Unable or unwilling to repress desire, the master silences the violation of the border and refuses to recognize, through any form of analytic discur-

20 See Laplanche and Pontalis:
   In so far as desire is articulated in this way through phantasy, phantasy is also the locus of defensive operations: it facilitates the most primitive of defense processes, such as turning around upon the subject's own self, reversal into the opposite, negations and projection (318).
21 Not in Parliament, but elsewhere in abolitonist rhetoric, one frequently finds the sadistic mistress, beating a female slave in a rage of sexual frenzy (usually coded as jealousy). Both Stedman, *Five Year's Narrative* and Mary Prince have extraordinary versions of this scenario.

sivity, the results of the infraction. . . . Sexuality on the border was not a construct that could be administered through analytic discourse.[22]

In the discourse of abolition in the romantic era, racialized sexuality was constructed not analytically, but rather through repeated fantasies that drew on childhood memories as well as familiar contemporary erotica. More 'analytic' voices in Parliament would decry these representations as excessive, fictional, and themselves wanton. In the Kimber case especially, they charged that Wilberforce's 'exaggerated account' of the flogging had destroyed the reputation of an 'honourable' Englishman (Cobbett 30:515ff). In fact, as a result of Wilberforce's tactics, the difference of race now informed representations of 'the English vice' as well as the passions associated with it. By fusing slavery with sexual passion, moreover, the speakers for abolition made the definition of slave as volatile as individual desire. And by focusing all eyes upon scenes of flogging conducted on the sexual-racial border (most flagrantly symbolized by the pregnant body of Capt. Kimber's victim) abolitionist rhetoric threatened to strip away the definitions that maintained that border.

Such a threat demanded an active redefinition of English male sexuality and subjectivity, one that would eventually banish both passion and the body in order to embrace self-possession through intellectual – not physical – action.

Hands Prompt to Relieve

Before we consider the role of intellectual activity in response to scenes of flogging, we need to look again at JanMohammed's claims about the 'open secret' of the white man's desire for the slave woman. The foregoing discussion of the debate in Parliament suggests that the fantastic, violent heterosexual desire portrayed in such as episodes as the Kimber affair substitutes for and yet calls forth the more familiar, often homoerotic, scene of the boy being whipped. In his discussion of the 'undermining' threat posed by racialized sexuality, JanMohammed ignores the chance of homoerotic crossings of the divide, and thereby the possibly compensating difference of gender written into the slave woman's body.

[22]   Abdul R. JanMohammed, 'Sexuality on \ of the Racial Border: Foucault, Wright and the Articulation of "Racialized Sexuality" ', in Domna C. Stanton, ed., *Discourses of Sexuality: from Aristotle to AIDS*, 104–5.

When men whip men, the confusion of racialized sexuality is particularly acute, in that the white man is potentially unmanned by his feelings for and his interchangeability with the other.[23] But when a man flogs a woman, he reasserts the masculine prerogative to act. The spectacle of the woman flogged ordains the aggression of masculine heterosexual desire, where gender makes clear the different roles even after the defining layer of skin is gone. One anxious sign of this gendered difference, one which remains intact after the stripping of skin from the body, is the repeated reference to what Wilberforce calls 'a situation incident to her sex', or the victim's pregnancy. The pregnant woman's body attests to a prior violation that reinforces her status as woman, victim and property. It also serves as a reminder of normative, reproductive sexuality in the midst of flagrantly non-reproductive sexual activity. In fact, the white man who whips (or rapes) the slave woman expresses his power over her at least as much as, if not more than, his levelling desire for her. The pregnant slave woman flogged is thus scandalous but at the same time the safest whipping fantasy for a group of gentlemen to entertain.

For the abolitionists especially, the insertion of a woman's body into the place of whipping boy allows the call for some physical response to be coded as chivalry. The white man may be subjected to disturbingly erotic images of flogging, arousing from him a physical response, but his difference from the female victim – the dis-identification offered by her naked body – reminds him, contrarily, of his ability to rouse himself to action. In the literature of the abolition movement, that self-determined action gets displaced from the physical to the mental, further emphasizing the abolitionist's (or the viewer's) distance from the body, and further linking the abolitionist with the voyeur. Even as they opened up the racial \ sexual border, the leading abolitionists worked hard to rebuild it, using their own intellectual labor as the antidote to fleshly transport. This more active stance became available in part through the solicitation of an aggressively heterosexual response to flogging, and in part, through the creation of a 'manly mind' unchained from physical sensation.

Thus Wilberforce's *Letter on the Abolition of the Slave Trade* reveals a strategy different from his sensational speeches in Parliament: ' "True humanity insists not in a squeamish ear. It consists not in starting or shrinking at such tales as these. . . . True humanity appertains rather to

---

[23] I am grateful here to Robyn Wiegman's 'Anatomy of Lynching' in her *American Anatomies: Theorizing Race and Gender*.

the mind than the nerves, and prompts men to use real and active en-
deavors to execute the actions which it [true humanity] suggests." '[24]
The trick of 'true humanity' lies in the leap from mind to action, somehow bypassing the nervous system, and sloughing off the ('starting',
'shrinking') sensitivity of skin as you go.

Most (not all) early anti-slavery literature was written by men and
even when appealing to women, positioned men as the primary spectators of scenes of violence. In most accounts of flogging, the male viewer
provides the fulcrum of our attention as he stands amidst a swirling con-
figuration of intense emotion and woeful impotence. The anxiety inherent in this situation is made explicit in William Cowper's poem on
the slave trade, which Thomas Clarkson cites in his influential *History
of the . . . Abolition of the Slave Trade* (1808):

> *My ear is pain'd,*
> *My soul is sick* with every day's report
> Of wrong and outrage with which this earth is fill'd.
> *There is no flesh in man's obdurate heart,*
> *It does not feel for man.* The nat'ral bond
> Of brotherhood is sever'd as the flax
> That falls asunder at the touch of fire.
>
> And worse than all, and most to be deplor'd
> As human Nature's broadest, foulest blot,
> [Man] Chains him, and tasks him, and exacts his sweat
> With stripes, that *mercy with a bleeding heart*
> *Weeps,* when she sees inflicted on a beast.
> Then what is man? and what man, seeing this,
> *And having human feelings, does not blush*
> *And hang his head to think himself a man?*[25]

What man sees are the sufferings of the male slave transferred onto a
feminized mercy who 'weeps with a bleeding heart' while man's [white
man's] fleshless heart refuses to feel. The flesh and blood of the slave
man are absorbed by the allegorized female figure, while the liberal male
subject is torn against himself, the spectacle of slavery threatening to
unman him. If he melts into the blood, sweat and tears of feeling for the
slave, he may lose that solid autonomy that distinguishes him from the

[24] 3rd edn, p. 38.
[25] Thomas Clarkson, *History of the . . . Abolition of the Slave Trade* (1808), 1:90.
Hereafter cited as Clarkson (italics added).

slave (always a 'he' but never a 'man' in these lines). He shows no broth-
erly feeling, but contemplation of the suffering feminine figure does allow man to feel, and more importantly, *think* about his role as a man.
(Cowper would later refuse to write about slavery; he could not 'contemplate the subject,' he wrote, 'without a degree of abhorrence' that
made it impossible for him to write.)[26] Clarkson himself, though 'seriously affected' and 'disconsolate' with questions about slavery, was able
to face the 'truth' of its abuses when he decided to 'interfere' by writing.
He wanted his essay on the evils of slavery 'to find its way among useful
people, and among such as would think and act with me' (Clarkson,
1:171–72).

The unmanly or, as Clarkson would say, 'vitiating' image of slavery,
epitomized by flogging, would spread like a disease unless man – that is,
the liberal subject with access to the public sphere – acted.[27] Still, the
representation of violence in slavery would debilitate a man if the
boundaries of racial identity were not boldly and repeatedly underscored through gendered and sexual difference. For the public the ico-
nography of flogging had to be carefully calibrated so that the identity of
the viewer, the autonomous and bodiless liberal subject, remained both
secure and unthreatening. James Grahame's 'Africa Delivered', included in the 1809 collection, *Poems on the Abolition of the Slave Trade*,
echoes Wilberforce's *Letter*, insists upon the division between bodily
sensation and the mind of the viewing subject.

> Let selfish sensibility wink hard,
> And bar both ears against the rude assault;
> There still are manly minds who bend a look
> Steadfast on guilt in all its hideous forms,
> Who misery firm survey with tearless eye,
> Yet melting heart, and hand prompt to relieve.

[26] After his initial poems on the subject, Cowper refused to write anymore:
' "I cannot contemplate the subject . . . without a degree of abhorrence that affects my spirits and sinks them below the pitch requisite for success in verse." '
Later he confessed that, 'when the case of the poor negroes occurs to me, . . .
Then I feel – I will not tell you what – and yet I must. A wish that I had never
been. A wonder that I am. And an ardent but hopeless desire not to be.' Quoted
in D.L. Macdonald, 'Pre-Romantic and Post-Romantic Abolitionism', *European Romantic Review*, 166, 172.
[27] 'But there [in moments of solitude] the question still recurred, "Are these
things true?" Still the answer followed as instantaneously "They are." Still the
result accompanied it "Then surely some person should interfere" ' (Clarkson
1:171).

> Truth, gloomy truth, tho' robed in weeds deep drench'd
> In blood, should meet unveil'd the public view.   (58)

Truth here is the flagellated corpse, unveiled to public view and still wearing its bloody, tattered weeds. Unlike Fox's or Pitt's speeches in Parliament, this poem asks the audience not to 'open' itself up masochistically to suffering, but rather to stand 'firm' against the 'rude assault' and extend a hand – the sign of agency. A choreography of flesh, the thinnest veneer of identity; heart, the basis of sentimental humanity; and hand, the emblem of physical action, performs here for the benefit of the intellectual gaze. When the calibration went awry, English manhood suffered.

In Grahame's 'Africa Delivered', as in other abolitionist tracts, flogging threatened to become a contagion on board slave ships, lashing out at English seamen as well as slaves.[28] The trigger for contagion, more often than not, was a mistaken 'look', one that failed to make the proper distinctions between flesh, heart, and hand; between women and men, blacks and whites. In the poem, a young sailor is flogged to death for refusing to whip a slave woman who resembles his 'true love' back home. Recalling 'that sad look! that turning farewell look!' of his beloved, the sailor (and momentarily the poem) mistakenly confuse the slave with the Englishwoman. He pays the price both for failing to see the difference and for failing to separate feeling from action:

> . . . the pitying youth persists
> To spurn the offered instrument of blood.
> 'Sheer mutiny!' vociferates the wretch,
> The self-appointed judge; 'haste, bind him up,
> And let the trenching scourge at every stroke
> Be buried in his flesh, until the ribs,
> Laid bare, disclose the pausing wheels of life.'
>
> (Grahame, 74)

The episode ends here, where all distinctions – between black slave woman and white freeborn Englishman, bleeding heart and mechanized

---

28 On the 'contagion' of flogging, Grahame quotes from *Stanfield's Letters, Appendix to his poem entitled the Guinea Voyage*: 'It no sooner made its appearance but it spread like a contagion. Wantonness, misconception, and ignorance, inflicted without appearance of remorse, and without fear of being answerable for the abuse to authority.'

'wheels of life', inside and outside, life and death are laid bare to the viewing eye.

In this regard, the poem mirrors – indeed adapts – the discourse of slavery in Parliament.[29] Grahame's poem also retells an episode from Fox's 1791 speech on the slave trade, narrating the experience of a male traveller in the West Indies. Walking through the dark, the traveller is strangely drawn toward a dreadful, torch-lit scene where a slave woman, having been strung up and flogged, is being tortured:

> O what a sight o'erpowers
> The shuddering sense! a youthful female writhes,
> Hung by one hand, while the other still strives
> To ward, with shrivelling grasp, the blazing torch;
> But soon, the hand, sealed up in moveless clutch,
> Avails not for defense; and now the flame
> With hissing noise clings round her heaving breast;
>
> (Grahame, 81–2)

The woman's unavailing hand displaces the ineffectual (and invisible) hand of the male viewer, 'the hand prompt to relieve' upon which Wilberforce and Clarkson rely. But the man's hand also figures in the anthropomorphised torch, which hissing, 'clings round her heaving breast'. In the syntax of Fox's speech, the metonymy of torch and hand is inescapable: there the gentleman 'perceived a young female . . . entirely naked, and in the act of involuntarily writhing and swinging, while the author of the torture was standing below her with a lighted torch in hand, which he applied to all parts of her body as it approached him' (Cobbett 29:350–51; also Grahame 100n.). This obsession with hands (or arms) in representations of flogging is hardly unique. (Often we read of the extremely vigorous arms needed for an effective flogging or of men taking turns, relieving each other at whipping, as each one exhausts himself in the work.)[30] In this instance, however, the insistence upon fusing vision with action, torchlight and hand also requires keeping the

[29] For a similar dynamic see also Clarkson's account of Peter Green's flogging in his History, and 'The Sailor Who Had Served in the Slave-Trade', The Poetical Works of Robert Southey, 2:70–76.
[30] Compare Mieke Bal's observation that in Western art, the hand 'is not only the organ of painting [or in this case, writing] but also . . . the sign that links looking with sexual violence'. 'Dead Flesh, or the Smell of Painting', in Bryson, Visual Culture, 165.

hands of the viewer (and the author?) out of sight. When the image and the argument stake themselves upon an appeal to sexual difference through heterosexual desire, just what sort of action, what sort of relief should the mentally active, viewing subject be performing with his hands?

The representation of a young, naked slave woman being tortured proved rhetorically effective in prompting the men of England to recognize their power – and desire – to act. Clarkson's *History of the Abolition of the Slave Trade* follows this strategy; it relates a history of how the 'passions' aroused by contemplating the naked 'truth' of slavery convert to manly action. But he is careful to define the action of a freeborn Englishman not as physical intervention (he will not raise his hand to touch the naked truth) but as intellectual labor deflected from passion – researching and writing about the slave trade and its abuses.

> But as the passions, which agitate the human mind, when it is greatly inflamed, must have a vent somewhere, or must work off as it were . . . so I found the rage, which had been kindling in me, subsiding into the most determined resolutions of future increased activity and perseverance. I now began to think that the day was not long enough for me to labor in.   (Clarkson 1:255)

As we have seen, the violent spectacle of flogging threatens to expose the undifferentiated truth of humanity, the truth that lies beneath the visible (and racially marked) surface of skin and that binds the freeman with the slave. The passions elicited by such a spectacle drive even further the 'continuity of being' between two bodies. By locating the violence (and the truth) of slavery upon a woman's body, however, and by fixing the register of feeling with (hetero)sexual desire, the viewing subject reasserts his prerogative to act freely. In this regard, the rhetoric of abolition participates in a sadistic logic; it writes pornography. That 'the author of this torture' picks up his pen – rather than a whip or a torch – to prove his capacity to act freely hardly distinguishes the abolitionist's work from the pornographer's. The representation of heterosexualized, racialized violence frees him, as long as the activity of his own body remains out of sight.

What education did the stripped and striped body of a slave offer to Englishwomen? For the white woman was repeatedly invited to view the representation of racial and sexual violence. The notorious and widely depicted 'case of Captain Kimber', the case portrayed in our cartoon, was the centerpiece of the earliest appeals. Women readers were repeatedly asked to fix their eyes on 'the strong marks of slavery' thus violently engraved on the female slave's body. Such appeals, increasingly frequent in the subsequent decades, 'recognized [white women] as constituents of the public' on the basis of 'their humanity, benevolence and compassion'.[31]

But white women were carefully instructed how they were to look at these scenes. It was assumed they would resist looking, because the images presented some danger to them: 'Be not afraid', wrote one tract, 'we do not ask you to do anything, to incite in anything unbecoming to your sex.' If, as I have tried to show, the potentially improper incitements were targeted at a male audience, then the women were invited into the spectacle of sexualized violence in order to filter the pornographic gaze. The Manchester *Mercury* argues in an early appeal,

> If . . . it be what Nature requires and mankind expects, that Women should sympathize with women; that if the brutality of men should at any time reverse in his practice the Obligation of his Species, a female may meet, from the Pity of her Sex, that assistance which the Inhumanity of the other may deny.[32]

The 'interference' demanded of women supposed that they would look differently from men – with Pity and Humanity, now feminine attributes. The abstracted and violent gaze of the 'manly mind', his 'torch', so to speak, would, according to commonplaces of anti-slavery propaganda, be mediated by the 'concentrated radiance of light and love' which the Christian woman would shed 'on the darkness of the slave'.[33] The radiant look of the white woman, in other words, would highlight racial difference, insisting upon her own distance from the slave woman even while it introduced an atmosphere of chaste virtue into a potentially lurid scene. By appealing to the white woman in the general public, the male abolitionists forestalled pornography, thereby legitimating their own writing.[34] Her white light made the representation of racial,

---

[31] Clare Midgley, *Women Against Slavery: the British Campaigns, 1780–1870*.
[32] Midgley, 21–22.
[33] Vron Ware, *Beyond the Pale: White Women, Racism and History*, 63–4, 61. See for example the finale of Hannah More's well-known poem, 'Slavery'.
[34] In his *The History of Sexuality*, according to Lora Romero, 'Foucault proposes that the rise of the micropolitical corresponds roughly with the displacement of narratives of [masculine] adventure by narratives of [feminine] sentiment.' If, Romero continues, 'we take seriously Foucault's comments about the involution of micro and macropowers around questions of race, then we would expect to

sexualized violence both visible and viable, cleaving the representation of violence from the violence of representation. And yet, as Karen Sanchez-Eppler has argued in the context of the American anti-slavery movement, the portrayal of the black slave women's sexual violation offered a fantasy scene to white women as well, an opportunity to participate vicariously in sexual excesses otherwise denied to proper gentlewomen.[35]

I hope I have not myself shed too much white light on this topic. My initial fascination with the image of flogging and the historical, romantic secrets it would reveal now seems like a desire to bathe the image of violence in a self-congratulatory or masochistic light, and prompt other minds to turn once again to research and writing, Clarkson's liberating labor. If nothing else, maybe now we might begin to recognize the articulation of our scholarly criticism, feminist or not, with erotic scenes of violence.

Works Cited

Bal, M. 1994. 'Dead flesh, or the smell of painting', in Bryson 1994, 365–383.

Bataille, G. 1986. *Erotism: Death and Sensuality*, trans. Mary Dalwood, San Francisco: City Lights Books.

Breval, J.D., a.k.a. Joseph Gay, 1732. 'The lure of Venus, or the harlot's progress'. Reproduced from the English Poetry Full-Text Database, Copyright © [1992–1995] Chadwyck-Healey, Ltd.

Bryson, N. et al., ed. 1994. *Visual Culture: Images and Interpretations*, Hanover and London: Wesleyan UP, printed by the University Presses of New England.

Clark, E.B. 1995. ' "The sacred rights of the weak": pain, sympathy and the culture of individual rights in antebellum America', *The Journal of American History*, September, 463–493.

Clarkson, T. 1808. *The History of the Rise, Progress, and Accomplishment of the Abolition of the Slave-Trade by the British Parliament*, 2 vols, Philadelphia: James P. Parke.

uncover not the superannuation of heroism by sentiment but rather their simultaneity and complication' (118).

[35] Karen Sanchez-Eppler, *Touching Liberty: Abolition, Feminism, and the Politics of the Body*, 106. In her analysis of the writing of anti-slavery women in America, Sanchez-Eppler finds that 'the racial and the sexual come to displace one another' in pairings 'that tend toward asymmetry and exploitation' (93).

Cobbett, W. 1818. *The Parliamentary History of England from the earliest period to the year 1803*, London: T.C. Hansard.

Feher, M. et al., ed. 1992. *Fragments for a History of the Human Body, Part Two*, New York: Zone Books.

Foucault, M. 1978. *The History of Sexuality, Volume 1: An Introduction*, trans. Robert Hurley, New York: Random House, Inc.

Freud, S. 1960. ' "A child is being beaten": A contribution to the study of the origin of sexual perversion', in *Collected Papers*, vol. 2, New York: Basic Books, Inc. by arrangement with The Hogarth Press, Ltd and the Institute of Psycho-Analysis, London, 172–201.

Gibson, I. 1978. *The English Vice*, London: Duckworth.

Hansard, T.C. 1812. *The Parliamentary Debates from the year 1803 to the present time*, London: Longman, Hurst, et al.

JanMohammed, A.R. 1992. 'Sexuality on\of the racial border: Foucault, Wright and the articulation of "racialized sexuality" ', in Domna C. Stanton, ed., *Discourses of Sexuality: from Aristotle to AIDS*, Ann Arbor: The University of Michigan Press, 94–116.

Kendrick, W. 1987. *The Secret Museum: Pornography in Modern Culture*, New York: Viking Penguin, Inc.

Laplanche, J. and Pontalis, J.B. 1973. *The Language of Psycho-Analysis*, trans. Donald Nicholson-Smith, New York: W.W. Norton and Co.

Locke, J. 1764. *Two Treatises of Government*, 3 vols (1689 rpt.; London: A. Millar.

McCalman, I. 1988. *Radical Underworld: Prophets, Revolutionaries, and Pornographers in London, 1795–1840*, Cambridge: Cambridge UP.

Macdonald, D.L. 1994. 'Pre-romantic and post-romantic abolitionism', *European Romantic Review* 4, 156–75

Midgley, C. 1992. *Women Against Slavery: The British Campaigns, 1780–1870*, London, New York: Routledge.

Montgomery, J. 1970. *Poems on the Abolition of the Slave Trade*, ed. with intro. Donald H. Reiman, 1809 rpt., New York: Garland Publishing.

Perniola, M. 1989. 'Between clothing and nudity', in Feher 1992, 236–265.

Pinch, A. 1994. 'Learning what hurts: "The Schoolmistress", the rod, and poetry', paper given at the annual North American Society for the Study of Romanticism Conference, Durham, North Carolina.

Pinch, A. 1996. *Strange Fits of Passion: Epistemologies of Feeling, Hume to Austen*, Stanford: Stanford UP.

Pinckard, J. 1809. *Pinckard's Notes on the West Indies*, in Grahame 1809, 99.

Pollack, G. 1994. 'Feminism\Foucault – surveillance\sexuality,' in Bryson 1994, 1–41.

Prince, M. 1987. *The History of Mary Prince, A West Indian Slave, Narrated by Herself*, ed. Moira Ferguson, 1831; rpt. London: Pandora Press.

Pringle, M. 1987. 'A letter from Mrs. [Mary] Pringle to Mrs. [Lucy] Townsend . . .', in Prince 1987, 119–120.

Romero, L. 1992. 'Vanishing Americans: gender, empire and the new historicism', in Samuels 1992, 115–127.

Roscoe, W. 1808. 'The Wrongs of Africa', in Clarkson 1808, 1, 227.

Samuels, S. ed. 1992. *The Culture of Sentiment: Race, Gender and Senitmentality in Nineteenth-Century America*, New York, Oxford: Oxford UP.

Sanchez-Eppler, K. 1993. *Touching Liberty: Abolition, Feminism, and the Politics of the Body*, Berkeley: University of California Press.

Shenstone, W. 1974. *The School-Mistress, A Poem. In Imitation of Spenser*, London, R. Dodsley, 1742; rpt. Oxford: Clarendon Press.

Southey, R. 1878. *The Poetical Works of Robert Southey*, 10 volumes in 5, Boston: Houghton, Osgood and Company.

Stewart, W. 1972. *Progressives and Radicals in English Education, 1750–1970*, London: Macmillan.

Ware, V. 1992. *Beyond the Pale: White Women, Racism and History*, London: Verso.

Wiegman, R. 1995. *American Anatomies:* Theorizing Race and Gender, Durham, NC: Duke UP.

Young, R. 1995. *Colonial Desire: Hybridity in Theory, Culture, and Race*, New York, London: Routledge.

Barbauld, Romanticism, and the Survival of Dissent

WILLIAM KEACH

IN THE LAST OF his *Lectures on the English Poets*, given at the Surrey Institution on 3 March 1818 and entitled 'On the Living Poets', Hazlitt proclaims himself 'a great admirer of the female writers of the present day'. Eager to get an unavoidable but minor topic out of the way as briskly as possible before turning to more consequential matters (initially to Samuel Rogers, himself 'a very lady-like poet . . . an elegant, but feeble writer'), Hazlitt begins his survey of women poets with this account of Barbauld:

> The first poetess I can recollect is Mrs. Barbauld, with whose works I became acquainted before those of any other author, male or female, when I was learning to spell words of one syllable in her story-books for children. I became acquainted with her poetical works long after in Enfield's *Speaker*; and remember being much divided in my opinion at that time, between her Ode to Spring and Collins's Ode to Evening. I wish I could repay my childish debt of gratitude in terms of appropriate praise. She is a very pretty poetess; and, to my fancy, strews the flowers of poetry most agreeably round the borders of religious controversy. She is a neat and pointed prose-writer. Her 'Thoughts on the Inconsistency of Human Expectations', is one of the most ingenious and sensible essays in the language. There is the same idea in one of Barrow's Sermons.[1]

It is all Hazlitt can do here to raise himself, momentarily, above condescending dismissal. Even the praise of Barbauld's prose concludes with his minimizing the conceptual originality of what he takes to be her finest essay.

You would never know from Hazlitt's critical sketch that this 'very pretty poetess' had, some six years earlier (in 1812, the year in which Hazlitt became Parliamentary Reporter for the *Morning Chronicle*), published a magnificent anti-war prophecy that provoked vicious attacks from the Tory press; that her first volume of *Poems* (1773) contained a

---

[1] *Complete Works of William Hazlitt*, ed. P.P. Howe (London: J.M. Dent, 1935), 5: 146–7. The paragraph on Rogers follows on 5: 148–9.

fiery 200-line celebration of Corsica's struggle for national self-determination; that her poems of the 1790s included such agreeable strewings of 'the flowers of Poetry' as the 'Epistle to William Wilberforce, Esq. on the Rejection of the Bill for abolishing the Slave Trade' and a celebratory challenge to revolutionary France, 'To a Great Nation':

> Rise mighty nation! in thy strength,
> And deal thy dreadful vegeance round;
> Let thy great spirit rous'd at length,
> Strike hordes of Despots to the ground.[2]   (1–4)

Barbauld's publisher was Joseph Johnson. Poems such as the ones I have just glanced at are entirely at home among the writings of Paine, Wollstonecraft, and Blake, however distant Barbauld may be from their radicalism at other moments of her career, in other parts of her work.

From one point of view Hazlitt's offering such a constricted account of Barbauld's career is not surprising: he simply found it convenient on this occasion to participate in and take advantage of the most familiar way of representing her to early nineteenth-century readers. When Barbauld's niece Lucy Aikin put together an anthology of Barbauld's writings shortly after her death in 1825, she entitled it A Legacy for Young Ladies. The Preface begins: 'The late Mrs. Barbauld was one of the best friends of youth. In her "Early Lessons", and "Prose Hymns", she has condescended to apply her admirable genius to the instruction even of infant minds.'[3] It is easy to see where Hazlitt's emphasis comes from. Yet one expects a more comprehensive and acute perspective from him – not just because he is a powerful and independent-minded critic, but because his distinctive critical resources were shaped in important respects by a background that he shared with Barbauld in activist Dissent.

Eighteenth-century Dissent was, as E.P. Thompson and others have insisted, extremely diverse.[4] Within that diversity, Hazlitt has a good deal in common with Barbauld in terms of family influences and

---

[2] All quotations of Barbauld's poems are from The Poems of Anna Laetitia Barbauld, ed. William McCarthy and Elizabeth Kraft (Athens and London: University of Georgia Press, 1994).
[3] A Legacy for Young Ladies, Consisting of Miscellaneous Pieces, in Prose and Verse, by the Late Mrs. Barbauld (Boston, 1826), p. iii.
[4] See The Making of the English Working Class (New York: Vintage Books, 1963), esp. chapter II, 'Christian and Apollyon', pp. 26–54. See also Raymond G. Cowherd, The Politics of English Dissent (New York: New York University

education. 'Like Priestley, Paine, Godwin and Blake', Marilyn Butler says of him, 'he came from the classic stock of the English left, the Dissenters: his father was a unitarian minister . . . rather in Priestley's mould.'[5] The year before he died Hazlitt wrote a keen appreciation of Priestley for *The Atlas*; his admiration for 'the little Presbyterian parson' with 'his sharp Unitarian foil' conveys a sense of undiminished admiration and gratitude.[6] Though a generation younger than Barbauld and positioned by gender in very different relation to the formal institutions of Dissent, Hazlitt absorbed, as a student at Hackney College, many of the intellectual and political influences that Barbauld had been exposed to at Warrington more than thirty years earlier. Both experienced the revival of Dissenting political activism in the early 1790s; both also lived through the crisis into which Dissent was thrown during these years, first by the defeat in Parliament of legislation to repeal the Corporation and Test Acts, then by the Pitt government's systematic political suppression of revolutionary and reformist opinion. Hazlitt was very well positioned, then, to appreciate Barbauld's achievements as a political poet and controversialist. But he recognizes her only as a versifying school-mistress, an influential but conventional domestic moralizer.

Thinking further about Barbauld's relation to the politics of Dissent, and about Hazlitt's failure to acknowledge this crucial dimension of her work, may help establish a fresh perspective on some unfamiliar strengths in her writing – and on some familiar problems, such as her notoriously disappointing poem 'The Rights of Woman'. This approach will also, I hope, open up broader questions about the place of Dissenting culture in Romanticism. Part of what I want to do in this essay is encourage a fresh awareness of how many important writers from the period 1770–1830 came from Dissenting backgrounds. We are used to recognizing Dissent (in various of its traditions and practices) as central to our readings of Paine, Wollstonecraft, Blake, Coleridge, Godwin, Hazlitt himself. But the case of Barbauld urges us to enlarge the picture to include a range of other women writers whose relation to Romanticism has recently come into critical view: Mary Hays, Helen Maria Williams, Amelia Opie, Jane Taylor.

Marlon Ross has taken important steps in this direction in a recent

Press, 1956) and Michael R. Watts, *The Dissenters* (Oxford: Clarendon Press, 1978).

[5] *Romantics, Rebels, and Reactionaries: English Literature and its Background 1760–1830* (New York and Oxford: Oxford University Press, 1982), p. 169.

[6] 'The Late Dr. Priestley', *Complete Works*, 5: 236–9.

essay called 'Configurations of feminine reform: the woman writer and the tradition of dissent'. When Ross says that 'women's political discourse' during the 'early Romantic period . . . occupies a position of dissent', he means primarily that, for a woman, 'to speak about politics is to place onself *against* the political establishment'.[7] This maximally generalized conception of 'dissent', ironically available to women precisely because they were excluded from the explicitly political sector of the public sphere, stands in complicated relation to the tradition of Nonconformist religious Dissent, which both encouraged women to think of themselves as spiritual equals with men and yet continued to subordinate them socially to fathers, brothers, ministers (Barbauld herself was not formally enrolled as a student at the Warrington Academy, where her father and brother taught). Like other women writers from her background, Barbauld produced poetry marked by what Ross characterizes as the 'status of double dissent'.[8] In readings of such chronologically and thematically divergent poems as *Eighteen Hundred and Eleven* and 'The Mouse's Petition', Ross draws out the complex generic and stylistic responses arising from this position of 'double dissent' – a position that allowed and even encouraged, for instance, distinctive combinations of sentimental pathos and satirical polemic. There is much more work to be done in this direction. The excellent new edition of Barbauld's *Poems*, edited by William McCarthy and Elizabeth Kraft, makes it possible to follow and assess the full significance of Barbauld's achievement as never before.

Barbauld's earliest poems often display an intriguing balance of warm attachment to and witty independence from the environment at Warrington Academy. Barbauld's family moved to Warrington in 1758, when her father John Aikin accepted a position there as tutor in languages and *belles lettres*. When John Aikin was promoted to tutor in divinity in 1761, his successor in languages and *belles lettres* was Joseph Priestley, already well-known as the founder of a dissenting school for thirty boys and five or six girls in Nantwich, Cheshire. Priestley and his wife left Warrington for Leeds in June 1767, just as Barbauld was turning twenty-four. And opening the new edition of Barbauld's *Poems* are the previously unpublished couplets 'On Mrs. P{riestley}'s Leaving

---

7   *Re-visioning Romanticism*, ed. Carol Shiner Wilson and Joel Haefner (College Park: University of Pennsylvania Press, 1994), p. 92.
8   'Configurations of feminine reform', p. 93.

Warrington'. The qualities Barbauld celebrates in her older friend and teacher reflect on the tone and stance of the poem itself:

> So cool a judgment, and a heart so warm.
> A soul refined, exalted far beyond
> The common level of a blameless mind . . .   (26–8)

It is hard not to read in Barbauld's tribute an implicit comment on the habits and demeanor of Mrs Priestley's famous husband, who (as Hazlitt recalls) 'in going to any place . . . walked on before his wife (who was a tall, powerful woman) with a primitive simplicity, or as if a certain restlessness and hurry impelled him on with a projectile force before others'.[9] In other poems from the Warrington period, Barbauld's admiration for Dr Priestley's powerful influence is delicately balanced by a penchant for wry, even teasing, observation. In another previously unpublished poem, 'Verses written on the Back of an old Visitation Copy of the Arms of Dr. Priestley's Family, with Proposals for a new Escutcheon', she boldly but playfully confronts the eminent Enlightenment intellectual with the trappings of his own class origins:

> Armorial ensigns crested conquerors use
> Ill-suit the sons of science, and the Muse. . .
> Shall Gothic towers their odious pomp display,
> And monsters grin in the fair face of day –
> Monsters uncouth, not form'd by Nature's law,
> Which this, nor any other world e'er saw –
> Chimaeras dire of some distemper'd brain –
> Where truth and freedom fix their chosen reign?
>   (3–4, 9–14)

Barbauld rhetorically redesigns the arms of the Priestley family with more appropriate – and feminine – figures:

> For the plum'd helmet, and the broken lance,
> Let Liberty her cap and spear advance. . .
> Instead of lions guarding hostile towers
> Let Science beckon to her laurel'd bowers.   (21–2, 25–6)

In the best known, and the best, of these early private poems evoking Priestley and his intellectual milieu, 'An Inventory of the Furniture in

---

9   'The Late Dr. Priestley', *Complete Works*, 5: 236.

Dr. Priestley's Study', Barbauld shortens the lines and sharpens the observational focus to put a fine and congenial satirical edge on what might at first appear to be deferential adulation. The verse catches by enacting the remarkable range and fluency of Priestley's intellectual labor. His study contains, among other things,

> A rare thermometer, by which
> He settles, to the nicest pitch,
> The just degrees of heat, to raise
> Sermons, or politics, or plays.   (25–8)

The study is strewn with new, even unfinished books, which Barbauld compares to 'Cadmus' half-formed men':

> And all, like controversial writing,
> Were born with teeth, and sprung up fighting.   (53–4)

This culminating image of intellectual and political combat is followed by an envoy in which the poet, seeming to apologize for her anoymous efforts, in fact speaks for Priestley and has him acknowledge her audacity:

> 'But what is this,' I hear you cry,
> 'Which saucily provokes my eye?' –
> A thing unknown, without a name,
> Born of the air and doomed to flame.   (55–8)

Barbauld knew that Priestley would not throw her poem in the fire; what she could not have known was that it, along with the other poems she gave to the Priestleys, would be destroyed in the Birmingham Riot of July 1791.[10]

The convergence in these early private poems of allegiance and independence, deference and audacity, reflects the distinctiveness of Barbauld's position within the Warrington milieu. If 'Barbauld is ambivalent in her relation to Dissent', as William McCarthy has recently argued, it is not primarily because 'she resents its self-denial, rationalism, and emotional low temperature'.[11] Rather it is because

---

10 See *Poems*, p. 204.
11 ' "We hoped the *woman* was going to appear": repression, desire, and gender in Anna Letitia Barbauld's early poems', *Romantic Women Writers: Voices and*

Dissent has taught her to claim a critical freedom for herself that has to coexist both with intellectual and political solidarity and with the continuing relegation of women to the realm of nurturing domesticity.

These ideological forces play themselves out differently in the more public poems included in the five editions of Barbauld's early verse to appear between 1773 and 1777. 'The Mouse's Petition' seems at first just the kind of performance that provoked Hazlitt's condescension. Written during a 1767 visit to the Priestleys in Leeds, the poem gained an impressive popular readership: it was reprinted in Wollstonecraft's 1789 *Female Reader* and elsewhere, and according to McCarthy and Kraft 'became a set piece for children to memorize'.[12] This kind of reception was made possible, as Ross and others have shown, by Barbauld's transposing of liberatory politics into the deceptively familiar key of quasi-comic sentimentality. What is less familiar about this poem, however, is its scene of instruction: we are placed not, as in Burns's famous poem written almost two decades later, as an observer or bystander in the field of peasant labor, but as an intruder into the laboratory of Enlightenment science. While it may be childlike for a mouse to speak in quatrains, it is boldly undeferring, even unaccommodating, to have this voice address its 'petition of mercy against justice' (as Barbauld herself expresses her theme in a note added to the third edition) to the great humane scientist, identified in Barbauld's original footnote as 'Dr. Priestley'. Contemporary accounts say that Priestley let the mouse go free – not because he was persuaded to forego experimenting on animals, but, as we learn from Priestley's remarks on such experiments in his *History of Electricity* (1767), because he took the concerns dramatized in Barbauld's poem seriously. The poem articulates a political and moral vision that looks ahead to the Wordsworths and to Coleridge: 'The well taught philosophic mind . . . feels for all that lives' (25–8). What is peculiar about Barbauld's handling of such values is her enacting them within such an intimately rendered sphere of intellectual Dissent. It is this intimacy that allows the poem to speak, mock-heroically, of Priestley's 'strong oppressive force' (11) in one stanza, of his 'hospitable hearth' (14) in the next stanza – and then of his 'wiles' (15) in the next line.

We need to keep the specific scene of instruction evoked in 'The Mouse's Petition' in view if we are to see how Barbauld's position of 'double dissent' functions in this case. Ross argues that Barbauld's

Countervoices, ed. Paula R. Feldman and Theresa M. Kelley (Hanover and London: University Press of New England), p. 123.
[12] *Poems*, p. 245.

'liberal political language' is 'subtly transferred out of the sphere of topical satire and political factionalism', that the poem's universalizing appeal ('Let Nature's commoners enjoy / The common gifts of Heaven', 35–6) '*discourages* readers from viewing themselves as members of any political faction'.[13] Perhaps – but the rhetorical circumstances of addressing this petition to Priestley mean that the implied debate between mercy and justice, between the claims of moral sympathy and the claims of science, is conducted within Dissent as a specific formation, if not a faction. It is by drawing us into a quite distinctive and historically particular formation in British intellectual and political life – not by diverting our attention from it – that the poem lays claim to a relevance beyond its immediate occasion. Even to grasp the force of Barbauld's motto from *The Aeneid – Parcere subjectis, & debellare superbos*; 'To spare the humble, and to tame in war the proud!' – depends upon our thinking about the ambiguous relation between subjection and pride for the aspiring woman writer from Warrington.

To move from Barbauld's Warrington poems of the 1760s and early 1770s to the verse she wrote in London (Hampstead) in response to the political ferment of the early 1790s is to be struck as much by continuity as by difference. The best introduction to Barbauld's political poetry from this period is the essay she published in March 1790, *An Address to the Opposers of the Repeal of the Corporation and Test Acts*. Writing in the immediate aftermath of Parliament's refusal to extend the rights of Dissenters, Barbauld uses the occasion to link the cause of religious freedom in Britain to the tide of revolutionary change surging forth from France. Here her political kinship with Paine, Blake, and Wollstonecraft is unmistakeable. 'Can ye not discern the signs of the times?' she asks the defenders of the establishment:

> The minds of men are in movement from the Borysthenes to the Atlantic. Agitated with new and strong emotions, they swell and heave beneath oppression, as the seas within the polar circle, when at the approach of spring, they grow impatient to burst their icy chains. . . . Whatever is loose must be shaken, whatever is corrupted must be lopped away; whatever is not built on the broad basis of public utility must be thrown to the ground. Obscure murmurs gather, and swell into a tempest; the spirit of Inquiry, like a severe and searching wind, penetrates every part of the great body politic; and whatever is un-

---

[13] 'Configurations of feminine reform', pp. 99–100.

sound, what is infirm, shrinks at the visitation. Liberty, here with the lifted crosier in her hand, and the crucifix conspicuous on her breast; there, led by Philosohy, and crowned with the civic wreath, animates men to assert their long-forgotten rights.[14]

This is the prose of Hazlitt's 'pretty poetess', prose which he characterizes generally as being 'neat and pointed'. Barbauld's *Address* signals the most confident and assertive moment of her career – a confidence and assertiveness that spring as much from an identification with the historical moment as from the momentum of Barbauld's own accumulating literary and pedagogical successes. The essay is signed, simply, 'A Dissenter'.

In Barbauld's poetry of the early 1790s the figure of Priestley remains, explicitly and implicitly, a fundamental point of reference. 'To Dr. Priestley, Dec. 29, 1792' was written four months before the publication of *Sins of Rulers, Sins of the Nation*, Barbauld's powerful pamphlet denouncing England's declaration of war against the French Republic. The poem reflects a period when pressure against individuals and groups sympathetic to the Revolution was intensifying daily. She begins not with the 'hooting crowds' (7) in Birmingham that had destroyed Priestley's house and laboratory in the summer of 1791, but with those members of London's Protestant Dissenting Ministers association who had just issued a Burkean declaration of loyalty to 'that excellent Form of Government, by King, Lords, & Commons, which hath obtained from Time immemorial in this Country':[15]

> Stirs not thy spirit, Priestley, as the train
> With low obeisance, and with servile phrase,
> File behind file, advance, with supple knee,
> And lay their necks beneath the foot of power?   (1–4)

After posing three such defiant questions, Barbauld quotes Milton's recovery of purpose and defiance of restored monarchical oppression at the beginning of Book 7 of *Paradise Lost* – 'On evil days though fallen and evil tongues' (12) – to turn her poem from disgust to renewed commitment, and to the future:

> To thee, the slander of a passing age
> Imports not. Scenes like these hold little space

---

[14] *The Works of Ann Laetitia Barbauld*, ed. Lucy Aikin (Boston: David Reed, 1826), 2: 253–54.
[15] Quoted in *Poems*, p. 292.

In his large mind, whose ample stretch of thought
Grasps future periods.   (13–16)

'[P]eriods' here are syntactical as well as historical: stretching her verse
past dramatically enjambed line-endings worthy of Milton, Barbauld
sees Priestley forging ahead into new political possibilities and a new life
of writing. The poem ends with a convergence of theological and political redemption characteristic of Dissent, with 'that distant day, / If distant', when Priestley will receive 'the thanks of a regenerate land'
(20–1).

Other poems from 1791–92 display, through a variety of stances and
tones, Barbauld's dissenting commitment to the revolution in France as
a harbinger of expanded freedom in Britain. On the eve of Bastille Day,
1791, she sent six quatrains in a letter to Samuel Rogers, who was away
at the time on holiday savoring the sublimities of north Wales.[16] With a
wittiness that enhances rather than disguises her political seriousness –
and in a gesture that reflects ironically on Hazlitt's view of Rogers as 'a
very lady-like poet' – Barbauld upbraids Rogers as a truant 'youth' (he
was twenty-eight in 1791, some twenty years younger than Barbauld)
indulging himself in 'poetic dreams' 'While dungeons burst, and despots
fall' (6–8). Barbauld aggressively transposes the imagery of timeless pas-
toral retreat to the sphere of immediate political struggle:

> Shall peals of village bells prevail
> Floating on the Summer gale,
> While the Tocsin sounds afar,
> Breathing arms, and glorious War?
>
> Think, when woods of brownest shades
> Open bright to sunny glades;
> Such the gloom, and such the light,
> Of Freedom's noon, and Slavery's night.   (9–16)

In the poem's concluding stanza, there may be an allusion to one of the
finest political poems from an earlier era of Dissent, Marvell's 'An Horatian Ode Upon Cromwell's Return from Ireland':

> Now stretched at hoary Snowden's base,
> Hide in shades thy long disgrace,

---

16 See *Poems*, p. 289.

> And blush that Freedom's child should be,
> Far from Freedom's jubilee.[17]   (21–4)

Rogers had Barbauld's own letter to help him know how to take her poetic rebuke:

> But pray Sir, what have you to say in your defence for rambling amongst fairy streams & hanging woods instead of being at the Crown & Anchor as you & every other Patriot ought to be on the 14th of July. . . . Do not you deserve at least as severe a Philippic as the Welsh farmer gave his Cow?[18]

That Barbauld was evidently at home in the Crown & Anchor as well as in the schoolroom and the bluestocking salon is part of what Hazlitt later obscures or forgets.

Barbauld's stanzas to Rogers may well have had the desired effect. A year later he was conspicuously among those who signed a subscription fund sent to Paris to help the young Republic in a moment of extreme crisis following the overthrow of the monarchy in August 1792: the Duke of Brunswick's allied armies had invaded; the September prison massacres registered the heightened internal tension and suspicion; numerous counter-revolutionary plots to subvert the National Assembly had been discovered. It was very likely at this critical moment that Barbauld wrote 'To a Great Nation', though the poem was not published until more than a year later (2 November 1793) in the *Cambridge Intelligencer*. The poem begins, as I have already indicated, with a militant call for solidarity in defense of the revolution, and with a keen sense of what will have to be sacrificed:

> Nor virgin's plighted hand, nor sighs
> Must now the ardent youth detain.
> Nor must the hind who tills thy soil,
> The ripen'd vintage stay to press,
> 'Till rapture crown the flowing bowl,
> And Freedom boast of full success.   (11–16)

---

17 Marvell's 'Horatian Ode' begins: 'The forward youth that would appear / Must now forsake his Muses dear, / Nor in the shadows sing / His numbers languishing' (*Poems and Letters*, edn H.H. Margoliouth; 3rd ed. revised by Pierre Legouis and E.E. Duncan-Jones, Oxford: Clarendon Press, 1971).

18 Quoted in *Poems*, p. 289.

Only when the need for fiercely determined resistance against the forces of counter-revolution has been established does Barbauld shift her perspective to look unflinchingly at the excesses of revolutionary self-defense and revenge – and to issue a call for compassionate generosity:

> Then fold in thy relenting arms,
> Thy wretched outcasts where they roam;
> From pining want and war's alarms,
> O call the child of Misery home. (24–7)

The principle on which the poem's culminating exhortation depends – 'Obey the laws thyself hast made' (35) – is an elaboration of Protestant self-reliance into a model of republican virtue: 'And rise – the model of the world!' (36).

Barbauld's principle of revolutionary integrity would be severely put to the test in 1793 and 1794. Like most of those in Britain who sympathized with the Revolution from a distance, she drew back from and condemned the Jacobin Terror. Her 'Hymn' to compassionate reformers ('Salt of the earth, ye virtuous few', written during the summer of 1794) articulates a disillusionment and a desire to transcend the bitter actualities of history that have become hallmarks of British Romanticism.

> E'en yet the steaming scaffolds smoke
>   By Seine's polluted stream;
> With your rich blood the fields are drench'd
>   Where Polish sabres gleam. (41–4)

The shift in focus from the Terror in France to the defeat of Kosciuszko's nationalist uprising in Poland is important: Barbauld's disillusionment in this poem is defined as much by the successes of the old order in thwarting liberatory change as by the excesses of the new order's fight for survival. The historical and political developments of the mid and late 1790s weigh heavily on Barbauld's writing. After the burst of assertively public verse in the early part of the decade, she returns to more private, domestic, meditative topics. 'Peace and Shepherd', Barbauld's response to France's invasion of Switzerland in February 1798, appears an exception, but even here the allegorical mode and tone of exhausted resignation contrast sharply with poems written a few years earlier. 'Peace' appears in an Alpine vale with 'scatter'd tresses torn', 'bleeding breast', and 'bruised feet' (1–8); she commiserates with the threatened shepherd but tells him,

> I hear the human wolves approach;
> I *cannot* shelter thee.   (43–4)

I have emphasized the consistently liberatory and democratic com-
mitments of Barbauld's poetry of the 1790s because this dimension of
her work, including its movement from enthusiastic assertiveness to
pessimistic resignation, links it and the Dissenting tradition from which
it springs to the most deeply characteristic trajectory of British Romanticism's first phase of cultural production. It is from this perspective, and
within this context, that Barbauld's more cautious and circumspect poems from the 1790s need to be read. Her response to Wollstonecraft in
'The Rights of Woman' exuberantly embraces the impulse towards radical self-emancipation ('Yes, injured Woman! rise, assert thy right!') but
immediately turns this impulse towards the accepted feminine sphere of
empathic sensibility and domestic nurture. Barbauld's unusual access at
Warrington to the kind of intellectual culture that Wollstonecraft complained women had been deprived of made her hesitant to generalize
her own educational experience in the direction of institutional reform.
This is clear in the most interesting of the reasons she gives for opposing
Elizabeth Montagu's proposal in 1786 for establishing 'A kind of Literary Academy for ladies':

> Perhaps you may think, that having myself stepped out of the bounds
> of female reserve in becoming an author, it is with an ill grace I offer
> these sentiments [against founding such an academy]. . . . My situa-
> tion has been peculiar, and would be no rule for others.[19]

The limits of Barbauld's position of 'double dissent' are evident here and
throughout 'The Right of Woman': her own active participation in the
public sphere of political as well as literary discourse, based again and
again on an appeal to 'common' human nature and universal human
rights, falters when faced with the prospect of breaking from middle-
class norms of gender.

And from the norms of class relations. 'To the Poor', written in 1795,
offers a message of resignation and acceptance that sounds more like
Hannah More than Barbauld or Priestley:

> Bear *thy* afflictions with a patient mind .   .   .
> Bear, bear thy wrongs, fulfil thy destined hour,
> Bend thy meek neck beneath the foot of power!   (6, 11–12)

---

[19] Quoted in Lucy Aikin's 'Memoir', *Works*, 1: xiv–xvii.

What is striking about Barbauld's conservatism in this poem is that it is linked to a sharply sarcastic denunciation of ruling-class superiority and established religious authority:

> Think not their threats can work thy future woe,
> Nor deem the Lord above, like Lords below.
> Safe in the bosom of that love repose
> By whom the sun gives light, the ocean flows,
> Prepare to meet a father undismayed,
> Nor fear the God whom priests and kings have made.
>
> (17–22)

The last line reminds one of Blake or P.B. Shelley – or Milton. Quoting this passage, an anonymous reviewer of Barbauld's 1825 *Works* wrote: 'Mrs. Barbauld's fiery democracy sometimes carried her almost the length of profanation.'[20] Even at its most conservative, Barbauld's poetry of the 1790s declares its allegiance to the cause of Dissenting republicanism and reform.

Barbauld was sixty-eight and still intensely productive as an editor and journalist when, near the end of the first year of the Regency, she completed *Eighteen Hundred and Eleven*, her most remarkable piece of writing and one of the major political poems of its time. The poem was savagely attacked by Tory reviewers, and even Barbauld's friends among the reformers were taken aback by its uncompromising denunciation of the war and its prophecy of British ruin and the migration of liberty and progressive enterprise across the Atlantic.[21] The most striking thing about the reception of *Eighteen Hundred and Eleven* is that readers on both sides of the political spectrum treated it as a disturbing departure from Barbauld's previous work. It is as if everyone assumed that Barbauld's perspective and commitment had shifted since the early 1790s in the direction of a concessive patriotism, as most of theirs had done. Such are the dangers of a career extending into its fifth decade.

But in fact, *Eighteen Hundred and Eleven* realizes impulses that are apparent in Barbauld's poetry from the beginning. They are most fully evident in *Corsica*, the first and most ambitious poem in Barbauld's 1773 collection. McCarthy and Kraft provide an informative account of the immediate context of *Corsica* – its relation to 'antigovernment ideology' of the late 1760s ('The cause of Corsica' was 'one more example of

---

20 Quoted in *Poems*, p. 295.
21 See my 'A regency prophecy and the end of Anna Barbauld's career', *Studies in Romanticism* 33 (1994), 569–77.

failure by the duke of Grafton's administration to respect the principles of liberty that Britain was supposed, in Whig tradition, to champion'), its place in 'the general ferment over "the state of public liberty" as well as the particular issue of Corsica'.[22] In its opening reference to 'this sickly age' (5) and its call for Britons to 'catch / The warm contagion of heroic ardour, / And kindle at a fire so like their own' (15–17), *Corsica* anticipates much of the argumentative structure and rhetorical unfolding of *Eighteen Hundred and Eleven*.

One of Barbauld's major challenges in the latter text, as Julie Ellison argues, is to move from 'the logic of systematic moral correction', with its vantage point of critical elevation, to a posture of sympathetic political engagement. Barbauld accomplishes this modulation, Ellison observes, by having 'Fancy materialize[ ] both to suffer and to stage the show, and finally to offer commentary on it'.[23]

> Where wanders Fancy down the lapse of years,
> Shedding o'er imaged woes untimely tears?
> Fond, moody power! as hopes – as fears prevail,
> She longs, or dreads, to lift the awful veil,
> On visions of delight now loves to dwell,
> Now hears the shriek of woe or Freedom's knell.   (113–18)

'Fancy' is the uncertain but indispensible power to which Barbauld turns here – not, as Hazlitt affects to be the case, 'to [his] fancy', in order to 'strew[. . .] the flowers of poetry most agreeably round the borders of religious controversy' – but to register the decay of British cultural progress and its vestigial survival and future revival. She evokes an 'ingenuous youth whom Fancy fires / With pictured glories of illustrious sires' (126–7), wandering through the ruins of London with 'mingled feelings' (157) and 'throbbing bosom[. . .]' (177), led by 'some Briton, in whose musing mind / Those ages live which Time has cast behind' (187–8). This extended drama of redemptive emotion is prefigured near the beginning of *Corsica*, which acknowledges its indebtedness to Boswell's *An Account of Corsica* (1768) with its 'views beyond the narrow beaten track / By trivial fancy trod' (20–1), before launching forth on its own impassioned appeal for Corsican freedom:

> How raptur'd fancy burns, while warm in thought
> I trace the pictur'd landscape; while I kiss

22 *Poems*, p. 232.
23 'The politics of fancy in the age of sensibility', *Re-visioning Romanticism*, ed. Wilson and Haefner, p. 238.

> With pilgrim lips devout the sacred soil
> Stain'd with the blood of heroes.   (31–4)

Barbauld's early pilgrimage from Britain to a Corsica fighting for its independence in the middle of the Mediterranean is mirrored in the pilgrimage back to Britain from newly independent lands across the Atlantic in *Eighteen Hundred and Eleven*. Both poems enact a necessary dependence on rectified 'fancy', on a political imaginary that has to be sustained in the face of historical contradiction and defeat.

The history and politics of Dissent are a central part of this process and reveal themselves most obviously in *Eighteen Hundred and Eleven*'s links to a tradition stretching back to the seventeenth century, to Dissenting visions of a corrupt monarchical and ecclesiastical establishment at home and a new land of religious and political freedom elsewhere. Once again, Priestley is given a dramatic place in Barbauld's vision of a degraded present waiting to be redeemed by its own abandoned and displaced potential. She pictures a future London lying in decay, with visitors from across the Atlantic – 'From the Blue Mountains, or Ontario's lake' (130) – wandering through the ruins of empire.

> Perhaps some Briton, in whose musing mind
> Those ages live which Time has cast behind,
> To every spot shall lead his wondering guests
> On whose known site the beam of glory rests . . .
> Point where mute crowds on Davy's lips reposed,
> And Nature's coyest secrets were disclosed;
> Join with their Franklin, Priestley's injured name,
> Whom, then, each continent shall proudly claim. (187–204)

Priestley's position is pivotal. Having been driven out of Britain by the forces of reactionary ignorance to live among the Blue Mountains of Pennsylvania, he now returns posthumously, in the company of his fellow American scientist Franklin and with the help of imaginative descendents from both sides of the Atlantic, to reclaim an honor previously denied. It is one of the main gestures of hope the poem offers towards a recovery of British cultural and political integrity – and its implications were not missed by the Tory reviewers. 'Instead of being *proudly claimed* by *each* Continent', wrote the *Anti-Jacobin Review*, '[Priestley] is almost *disowned* by BOTH.'[24] By 1812, when *Eighteen*

---

[24] Quoted in *Poems*, p. 315.

Hundred and Eleven was published, Britain was already at war again with her former colonies, and Tory chauvinists were in no mood to accept a renegade Dissenter such as Priestley back into the fold of national greatness, even after his death and despite his scientific eminence.

Priestley is crucial to the complex transatlantic politics of *Eighteen Hundred and Eleven*, as a figure for the imagined future return to Britain of a rejected and expelled potential through a process that counters the otherwise prevailingly westward progress of liberty and genius. He may also be a source and point of departure for the deployment of 'fancy' in Barbauld's tragic yet redemptive rhetoric of historical change. Priestley's *Course of Lectures on Oratory and Criticism*, first delivered when he was a tutor at Warrington in 1762 and published by Joseph Johnson in 1777, contains extended discussions 'Of the Tendency of strong Emotions to produce Belief, and the transferring of Passions from one Object to Another' (Lecture XIII), 'Of the Influence of the Passions on each other, and other Circumstances relating to strong Emotions of Mind' (Lecture XIV), and 'Of the Pleasures of Imagination in general' (Lecture XVII). The pertinence of Priestley's lectures to Barbauld's turning to 'raptur'd fancy' in *Corsica* and then much later in *Eighteen Hundred and Eleven* may be seen in his remarks about the mind's engagement in reading history: '. . . unless history be read . . . with a view to gain a knowledge of mankind, in order to form our own conduct . . . it is nothing better than reading romance. By reading history with some farther view, as a *means* to a farther end, we make it a *science*. It then engages our active powers . . . and is capable of being pursued with continued and increasing ardour' (Lecture XVIII).[25] The link here between 'ardour' and 'reading history with some farther view' had been cast into an elegiac key by Barbauld herself in an essay 'On the Uses of History', where she anticipates the functions of historical imagination in *Eighteen Hundred and Eleven* by projecting her reader into a moment of political decline:

> . . . should he observe the gathering glooms of superstition and ignorance ready to close again over the bright horizon; should Liberty lie prostrate at the feet of a despot, and the golden stream of commerce, diverted into other channels, leave nothing but beggary and wretchedness around him; – even then, in these ebbing fortunes of his

---

[25] *Course of Lectures on Oratory and Criticism* (1777), pp. 144–5; quoted from the text reprinted in the Landmarks in Rhetoric and Public Address series, ed. Vincent M. Bevilacqua and Richard Murphy (Carbondale: Southern Illinois University Press, 1965).

country, History, like a faithful meter, would tell him how high the tide had once risen; he would not tread unconsciously the ground where the Muses and the Arts had once resided, like the goat that stupidly browses upon the fane of Minerva.[26]

This is one side of the prophetic dialectic enacted in *Eighteen Hundred and Eleven* – historical knowledge as a stay against political despair and a repository of political desire. The other side, as we have seen, requires crossing and double-crossing the Atlantic in a process that is inevitably a matter of 'fancy' as well as of history, extending and challenging – as Priestley's very life had done, following the trajectory of emigrant Dissent – the notion of a privileged British national identity. Barbauld's last public writing constructs a Dissenter's vision of what it means, in Demogorgon's words, 'to hope, till Hope creates / From its own wreck the thing it contemplates'.[27] It is one of the surprises of Romantic literary history – or instead one of its predictable disconnections – that neither Shelley nor Hazlitt seems to have been able to hear her.

26 *A Legacy for Young Ladies*, p. 74.
27 *Prometheus Unbound* IV. 573–4; quoted from *Shelley's Poetry and Prose*, ed. Donald H. Reiman and Sharon B. Powers (New York: W.W. Norton, 1977).

Barbauld's Domestic Economy

JOSEPHINE MCDONAGH

THE SWINGEING ATTACKS ON Anna Letitia Barbauld's late poem, *1811*
(1812) – her devastating account of the ruined state of the British
nation in the midst of the Napoleonic wars – have acquired lasting
notoriety. Croker's lambasting, in the Tory magazine, the *Quarterly*, of
the 'fatidical spinster' whom he pictured 'dash[ing] down her shagreen
spectacles and her knitting needles . . . to sally forth',[1] is held to have
been responsible for the silencing of Barbauld for the rest of her life.
Standing accused of abandoning her proper, domestic role, the 'knitting' lady retreated forthwith: *1811* was the last work she published, although she continued to write. As William Keach has observed, however, more striking even than Croker's attack is the fact that criticism of
the poem came from all directions, not only from Tories. Even those
from whom she might have expected a more sympathetic response
found room for complaint.[2] In the *Eclectic Review*, a magazine to which
Barbauld had contributed, the tone is one of apologetic embarrassment:
'[d]isposed as we are to receive every performance of Mrs Barbauld with
peculiar cordiality, yet her choice of a subject in this instance, as well as
her manner of treating it, is so unfortunate that we scarcely ever read a
poem of equal merit with so little pleasure'.[3] Her friend Crabb Robinson
wrote in his diary, 'I certainly wish she had not written it. . . . For the tone
and spirit of it are certainly very bad.'[4] In the *Monthly Review*, a magazine
to which her brother, John Aikin, was a regular contributor and for
which she wrote herself from 1809 to 1815, an otherwise admiring reviewer wrote that, 'the first thought which occurred to us, after our pe-
rusal of her poem, was that, instead of purporting to be descriptive of the
year 1811, it should have been made to refer to a subsequent period'.[5]
Trying to be nice, the reviewer unfortunately misses the point: *1811*

---

1   John Wilson Croker, *Quarterly Review* 7 (1812): 309–13, 309.
2   William Keach, 'A Regency Prophecy and the End of Barbauld's Career',
Studies in Romanticism 33 (Winter: 1994): 569–577.
3   *Eclectic Review*, 8 part 1 (December 1811): 474.
4   *Henry Crabb Robinson on Books and Their Writers*, ed. Edith J. Morley (London: J.M. Dent, 1938), 1:64. Cited in Keach, 570.
5   *Monthly Review*, new series, 67 (1812): 428. On the Aikin family's contributions to the periodical press, see J.O. Hayden, *The Romantic Reviewers
1802–1824* (London: Routledge & Kegan Paul, 1969), 52–58.

does contain a warning about the future – national decline and the transfer of wealth and moral virtue to the New World – but one based on its assessment of the lamentable current state of England.

Barbauld's poem and its gloomy predictions seemed palatable to no one. Its reception, however, provides a useful commentary on the gendered terrain of public discourse in the early decades of the nineteenth century. Throughout the reviews, the tone was one of irritation and embarrassment. The message was emphatic: Mrs Barbauld had spoken out of line, out of place and out of time. In doing so she had exposed herself to criticism, but also, in a more particular sense, exposed *herself*. The criticisms in the reviews tended to focus on her gender and her sex. Nowhere is this more evident than in Croker's review, which concentrates its attacks specifically on the aberrant femininity of this 'spinster' (who was in fact a widow), the 'fair pedagogue' and so forth: she had 'wandered from the course in which she was respectable and useful'.[6] Maria Edgeworth, Barbauld's friend and correspondent, understood the nature of the insults, the lurking suggestion throughout that, by behaving with impropriety, she had encouraged the various assaults she received – the literary equivalent of dressing provocatively.[7] In a private letter to Barbauld, she declared that 'it is not their criticism of your poem which incenses me, it is the odious tone in which they dare to speak of the most respectable and elegant female writer that England can boast'. She called on a chivalric 'public' to redeem Barbauld's soiled reputation: 'The public, the *public* will do you justice!'[8]

The *Eclectic Review*, however, gives another sense of her transgression. The figure of exposure here is different from that in Croker's account – and in fact much more violent. The disturbing image conjured is of Barbauld, not as an ineffectual spinster, but as a matricidal anatomist:

> The whole tone of it is a most extraordinary degree unkindly and unpatriotic – we had almost said unfilial. Such is her eagerness to read a lecture in morbid anatomy, and display her knowledge of the body of

6   Croker, 309. On the sexual character of the criticisms, see Keach, 569–71.
7   Previously she had been admired precisely for her 'propriety'. Coleridge, for instance, wrote: 'The more I see of Mrs Barbauld the more I admire her – that wonderful *Propriety* of Mind!' Coleridge to Estlin, 1 Mar. 1800; Letters, 1:578. Cited in William McCarthy and Elizabeth Kraft, *The Poems of Anna Letitia Barbauld* (Athens: University of Georgia Press, 1994), 296. However, later he descended to lewd name calling: 'Mistress Bare and Bold'. See Coleridge, *Notebooks*, 3: 3965. Cited in McCarthy and Craft, xxxiv.
8   Anna Letitia Le Breton, *Memoir of Mrs Barbauld: Including Letters and Notices of her Family and Friends* (London: George Bell, 1874), 157.

her venerable parent, while she is yet in very tolerable health; and in doing this preserves all the while such perfect composure, as is to us absolutely astonishing.[9]

Barbauld has found disease where there was none, and indecently displayed her findings. Another female body is exposed – but this time it is the mother's (England's) body, flayed, its interiors ripped apart.

Interesting here is the way in which emphasis is placed on what is deemed to be Barbauld's excessive, fanatical, and thus unfeminine claims to knowledge. Through the anatomical metaphor, the reviewer draws attention to the poem's inclusion of a realm of knowledge of public affairs that it is clearly inappropriate for a woman to possess, but also for a poem to evince. Concluding, the reviewer judges the poem to be 'not so much a work of genius as of art and industry; not an emanation, but an edifice of the mind: its words more poetical than its imagery, and its imagery than its sentiment'.[10] The judgement recalls the antidiscursive critical values of Wordsworth – the idea that poetry should be an 'emanation', a powerful overflow of feeling – rather than a sustained engagement with or display of knowledge. Later the notoriously undisciplined writer, Thomas De Quincey, whose obsessions with disciplinary boundaries I have discussed elsewhere, further developed Wordsworth's terms into the idea of two distinct kinds of literature: the 'literature of power' and 'literature of knowledge', the former characterised as the outpourings of poetic genius, while the latter assumed a more expository function, designed to impart information, to instruct rather than to move.[11] De Quincey's terms were influential in the construction and dissemination in Britain of a notion of 'literature' ('the literature of power') as a transcendent category which took hold throughout the century: a depoliticised discursive space for the outpourings of subjective feeling in particular generic forms (especially poetry), in the construction of what would come to be known as the 'Romantic Ideology'. In the *Eclectic*'s critique, Barbauld's mechanical poetry, the work of 'art and industry', rather than effortless 'genius', designates her as a writer of the qualitatively lesser 'literature of knowledge', rather than the superior 'literature of power'.

9 *Eclectic Review*, 8 part 1 (December 1811): 474.
10 Ibid., 478.
11 Thomas De Quincey, 'Letters to a Young Man' (1823) and 'The Poetry of Pope' (1848), in *Works*, ed. David Masson, 14 vols (Edinburgh: Adam and Charles Black, 1889–90), 10: 47–49, 11: 54–48; Josephine McDonagh, *De Quincey's Disciplines* (Oxford: Clarendon Press, 1994), 72–81.

According to this account, then, Barbauld's misdemeanour is a double one: a gender *and* a genre offence. By displaying a too technical – 'anatomical' – knowledge of the state of the nation within the form of poetry, she transgresses the generic rules of the 'literature of power'. But by aspiring to the 'literature of knowledge' as a woman, displaying a knowledge that she should not have, and certainly should not reveal, she transgresses the limits of appropriate female utterance. This observation is a useful one because it points to a distinction in the modes of public discourse available to women in this period. Feminist revisions of Romanticism have shown the amount of poetry by women at this time which was published, circulated and highly regarded, as a conclusive corrective to the received view that, in some vaguely defined 'past', women were excluded from most forms of literary expression – and certainly all public ones. Recent critics have offered a more nuanced and historically convincing account of women's relation to public discourse through using the Habermasian model of the public sphere of letters, which in the eighteenth century was still relatively ungendered. In this respect, Keach usefully comments on Edgeworth's letter to Barbauld, and her application to an undesignated 'public' to redeem Barbauld's soiled reputation. He reads this as an indication of the 'moment in cultural history when, as Habermas puts it, "the sphere of the conjugal family became differentiated from the sphere of social reproduction" '.[12] Other models, however, can also be illuminating in explaining the awkward position of women in relation to public utterance. If women were not excluded from the production of literary works, it is true that they are strikingly and increasingly absent from other kinds of public discourse. This is markedly the case within the new and developing disciplines, the emergence of which, around the beginning of the nineteenth century, Michel Foucault analyses in *The Order of Things*, as indicative of the epistemic shift that characterises modernity.[13] The absence of women as producers of knowledge in the new disciplines of (following Foucault) the biological sciences, political economy and linguistics, is

[12] Keach, 571. Citing Jurgen Habermas, *The Structural Transformation of the Public Sphere: An Inquiry into a Category of Bourgeois Society*, trans. Thomas Burger with the assistance of Frederick Lawrence (Cambridge, MA: MIT Press, 1991), 28. Essays by Mary Favret and Ann Mellor in the same *Studies in Romanticism* edition (33[winter 1994]) also offer useful developments of the Habermasian model.
[13] Michel Foucault, *The Order of Things*, trans. Alan Sheridan (London: Tavistock Press, 1970).

explicable in terms of women's lack of education at the higher levels, and the development of a gendered division of labour in which middle-class women's roles were restricted to the domestic arena.[14] But their presence as producers of *literature* indicates the particular discursive space that literature provides, straddling public and private in intricate and interested ways, but ones in which the exact division is still to be negotiated.

In its critique of *1811*, the *Eclectic Review* alights on the poem's disciplinary transgression – displaying too much knowledge of the wrong kind and in the wrong way. I want to suggest that one way in which we might understand the critical failure of the poem – its out-of-placeness and its consequent exposures – is through its evident inability to observe the strictures of an emerging economy of knowledge, which has precise implications for the gendered division of intellectual labour. To this end, I want to look at Barbauld's work within, or more accurately *around*, one of the newly emerging disciplines – that of political economy. In some ways the choice of political economy is somewhat arbitrary, and at first sight marginal to the poem *1811*. Only in a loose sense does this text engage with issues in political economy; for instance, in its invocation of 'Commerce' as a self-propelling system, dissociated from any particular geographical or social location, able to abandon the shores of England for more hospitable American climes ('The golden tide of Commerce leaves thy shore' [line 62]). However, in this looser sense, *1811*, and many of Barbauld's other writings, do engage with issues that overlap with political economy. In the following discussion, I will consider the implications of the development of a discipline like political economy as a gendered discursive space. For Barbauld, I will suggest, this process of disciplinisation amounts to a stricter regulation of the divisions between private and public utterances, which not only has profound effects for a woman writer, but, as we shall see, also ruptures the organisation of Barbauld's moral universe. This enhanced separation of spheres is seen by her as a lamentable privatisation of the domestic world, which renders it no longer capable of having the political and public function that it holds in the earlier work. By looking at her

---

[14] Foucault's analysis of the epistemic turn is useful in considering the *Eclectic Review*'s accusation that Barbauld is a 'morbid anatomist'. This would put her on the side of Marie-François-Xavier Bichat, the French anatomist whose works Foucault held up as ushering in a new, modern understanding of the human body as an organic unit. On this see Michel Foucault, *The Birth of the Clinic*, trans. Alan Sheridan (London: Tavistock, 1973)

treatment of the idea of home, in the final part of the essay I shall examine Barbauld's sense of the political and moral implications of this division, its impact on the formation of the idea of the nation. It is this wresting of public from private that in 1811, I shall suggest, is held responsible for Britain's sorry decline.

That Barbauld only latterly became aware of the changing epistemological landscape is evident in a passing remark in her correspondence with Edgeworth. In September, 1817, she writes to Edgeworth, 'I am just entering on "Mrs Marcet's Conversations on Political Economy", a new subject for a lady's pen.'[15] Jane Marcet's educational works, her 'Conversations' on subjects as diverse as, for instance, chemistry, natural philosophy, the evidence of Christianity, and the history of England were enormously successful in the first half of the century.[16] Ostensibly for children, but also designed to address women, specifically mothers, the works introduced this amateur audience to the technicalities of the new disciplines. Her *Conversations on Political Economy*, first published in 1816, ran to five editions within the space of eight years and came to be recognised as an accomplished and standard introductory work on the subject. J.R. McCulloch, for instance, in his comprehensive bibliography of political economy, wrote in 1845 that this was 'on the whole, perhaps, the best introduction to the science that has yet appeared'.[17] Moreover, Marcet is the only female name to appear in McCulloch's compendious work.

In this sense, Barbauld's observation that political economy is a 'new subject for a lady's pen' is an accurate observation. In other senses, however, this passing remark jars. First, the implication, that Marcet was opening up the field to more female interventions, is not borne out by subsequent works. Although Harriet Martineau consciously followed in Marcet's footsteps with her multi-volumed *Illustrations of Political Economy* (1832–34), women seem to have contributed very little to the expanding field of works of political economy.[18] Second, Barbauld and her

15 Le Breton, *Memoir of Mrs Barbauld*, 178.
16 Jane Marcet, *Conversations on Chemistry* (1806), *Conversations on Natural Philosophy* (1819), *Conversations on the Evidence of Christianity* (1826), *Conversations on the History of England* (1842).
17 J.R. McCulloch, *The Literature of Political Economy* (London: Longman, Brown, Green and Longman, 1845), 18.
18 Martineau's works on political economy did not gain the recognition from political economists that Marcet's did. For instance, Martineau did not receive an entry in McCulloch's bibliography. Goldstrum speculates that this was be-

correspondent Edgeworth were already no strangers to the discipline of political economy themselves. Both women were immersed in an intellectual culture in which political economy and political economists played a major part. This is evident, for instance, from Barbauld's relations with T.R. Malthus, who had been educated at the Warrington Academy, the dissenting school at which Barbauld's parents had been teachers, and who maintained close ties with the family from then on.[19] Edgeworth had received a thorough education in political economy from her father, Richard Lovell Edgeworth. Both writers' works are steeped in ideas from political economy, even if they sometimes adopt a critical stance in relation to them. In this respect we might note Edgeworth's discussions of rent and land improvement in *Castle Rackrent* (1800); or Barbauld's critique of 'Enfeebling Luxury and ghastly Want' (*1811*, line 64) in poems such as *1811*, and 'West End Fair'; or, as Isobel Armstrong has recently shown, her critique of Malthusian population theory in 'Inscription for an Ice-House' or her prose piece, 'Dialogue in the Shade'.[20]

Even more pertinent in this context is the fact that Barbauld's immensely successful work for children, *Evenings at Home* (1793), co-written with her brother, John Aikin, incorporates episodes illustrating themes from political economy. For instance, in volume one, we find 'A Dialogue on Different Situations in Life', a conversation in which Mrs

<hr />

cause of Martineau's Unitarian background. He also argues that the impact of both writers was much more limited than is sometimes claimed. Neither 'achieved anything like "household name" status', he argues, and both were overshadowed by the introductory works of Richard Whately which, by mid-century, had become part of the school curriculum. See Max Goldstrum, 'Popular Political Economy and the British Working-Class Reader in the Nineteenth Century', in *Expository Science: Forms and Functions of Popularisation*, ed. T. Shin and R. Whitley (Dordecht: D. Reidel, 1985), pp. 263–7. Symptomatically, Donald Winch, in his index to *Riches and Poverty: An Intellectual History of Political Economy in Britain, 1750–1834* (Cambridge: Cambridge University Press, 1996), makes an interesting hybrid of 'Harriet Marcet'.

19 See Donald Winch, *Riches and Poverty*, 255.

20 Isobel Armstrong, 'The Gush of the Feminine: How Can We Read Women's Poetry of the Romantic Period?', in *Romantic Women Writers: Voices and Countervoices*, ed. Paula R. Feldman and Theresa M. Kelley (Hanover, NH: University Press of New England, 1995), 13–32. For the context of Barbauld's critique of Malthus, see also Josephine McDonagh, 'Infanticide and the Boundaries of Culture, from Hume to Arnold', in *Inventing Maternity: Politics Science and Literature 1650–1865*, ed. Carol Barash and Susan Greenwood (Lexington, Kentucky: University of Kentucky Press, forthcoming, 1998).

Meanwell explains to her daughter, Sally, the nature of wealth and inheritance, the function of poor relief, and the greater virtues of industry and charity; in volume two, there is a conversation 'On Manufactures' between Father and Henry; and in volume three, 'The Landlord's Visit, a Drama', which dramatises the precept that 'good tenants deserve good landlords'.[21] Together these episodes teach the rudiments of economic exchange, production and consumption, and establish connections between wealth, social class and moral virtue, as the middle-class values of industry and sobriety, charity and quiescence are extolled. Thus Mrs Meanwell convinces her daughter of her moral advantages, over those of her daughter's aristocratic friend, the daughter of Sir Thomas, recipient of inherited wealth. 'Let it dwell upon your mind, so as to make you cheerful and contented in your station', she urges, 'which is so much happier than that of many and many other children.'[22]

While the strong moral agenda of Aikin and Barbauld's *Evenings at Home* is less evident in Marcet's work, there are striking similarities between the two works in their use of the Socratic form, in their episodic structure, and pedagogic content.[23] Given the popularity of *Evenings at Home*, it is hard to believe that Marcet was not aware of it when developing her own characteristic conversational form as a mode through which to instruct the uninitiated in political economy. *Evenings at Home* was of course a co-authored work, and indeed it is not the case that all the episodes on political economy themes were penned by Barbauld's 'lady's pen': Lucy Aikin in her memoir of her aunt corrects what she purports to be a widely held view, that all the contributions to *Evenings at Home* were by Barbauld, and lists only fourteen – including 'On Manufactures' – of the ninety-nine pieces as hers.[24] Nevertheless, despite this, the prominence of pieces on themes in political economy in this work in which Barbauld had a significant hand suggests a certain

21 John Aikin and Anna Letitia Barbauld, *Evenings at Home: or, the Juvenile Budget Opened, Consisting of a variety of Miscellaneous Pieces for Instruction and Amusement of Young Persons*, 6 vols (10th edition; London: Joseph Johnson, 1814), 3: 15.
22 Ibid., 1: 61.
23 On children's literature in this period, see Alan Richardson, *Literature, Education and Romanticism: Reading as Social Practice, 1780–1832* (Cambridge: Cambridge University Press, 1994), ch. 3, esp. 127–42.
24 Barbauld, *The Works of Anna Letitia Barbauld with a Memoir by Lucy Aikin*, 2 vols (London: Longman, Hurst, Rees, Orme, Browne, and Green, 1825), 1: xxxvi–xxxvii.

kind of forgetting on her part when she declares political economy to be 'a new subject for a lady's pen'.

Marcet's work, and Barbauld's recognition of it, however, coincided with a new phase in the growth of the discipline of political economy. The development of political economy as an academic subject can be located at around this time. Malthus's appointment to a chair in political economy in 1805, at the newly established college of the East India Company at Haileybury, marked the first use of political economy to designate an academic office, and demonstrated the discipline's growing prestige; this was further enhanced by the establishment of the Political Economy Club in 1821. Alongside its new institutional status, as Noel Thompson has observed, political economy also gained popularity in the post-war period with a general, unspecialised readership, as society saw the emergence of new economic phenomena which could not be explained in terms of local or natural factors: the activities of bad employers, or harvest failures, wars or plagues, 'factors exogenous to the functioning of the economic system'. In the early nineteenth century, Thompson argues, it became apparent that 'it was not shortage of physical produce which caused hardship . . . but rather the fact that markets were glutted with products which could not secure adequate remuneration for their producers'.[25] Hence political economy provided a widely endorsed explanation for social effects in the post- war period, both for middle-class and working-class audiences. Marcet's work, therefore, was timely in that it provided popular education in a subject of growing relevance to daily life – but also, paradoxically, a subject that was becoming increasingly specialised, abstract, and separate from the kinds of social effects it sought to explain. Indeed, one could see Marcet's work of popularisation as an adjunct to the discipline's new sense of itself as a discrete subject – a specialism, in need of interpretation and mediation.

Marcet's work as a female disseminator of the subject – addressing a distinctly female and infant readership – came at a time when the discipline was becoming institutionalised in ways that, in fact, initiated a more formal exclusion of women, as both producers and consumers of economic knowledge. Barbauld's passing comment, that Marcet wrote on 'a new subject for a woman's pen', thus marks this moment of women's exclusion from the subject in its institutionalised form – from

[25] Noel W. Thompson, *The People's Science: The Popular Political Economy of Exploitation and Crisis 1816–1834* (Cambridge: Cambridge University Press, 1984), 56–7. See also Winch, *Riches and Poverty*, ch. 13.

the universities and the Political Economy Club, for instance. Barbauld's comment demonstrates a recognition of a new specialisation in the fields of knowledge that had specific implications for women writers. For the developing academisation, or professionalisation of the disciplines brought with it the increasing separation of spheres and what was imagined as an increasing confinement of women to the private realm of the domestic.

The fundamental irreconcilability of private and public, domestic and national, within the development of political economy, was a problem of wider scope than might at first be apparent. While its original conceptual model was that of the household economy, as is reflected in the derivation of the word economics from the Greek term for the household, οιχοσ, nevertheless, in its developed form, it engendered a conflict between domestic or private interests and those of the state and the larger society.[26] As Kurt Heinzelman points out, while the economic theorists of the late eighteenth and early nineteenth centuries modelled 'economic production on a household that attains self-sufficiency primarily by means of agricultural labour', they also conceptualised economic consumption on a model of 'individualistic decision-making within a society of duly constituted individuals acting in generally similar, self-interested ways'.[27] The mutual co-operation implicit in the model of production was thus fundamentally at odds with the idea of the competitive market place in which individuals were motivated only by self interest. The moral problem presented by political economy, then, emerged out of the conflict between domestic mutuality and an aggressively individualistic market place. This structure of antagonism is repeated in many other aspects of eighteenth-century and early nineteenth-century culture, in particular in the long tradition of civic humanism that it inherited, in which individuals were considered at risk from the corrupt state.[28]

This intellectual context is useful for understanding an increasingly intense anxiety in Barbauld's work around the divisions between public

---

26 See J.G.A. Pocock, 'The Mobility of Property and the Rise of Eighteenth-Century Sociology', in *Virtue, Commerce, and History: Essays on Political Thought and History, Chiefly in the Eighteenth Century* (Cambridge: Cambridge University Press, 1985), 103 ff.

27 Heinzelman, 'The Cult of Domesticity: Dorothy and William Wordsworth at Grasmere', in Anne K. Mellor (ed.), *Romanticism and Feminism* (Indiana: Indiana University Press, 1988), 58.

28 Pocock, *Virtue, Commerce and History*, 43–45, 70–71, 114 ff.

and private. In her political writings, it is this division that she holds responsible for the political and moral problems of the state. In 'Sins of the Government, Sins of the Nation' (1793), for instance, her response to England's declaration of war against the French Republic in February of the same year, she writes: 'the united will of a whole people cannot make wrong right, or sanction one act of rapacity, injustice, or breach of faith. The first principle, therefore, we must lay down is, that we are to submit our public conduct to the same rules by which we are to regulate our private actions . . .[29] What has been lost, and must be retrieved, is a fundamental congruity between private and public action.

This separation of private and public acts represented a rupture in Barbauld's moral universe. For her, the domestic provided a model for conceptualising social and economic relations within the nation, and beyond. In Hymn VIII of *Hymns in Prose for Children* (1781), she presents a picture of the cosmos, beginning with the 'cottage of the labourer covered with warm thatch'. Scanning the scene, we are next introduced to 'the mother [who] is spinning at the door; the young children [who] sport before her on the grass; . . . the father [who] worketh to provide them food. . . . The father is the master (of the family).' This harmonious family unit then provides the basic social building block for the construction of a wider society: '[m]any homes are built together'; '[i]f there are many houses, it is a town – it is governed by a magistrate', who within the symmetry of the vision, occupies the same position as the father. The town is both the aggregate of many families, and an enlarged version of the family. On the same basis, she envisages a kingdom made up of many towns, and a universe made up of many kingdoms, over which God rules like the father, the magistrate or the king over each of their respective domains. 'All are God's family', she goes on, returning us to the beginning, to the first and basic unit in the construction of the cosmos. This is a patriarchal universe, founded on a clear continuity and congruence between the domestic sphere and the public world of affairs of state, and religious belief. Significantly, there is no sense of a market or a developed economy here, except in the blandest sense of 'buy[ing] and sell[ing]' on the village green. Rather, what is represented is an agrarian society in which families are virtually self-sufficient.[30]

Barbauld returns to the idea of home in many of her poems, most

---

[29] *Works* 2:387. See J.E. Cookson, *The Friends of Peace: Anti-War Liberalism in England, 1793–1815* (Cambridge: Cambridge University Press, 1982), ch. 4.
[30] Barbauld, *Hymns in Prose for Children* (London: Joseph Johnson, 1781), 53–62.

famously perhaps in 'Washing-Day' (1797), a text that manages to find poetic material in the most mundane of domestic activities. Frequently it is the representative capacity of the home that interests her – its function as the basis for an exploration of wider social and political concerns. This is the case in her poem, 'To a Great Nation' (1793), the 'Nation' in question being France, on the occasion of the invasion of the new republic led by the Duke of Brunswick in September 1792. Although Britain had at this stage not yet declared war with France, nevertheless, Barbauld's continuing support for the revolution is striking at a time when general British opinion had turned against it. The point at issue here, is not, however, Barbauld's political allegiances; rather, more simply, her utilisation of the rhetorical category of the home. In the poem, Barbauld calls on France to '[r]ise', and '[s]trike hordes of Despots to the ground' (line 4) in order that it might 'rise – the model of the world' (line 36).[31] The focus of attention is the different ways in which the nation is represented and the kinds of transformations it must undergo to achieve this representative- 'model'-status: first it is a '*Briareus*',[32] a many-armed monster, crushing its enemies; then, after a period of penitence ('wash with sad repentant tears, / Each deed that clouds they glory's page' [lines 21–2]), it is transformed into an altogether more domestic image, as the arms of the monster are transformed into the arms of a mother, embracing 'wretched outcasts where they roam/ . . . / O call the child of Misery home' (lines 26–8). This 'home' then becomes a mausoleum, as they 'build the tomb' for those 'who bled in freedom's cause' (lines 29–30); a site of national mourning through which can be established the 'antient [sic] laws' of the state. In the end, in this more maternal and domestic cast, national and domestic values are conjoined, and the home, as the nation, achieves a representative capacity – 'thy tide of glory stay'd / . . . thy conquering banners furl'd, / Obey the laws thyself has made, / and rise – a model for the world' (lines 33–36).

In other poems, however, this reassembling of domestic and national, or private and public, is not effected; instead they are wrested apart, or come into conflict with each other. Her undated poem 'The Baby-house' is interesting in this respect.[33] The poem begins by admiring

---

31 All citations from the poems are from McCarthy and Kraft, eds, *Poems*.

32 '*Briareus* was a giant of ancient fable, represented with a hundred hands, and fifty heads.' Barbauld's note, reprinted in McCarthy and Kraft, 292.

33 McCarthy and Kraft remain uncertain as to the date of the poem, but suggest that it came after 'The Wake of the King of Spain' which they tentatively date

the 'baby-house' – or doll's house – of 'Dear Agatha', with its tiny luxu-
ries, its 'velvet couch', 'tiny cups' and 'sugared meat'. But what begins as
a miniature emblem of domestic bliss and bourgeois comfort is appropriated in the course of the poem by national cultures to become a means of
oppression of the poor and a tool for class division. As a toy, the Baby-
house is a totally different kind of 'model' to that of the home in 'To a
Great Nation'. Thus, the Egyptian pyramid, built by 'some mighty
nation's toil', is a 'baby-house to lodge the dead'. The baby-house of Ver-
sailles is nothing but a 'dome[. . .] of pomp and folly', the luxurious adjunct of a state in which 'The peasant faints beneath his load, / Nor
tastes the grain his hands have sowed.' And finally, the poem claims that
'Baby-houses oft appear / On British ground, of prince or peer':

> Where are they now?
> Gone to the hammer or the plough:
> Then trees, the pride of ages, fall,
> And naked stands the pictured wall;
> And treasured coins from distant lands
> Must feel the touch of sordid hands;
> And gems, of classic stores the boast,
> Fall to the cry of – Who bids most?
> Then do not, Agatha, repine
> That cheaper Baby-house is thine.   (lines 45–54)

Ultimately, the trappings of luxury are transient, will fall into decay, will
be wrested back into circulation ('gone to the hammer' of the auction-
eer), 'naked' and soiled. The decline of the baby-house in these final
lines is represented in striking terms as a kind of exposure, almost a sexual violation ('naked' and 'touched by sordid hands'), as the small domestic model is dissipated and recirculated back on the market. Agatha's
modest, or 'cheaper' baby-house, therefore, presents a preferable image
of moderation, but it is one in which the domestic has no public, or national face.

    What is described in these visions of national degeneracy is precisely
the opposite of the moral universe of the *Hymns*, and of what is achieved
in 'To a Great Nation'. Here – even though the home has only representative status and exists only as a model – it is divested of its representative capacity to become an empty emblem. No continuity is envisaged

---

c.1819. The post-1811 date for 'The Baby-house' would, however, suggest a progressive disillusionment with the possibility of reassembling private and public.

between the domestic and the national; it can only function as a sign of material excess and moral corruption.

A similar kind of disjunction between domestic and national domains is evident in 1811. Indeed, the crux of the poem is the realisation that the nation state in fact is responsible for the hardships of domestic life during the war: Britain must share a responsibility in the effects of the war ('Thou who has shared the guilt must share the woe' [line 46]). The 'woe[s]' represented throughout the poem are located in a feminine, natural, and specifically domestic realm, and are exacted by a masculine aggressor: 'famine', 'disease and rapine' are 'called' by 'man', the 'sword not the sickle, reaps the harvest now' and soldiers are seen as taking the 'scant supply' from the peasant, who 'retires to die' (lines 15ff.). The most striking images in the first passages of the poem are of the needless productivities of nature ('[b]ounteous in vain' [line 11]) and women ('[f]ruitful in vain,' [lines 23 and 27]): women's sons, brothers, husbands are slaughtered, their bodies like 'fallen blossoms strew a foreign strand' (line 26). Described here is something close to a Malthusian vision, in which excessive productivity brings only death in (for Malthus) a natural process of realignment between lives and resources. For Barbauld, on the contrary, the emphasis is on men's agency in war, rather than a natural or inevitable overproductivity.[34]

Rather than resolving this conflict between men and nations, on the one hand, and women and nature on the other, Barbauld predicts only their continuing disjunction and the continuing ruin of Britain – '[t]he worm is in thy core, thy glories pass away' (line 314). Instead, focus is shifted to the New World, whence the 'spirit' or 'genius' takes 'his awful form' (line 324) and can flourish. Britain remains scarred by its inability to realign national and domestic values. Images of disjunction abound in the poem: families are riven by a war in which men die in foreign lands; wealth has been accumulated through gathering 'gems' from 'the East' (line 307); luxurious but unnatural goods, like 'summer ices' and the 'winter rose' (line 306), abound; 'commerce' departs, leaving behind 'crime' and 'fraud', and 'grandeur' for the few in the midst of 'the mass of misery' (line 320). All of these images are ones that suggest profound disorder, as people and things are taken from their natural enviornment, or mixed in unnatural combinations. Within this disordered universe, there is no possibility of finding the cohesive symmetries of her moral universe described in the *Hymns*.

---

[34] On Barbauld's critique of Malthus, see n. 19 above.

Many of these images are ones which describe a kind of spatial disjunction: for instance, the splitting of families and the separation of mothers from their sons. This kind of dispersal, we might note, has some affinities with the structure of political economy, in which material effects such as hunger and poverty are explained in terms of geographically and conceptually remote economic causes. This kind of dissociation between local effects and their roots in the disinterested and abstract mechanisms of the market is one that in Barbauld's way of thinking would endorse the division between public and private; it makes the domestic household the inevitable and, to a degree, irrelevant, consequence of the larger abstract system, rather than, in her moral universe, the representative unit of social order, the basis of public life.

The importance of the domestic in Barbauld's work should not be under-estimated. Paul Hamilton rightly points out the optimistic cast of her cosmopolitan patriotism expressed in the poem, that 'the alternative [to 'self-serving nationalistic modes'] is to free identity from a fixed patriotism and tie it instead to a cultural centre of gravity that will settle wherever civilization renews itself'.[35] Within this we should remain aware of the structural necessity of the domestic unit in relation to the wider conception of the public and the national.

One of the many responses to the poem was Anne Grant's *1813: A Poem in Two Parts* (1814), designed as a specific rejoinder to Barbauld's 'unpatriotic' poem. One of its striking features is its reaggregation of the domestic and the national: for Grant, the family and the household regain the representative function within the conceptualisation of the nation that is lost in *1811*. Thus unlike Barbauld's uselessly productive mothers, Grant envisages a world populated by British babies, spawned from the great maternal body of the nation:

> Her children spread o'er Earth's remote extremes,
> Or by Columbia's lakes, or Ganges' streams,
> Whether they serve, or suffer, or command,
> Led by the Genius of their native land,
> Shall at their country's hallow'd altars bend,
> And truth and freedom o'er the world extend.[36]

---

[35] Paul Hamilton, 'The New Romanticism: Philosophical Stand-ins in English Romantic Discourse', *Textual Practice* 11 no. 1 (1997): 109–132, 127.
[36] Grant, *Eighteen Hundred and Thirteen: A Poem in Two Parts* (Edinburgh, 1814), 62.

The nation as a mother, no longer 'fruitful in vain', is the effective agent of colonisation, her offspring exporting national values to the 'remote extremes' of the world. Grant's form of maternal nationalism can be seen in a tradition of patriotic poetry written by women throughout the century, such as Felicia Hemans and Adelaide Proctor.[37]

For Barbauld, in 1811, however, this maternal role is sadly not available. The intellectual, social and political conditions for the domestic to maintain this representative capacity have, in her eyes, been lost. It amounts to a kind of displacing of women from a domestic function that provides a model for social relations, to one that is nothing other than a totally privatised one. This privatisation of the home is in fact an aspect of the degeneracy that she diagnoses in the state of the nation.

To a certain degree, therefore, we might agree with the *Eclectic Review*'s estimation that the poem is 'unfilial', for it recognised the decline of the domestic sphere in relation to the conceptualisation of the national. If Barbauld does kill the mother-nation through her morbid anatomising, as the review suggests, she does so because she finds her already dead – that is, in a context in which the representative bond between domestic and national, private and public has been broken; in which, in a sense, the domestic has lost its meaning. The severe criticisms of 1811 thus come in a context which is characterised by this splitting of private and public, in which women's voices in the public sphere will sound only shrill and shrewish. They mark a particular stage in the negotiation of public and private, and of the proper place for women. They also provide insight into the complex construction of the domestic ideology as it takes shape in the early decades of the nineteenth century, the conservative uses of which have been widely explored. Barbauld's works, however, remind us that shadowing this is a much more radical conception of the domestic.

---

37 There are evident links between this kind of maternal nationalism and the proto-eugenic arguments of the 1880s and 1890s in which women's role is defined specifically in terms of their reproductive capacity, to populate the empire with fine English bodies. See Anna Davin, 'Imperialism and Motherhood', *History Workshop Journal* 5 (spring 1978): 9–65; Sally Ledger, *The New Woman: Fiction and Feminism at the Fin de Siècle* (Manchester: Manchester University Press, 1997), ch. 3.

Commodities Among Themselves:
Reading/Desire in Early Women's Magazines

SONIA HOFKOSH

> It has to be made clear from the outset that consumption is an active form of relationship (not only to objects, but also to society and to the world), a mode of systemic activity and global response which founds our entire cultural system.
>
> Jean Baudrillard, *The System of Objects*[1]

I WANT TO BEGIN this discussion of the function of women's consumption in a romantic cultural system by juxtaposing two very different scenes of economic proliferation. In the first, from William Wordsworth's 1805 *The Prelude*, the poet describes his experience of London's 'endless stream of men and moving things':

> Here, there, and everywhere, a weary throng,
> The Comers and the Goers face to face –
> Face after face – the string of dazzling Wares,
> Shop after shop, with Symbols, blazoned Names,
> And all the Tradesman's honours overhead:
> Here, fronts of houses, like a title-page
> With letters huge inscribed from top to toe
> Stationed above the door, like guardian Saints.[2]

Signs taken for wonders, one after the other. Dazzled, the poet appears very nearly overwhelmed ('escaped as from an enemy', line 185) by sheer number and activity and desire ('the wealth, the bustle, and the eagerness', line 161), by the perceptual commingling of persons and commodities. This is a picture of 'a too busy world' (1850, line 150) that in Wordsworth's famous sonnet 'is too much with us'.

> The world is too much with us; late and soon,
> Getting and spending, we lay waste our powers:

---

[1] Jean Baudrillard, *The System of Objects*, trans. James Benedict (London: Verso, 1996), 199.
[2] William Wordsworth, *The Prelude*, ed. Mork L. Reed (Ithaca: Cornell University Press, 1991), Book 7, lines 158; 171–77.

> Little we see in Nature that is ours;
> We have given our hearts away, a sordid boon!

Such a representation of the world of and as commerce might be understood, in the terms of Robert Sayre and Michael Löwy, to figure Romanticism in its anti-capitalist spirit.[3] The poet laments the waste of power, the sordid excess which characterize the culture of accumulation. Further, he ambivalently perceives his own participation in the 'weary throng', registered in *The Prelude* passage in the huge letters on the houses that look 'like a title-page', at once depicting his own authorial aspirations (a blazoned name, and honour) and dwarfing them. Some lines later, the author's investment in commercial culture can also be read as writing on the wall.

> Here files of ballads dangle from dead walls;
> Advertisements, of giant-size, from high
> Press forward, in all colours, on the sight;
> These, bold in conscious merit; lower down,
> That, fronted with a most imposing word,
> Is, peradventure, one in masquerade.   (lines 209–14)

Pressed, depressed, dispossessed ('little we see . . . that is ours'), he resents the implication of aesthetic forms – symbols, ballads, title-pages, his own poetic words – in the purely material exchanges that alienate the heart, compromise the honour, press on the sight, and so overwhelm individual consciousness that the poet, looking up at 'giant-size' advertisements, must also behold himself belittled there, in a posture not unlike that of the 'travelling Cripple, by the trunk cut short', 'already met elsewhere', face (after face) 'turned up' looking at him (lines 216–19). In the writing on this wall, dead letters, yet exerting pressure, so 'imposing' – 'all too legible'[4] – the poet reads his own diminished stature in an economy of proliferation, a world too much.

---

3   Robert Sayre and Michael Löwy, 'Figures of Romantic Anticapitalism', *Spirits of Fire: English Romanticism and Contemporary Historical Methods*, eds G.A. Russo and Daniel P. Watkins (Rutherford, NJ: Fairleigh Dickinson University Press, 1990), 23–68. See also Michael Ferber's contribution to that volume, 'Romantic Anticapitalism: A Response to Sayre and Löwy' (69–84), which notes that 'the question of romanticism's resistance to, vulnerability to, and even collaboration with commodification remains (I think) to be explored' and suggests that one way to begin that exploration might be to look at the history of consumption (80).
4   Mary Jacobus, 'The Writing on the Wall', *Romanticism, Writing, and Sexual Difference: Essays on 'The Prelude'* (Oxford: Clarendon Press, 1989), 3–32; 21.

The second passage I want to look at briefly is a vision that transforms proliferation into its own kind of abundant recompense. In 'Commodities among Themselves', Luce Irigaray imagines the 'economy of abundance' that could obtain if women, who systematically function as transactive objects in patriarchal culture, enacted ' "another" kind of commerce, among themselves':

> Exchanges without identifiable terms, without accounts, without end . . . Without additions and accumulations, one plus one, woman after woman . . . Without sequence or number. Without standard or yardstick. *Red blood* and *sham* would no longer be differentiated by deceptive envelopes concealing their worth. Use and exchange would be indistinguishable. The greatest value would be at the same time the least kept in reserve. Nature's resources would be expended without depletion, exchanged without labor, freely given, exempt from masculine transactions: enjoyment without a fee, well-being without pain, pleasure without possession.[5]

As much as in Wordsworth's experience of the metropolis as marketplace, Irigaray's commercial phantasmagoria imbricates the constitutive economic, libidinal, and linguistic exchanges which shape (and might reshape) the social order.[6] Envisioning relations among women in a liberatory economy of excess, Irigaray theorizes the possibility of a 'too much' ('without end'; 'woman after woman') that would be enough to erase the very distinctions ('identifiable terms') that the dazzled Wordsworth loses sight of in the midst of the throng of faces, shops, and advertisements of London: between the person ('red blood') and the commodity masquerade ('sham'). In this vision ('utopia? perhaps') such erasure is the modality of desubjugation. Women, giving their hearts away, reclaim themselves as speaking, desiring, consuming subjects.

Intimations of some sort of shared anti-capitalist conception or concern, even despite the significant differences dividing the English Romantic poet's work from the French feminist philosopher's (among which are those of time and place and genre), can be discerned in the

---

[5] Luce Irigaray, *This Sex Which Is Not One*, trans. Catherine Porter (Ithaca: Cornell University Press, 1985), 196–97.
[6] For a discussion of the implications of this feminized economy for a sexual politics, see Elizabeth Grosz, 'The Hetero and the Homo: The Sexual Ethics of Luce Irigaray', *Engaging with Irigaray: Feminist Philosophy and Modern European Thought*, eds Carolyn Burke, Naomi Schor, Margaret Whitford (New York: Columbia University Press, 1994), 335–50.

verbal echoes resonating between them ('shop after shop' . . . 'woman after woman'). Such echoes as I hear them reverberating back from Irigary's text to Wordsworth's provoke a series of questions. One, about the historical development of the kind of structures of individuality and desire that Wordsworth's poetry posits, structures that are based as much on the exchanges (or exchangeability) of the person (the coming and the going; the getting and the spending; the seer as the seen; commodities among themselves) as on the writing that traces those circulations into narrative. Two, about the specific embeddedness of those psychologized structures in the empire of capital and consumption emerging through the eighteenth and nineteenth centuries and into the twentieth.[7] Three, about the effects of and consequences for gender and sexuality in relation to that emergence.

I juxtapose Irigaray's female economy of abundance with Wordsworth's considerably more anxious if also equally dazzling spectacle of urban commerce not exactly to draw a line from one to the other or to propose an explicit historical relation between them, however askew. I put the feminist's suggestive fantasy of women on the market next to the poet's uneasy sojourn there in order to evoke in our reading of Romantic writing the possibility that is implicit in Irigaray's vision: the possibility of looking from a different perspective at Romantic formulations of identity in the making of the (capitalist) world that is still with us, at the same time that we see how those formulations offer an ('utopian? perhaps') alternative to this world's coersive ('bold'; 'imposing') commodity culture. While one might surely construe the ideological momentum activating the writing of these two passages to be wholly unrelated if not at odds, it is perhaps through such peculiar, incidental couplings that powerful logics such as the one I want to explore can be challenged or revised. For the possibility of reading from the perspective of the commodity, as fanciful as that may seem, means that we can look at the practices of consumption ('getting and spending') as 'an active form of relationship', rather than simply as a laying waste of power; it means that we can consider the role of women in the emerging entrepreneurial dynamics of industrial capitalism, not only attending to 'some

7   Colin Campbell has offered one theory of the relation between romantic individualism and consumerism in *The Romantic Ethic and the Spirit of Modern Consumerism* (Oxford: Basil Blackwell, 1987). Also see Campbell's 'Understanding Traditional and Modern Patterns of Consumption in Eighteenth-Century England: A Character-Action Approach', *Consumption and the World of Goods* (see note 9), 40–57, which to some extent summarizes his earlier argument.

female Vendor' (line 198), whose shrill cry thrills the poet in the streets of London, but also to other discourses of desire articulated through the public sphere.

If it is not until the mid-nineteenth century, in the view of Thomas Richards in *The Commodity Culture of Victorian England*, that advertisers begin to become 'the minstrels of capitalism' and advertisements 'a distinctively capitalist form of representation',[8] the wandering poet of Wordsworth's *The Prelude* – 'peradventure, one in masquerade' – already registers the effects of the commercialization taking conspicuous place through the eighteenth century, as John Brewer, Neil McKendrick, and J.H. Plumb have established in *The Birth of a Consumer Society*, and many others have substantiated.[9] Following the poet as he surveys commodity culture in various of its textual or aesthetic embodiments, but with considerably less agoraphobia than he experiences, I want to shift, as he reluctantly does, the direction of our attention 'from high' to 'lower down'. I will be looking here not to Nature for the primary location and the legacy of Romanticism – that sense of self which is properly ours; nor do I want to focus on 'the trademan's honours' blazoned 'overhead' as the paradigmatic sign of a sordid commercial world that is too much with us. I want to look rather at a version of what the poet will later call the 'trivial objects' (1850; line 703) of 'men and moving things' that circulate through this commercial world, at the commonplace interaction of consumer and commodity, in order to explore the way Romantic aesthetics – an aesthetics of the subject, the individual, of being – is installed as, contends with, and accommodates itself to, a culture of consumption – a world of goods. This shift does not only highlight what troubles the poet so much in the conjunction of 'men and things' – faces that turn into shops, names that function as

8   Thomas Richards, *The Commodity Culture of Victorian England: Advertising and Spectacle, 1851–1914* (Stanford: Stanford University Press, 1990), 1; 12.

9   *The Birth of a Consumer Society: The Commercialization of Eighteenth-Century England*, eds Neil McKendrick, John Brewer, and J.H. Plumb (Bloomington: Indiana University Press, 1982). Recent work on early modes of consumption and (pre)capitalist formations by historians and scholars in a range of disciplines can be represented by the massive project on 'Culture and Consumption in the Seventeenth and Eighteenth Centuries' that issued in three volumes, to which I will have occasion to refer later in the essay: *Consumption and the World of Goods*, eds John Brewer and Roy Porter (London: Routledge, 1993); *The Consumption of Culture, 1600–1800: Image, Object, Text*, eds Ann Bermingham and John Brewer (London: Routledge, 1995); *Early Modern Conceptions of Property*, eds John Brewer and Susan Staves (London: Routledge, 1996).

advertisement, the subject conscious only of the endless pursuit of objects. Such a shift also points to what the age of Wordsworth shares with what McKendrick would call instead the age of Wedgwood: an entrepreneurial spirit that capitalizes on the motivations and mystifications of individual desire.

William Wordsworth the poet and Josiah Wedgwood the potter were alike producers, one interested in the reproduction of the common language of men as high art, the other in the reproduction of art into the material of the everyday, art for which any (monied) man might speak. Both propose to create the taste – for poetry or porcelain – by which they will be appreciated and their own cultural worth will accumulate. But here I am concerned with the way producers necessarily operate in the context of consumption, producing and consuming as 'aspects of a single cultural process',[10] and especially with the way women in particular function as consumers of literary and other goods and are thus read into or read the cultural economy that determines the integral properties – the meaning and value, the heart – of the world of 'men and things'. The shift I thus make, then, is from the entrepreneurial discourse of individualist production that either Wordsworth's poetics or Wedgwood's promotional strategies might be taken to exemplify for the period to the discourse of consumption in the early women's magazines of the late eighteenth and early nineteenth centuries. The magazines are indeed 'trivial objects' that nonetheless, or, rather, that therefore, provide one site for an exploration of an economy – and its attendant ideologies – in the process of formation. The magazines, stores of print, instantiate that process at the same time that they delineate, perhaps only at their inception, a potential counter or alternative to that process that is embedded in its history.

The evocative metaphor implicit in the title of the book, *The Birth of a Consumer Society*, indeed suggests that in the history of commercial culture women have been understood as so fundamental to the dynamic of consumption that the specificities of their involvement in that dynamic have until recently gone unexamined. Amanda Vickery has argued that 'historians have dismissed women's dealings with material things as a category of leisure, domestic material culture as an arena of female vanity, not skill, and shopping a degraded female hobby, not unpaid work'.[11] Female consumers have for the most part been conceived

---

10 T.H. Breen, 'The Meanings of Things: Interpreting the Consumer Economy in the Eighteenth Century', *Consumption and the World of Goods*, 249–260; 250.
11 Amanda Vickery, 'Women and the World of Goods: A Lancashire Con-

as 'decorative appendages confined to the private' sphere (Vickery, 295), primarily passive in the exchange between 'men and things', their desires innate or, even, pathological, rather than interested, emulative rather than engaged, buying what comes naturally to them as feminine bodies rather than making conscious choices. The early women's magazines I want to look at here complicate this conception of women as merely passive consumers, conflated with the commodities they don't really know why they buy. The very notions of leisure, vanity, hobbies, or decoration that are associated with femininity and the private sphere and therefore considered 'trivial' in the historical account of capital expansion are themselves informed in the magazines by issues of class and national as well as gender politics.

For example, a series of letters to the Editor of *The British Lady's Magazine*, called 'The French Revolution in Dress', frames its critique of the excesses of women's contemporary fashion as a crisis of national proportion, and its irony, like all irony, reaches beyond its avowed target of feminine frivolity. Published in 1815 in the first volume of *The British Lady's Magazine*, 'The French Revolution in Dress' ridicules English women's adoption of the latest French style of dress by depicting as if in a dream its clashing colors and exaggerated forms: the bonnet, resembling 'a reasonable tower', is light blue with pink ribbons and black feathers; the dress, yellow-green, with 'so many plaits, fillings, and stuffings' that the writer supposes that the wearer must be deformed. As it thus describes this 'gaudy' outfit in the detailed terms of aesthetics or taste, however, it links fashion not only to recent political events, but to matters of 'public policy' such as the interests of British manufacturers. A woman's choice of clothing, her fashion statement, also says something about the very fabric of the national and economic system.

Another contribution to *The British Lady's Magazine* which may be more familiar is Mary Lamb's letter to the Editor, 'On Needlework'. Writing as 'Sempronia', Lamb recognizes that one woman's merely 'lady-like amusement' is also at the same time another woman's means to earn a living wage. She argues that women who can afford to should employ a seamstress rather than do their own sewing at home. It is an argument that situates the feminine domestic work of the needle outside in the marketplace, fundamentally connected to political concerns about labor practices and gender inequities.[12] *The British Lady's Magazine*

sumer and Her Possessions, 1751–81', *Consumption and the World of Goods*, 274–301; 277.

[12] On the political position of Lamb's essay, see Jane Aaron, ' "On Needle-

and other early women's periodicals in fact implicitly address their women readers as active agents in a developing cultural economy, their consumption, like production, fully significant in the public sphere, even when all they do is put on a dress or sit at home and sew. One of the main points here is to remark the productive potential of the consumer that is a basic assumption of the early women's magazines. It is to suggest that instead of privileging the scene of production or the single, empowered producer – whether Wordsworth or Wedgwood – as the unique source of values in our account of early capitalism and of the (Romantic) texts that emerged out of its boon, sordid or otherwise, we recognize the consumption that is itself ' "cultural work", productive of "cultural capital", and grist for cultural "resistance" '.[13]   Further, if 'demand, hence consumption, [is] an aspect of the overall political economy of societies',[14] we also have to recognize the formative function of women' s desire – that historically, 'the acquisition of goods by women in this economy was an assertive act, a declaration of agency'.[15]

As *The Lady's Monthly Museum* put it in 1798, that magazine was intended as an antidote to 'the indolent habit of loitering away time in an unprofitable manner': reading the magazine was itself, in effect, a kind of woman's work, the labour of her leisure, inseparable from the consideration of profit and loss, power and waste, that ramifies through the culture of capital, in the public sphere as well as in the private, through the logic of production as well as consumption, linking those logics and so reconceiving the gendered terms conventionally elaborated to distinguish them.[16] We might see the women's magazines, then, not as

work": Protest and Contradiction in Mary Lamb's Essay', *Romanticism and Feminism*, ed. Anne K. Mellor (Bloomington: Indiana University Press, 1988), 167–84.
[13] Jean-Christophe Agnew, 'Coming Up For Air: Consumer Culture in Historical Perspective', *Consumption and the World of Goods*, 19–39; 30. Agnew is here drawing on the work of anthropologist Daniel Miller in *Material Culture and Mass Consumption* (Oxford: Basil Blackwell, 1987).
[14] Arjun Appadurai, 'Introduction: Commodities and the Politics of Value', *The Social Life of Things: Commodities in Cultural Perspective*, ed. Arjun Appadurai (Cambridge: Cambridge University Press, 1986), 3–63; 29.
[15] T.H. Breen, 'The Meaning of Things', 257.
[16] For a discussion of the gendering of public and private spheres, especially as those terms are developed in the work of Jürgen Habermas, see Joan B. Landes, *Women and the Public Sphere in the Age of the French Revolution* (Ithaca: Cornell University Press, 1988), and 'The Public and the Private Sphere: A Feminist Reconsideration', *Feminists Read Habermas: Gendering the Subject of Discourse*, ed. Johanna Meehan (New York: Routledge, 1995), 91–116.

exemplary 'imposing words' – manipulating individual readers into getting and spending, molding them into thoughtless, heartless consumers, but rather as a form, or forum, for cultural self-fashioning, as the commodity form that is not so much a sign of individual alienation as a site of social inscription, consolidation, and, even, potentially, challenge. In these magazines we can observe what has been called 'the middling sort' – an 'imprecise and fluid body of consumers'[17] – as it begins to sort itself out, articulate its aspirations, get dressed up, distinguished as a class, largely through the activity of women who desire to see themselves represented in its pages.

But as I will want to argue, even as the middle-class is coming to recognize itself in the pages of the magazines, those pages providing some of the discursive terms for the formation of a bourgeois public culture,[18] the magazines may also be read as presenting another possible mode of social action and interaction. That is, while the early women's magazines participated in the shaping of class identity (and women's role in that shaping is a crucial part of the point here), in the heterogeneity of their subject matter and address, in the assumption that readers are also writers, consumers producers, commodities (the magazines themselves) meaningful in a variety of ways to a variety of persons, and in their attention to the material as well as the moral forms of women's cultural situation, the magazines of the later eighteenth and early nineteenth centuries also offered their readers a transformative potential. The personal as well as the class identities the magazines helped formulate are in those magazines more fluid than fetishized, inflected and unstable rather than institutional. The magazines bear out Terry Lovell's observation about early commoditization that 'the culture of anarchic excess . . . is every bit as bourgeois' as more 'sober, rationalist forms of emergent cultural life'.[19] And in that the readers of the early women's magazines would all be only in a very broad sense incipiently middle-class, upwardly mobile, that class can be seen to allow the possibility of

---

[17] 'The "middling sort" is a broad and generous concept which takes in everybody above the proletariat and below the aristocracy.' David Levine, 'Consumer Goods and Capitalist Modernization', *Journal of Interdisciplinary History* 22 (Summer 1991): 67–77; 68. See, also, Lorna Weatherill, *Consumer Behaviour and Material Culture in Britain, 1660–1760* (London: Routledge, 1989).

[18] See Jon P. Klancher, *The Making of English Reading Audiences, 1790–1832* (Madison: University of Wisconsin Press, 1987).

[19] Terry Lovell, 'Subjective Powers?: Consumption, the Reading Public, and Domestic Woman in Early Eighteenth-Century England', *The Consumption of Culture*, 23–41; 26.

alternative self-definitions. If the magazines do not quite in themselves constitute a counterpublic sphere, their function as cultural commodities – advertising the contestations within a gendered economy as well as other kinds of conflicting desires – can be understood to represent a form of publicity through which women can define their opinions and aspirations towards some provisional sense of collective identity.[20]

Though the magazine format is introduced in 1731 as 'an entirely new type of journal containing material drawn from many literary sources',[21] 'a storehouse of miscellaneous writings',[22] it is not until the publication of *The Lady's Magazine* in 1770 that the genre finds an apparently fitting vehicle for women. *The Lady's Magazine or Entertaining Companion for the Fair Sex* combined the features of previous periodical literature – essays, extracts, stories, and original verse, with a new attention to women as individual bodies – not just how they look, or how they (should) behave, but also what they want: 'As your Sex is in this age more employed in reading than it was in the last', the opening address of *The Lady's Magazine* begins, this 'periodical production' will be

> calculated for your particular amusement, and designed to improve as well as delight . . . The subjects we shall treat are those that may tend to render your minds not less amiable than your persons . . . external appearance is the first inlet to the treasures of the heart, and the advantages of dress, though they cannot communicate beauty, may at least make it more conspicuous.

The magazine proposes that what women want is material – of the heart, the body, real goods. But even as it initiates features to fulfill this material desire such as fashion news, elaborate engravings, recipes, and fold-out patterns for embroidery, *The Lady's Magazine* acknowledges the economically embedded character of such desire:

[20] See Bruce Robbins, 'Introduction: The Public As Phantom', *The Phantom Public Sphere*, ed. Bruce Robbins (Minneapolis: University of Minnesota Press, 1993), vii–xxvi: 'Yet publicity can be a means of alternative self-fashioning for collectivities that may not otherwise or already enjoy "fact-to-face" identity' (xviii).
[21] Cynthia L. White, *Women's Magazines, 1693–1968* (London: Michael Joseph, 1970), 27.
[22] Alison Adburgham, *Women In Print: Writing Women and Women's Magazines from the Restoration to the Accession of Queen Victoria* (London: Allen & Unwin, 1972), 129.

> In this we consult not only the embellishment but likewise the profit of our patronesses. They will find in this Magazine, price only sixpence, among variety of other Copper-plates a Pattern that would cost them double the money at the Haberdasher.

Consulting at once female pleasure and profit, *The Lady's Magazine* appeals to women as a body – 'a new readership that cut across class lines'[23] – but also as bodies – as 'persons' with minds and hearts motivated by and motivating an economy of getting and spending and saving. Such mutual motivation suggests both the importance that a gendered account of individual interest ('for your particular amusement') played in developing standards of value in the marketplace, and also, obversely, the public interest operative in the privatized discourse that the women's magazines deploy.

Other magazines followed the model thus established by *The Lady's Magazine*, which itself had a successful run of almost 80 years: *The New Lady's Magazine* appeared in 1786; *The Lady's Monthly Museum* in 1798; *La Belle Assemblee; or Bell's Court and Fashionable Magazine* in 1806; and *The British Lady's Magazine* in 1815. All these had extended runs, some lasting well beyond 1832, one conventional limit of Romanticism. These magazines are distinguished (from their immediate predecessor, the essay-periodical, and from most modern magazines for women) in three ways that are important for my discussion. First, they are striking in the range and variety of their contents: from advice columns to analysis of foreign politics, from extracts of *Paradise Lost* to accounts of the latest styles in France, from line drawings after Raphael to portraits of famous contemporary women, from 'Medical Vulgar Errors Refuted', for 'such of our Readers as are Mothers, or have the Management of children'[24] to 'Epitome of Public Affairs', including the progress of parliamentary reform, riots, and prices on the New York markets ('wheat was at two and a quarter dollars per bushel, equal to eighty shillings per quarter').[25] In such a heteroglossia, high art consorts with commerce; domestic economy entails an international index of value.

---

[23] Kathryn Shevelow, *Women and Print Culture: The Construction of Femininity in the Early Periodical* (London: Routledge, 1989), 23. See also Cynthia L. White, *Women's Magazines*: 'This expanding readership was made up of new recruits from the commercial classes as well as a substantial number of domestic servants whose conditions of work gave them both facilities for reading and access to reading matter' (25).

[24] *The Lady's Monthly Museum*, July 1798.

[25] *The Lady's Monthly Museum*, Jan. 1817.

Second, these magazines depart from the essay-periodical archetype in their innovative attention to format and presentation of the text. In its premiere issue, *La Belle Assemblee* boasts, 'we flatter ourselves that we have introduced a material improvement, so far as method, arrangement, and elegance of display may be considered as enticements to readers',[26] and *The Lady's Monthly Museum*, which had been the first periodical to feature colored engravings,[27] acknowledges the terms of the competition: 'We are not insensible, that, in point of embellishments, we have been rivalled by works of a similar nature.'[28] That the magazines from their initial appearance understood themselves as commodities in a competitive market is underscored by such attention to self-advertising display. Appearance of the magazines themselves became one of their primary selling points, and the link to commercial culture is made even more conspicuous when, for example, Mr Bell of *La Belle Assemblee* produces an advertising supplement,

> which is intended to give a permanence and order to Advertisements, together with a grace and splendour in their display never before attempted; to make them coexistant with, and forming an integral part of the Work, to be bound up and preserved with it; to be refered to as Commercial Indexes, and to be regarded as a necessary link and portion of the whole.[29]

If in this early form, Bell's five-page supplement almost exclusively listed notices for recently published books (with one advertisement for John Dennet, Wine, Brandy, and Liqueur Merchant, and another for Desormeaux's Universal British Cement), by 1820 his 'Commercial Indexes' included corsets, depilatories, fruit lozenges, tooth powders, riding habits, macassar oil, water filtering machines, engravings of Bonaparte, and anchovy paste, many with elaborate graphics, illustrations, or royal seals. Something for everyone; not just, like books, 'intellectual storehouses',[30] but virtual department stores. As Edward Copeland has remarked, reading the magazines may well have served as an incipient kind of window shopping.[31] And shopping, it has been argued, admits

---

26 *La Belle Assemblee,* Feb. 1806.
27 On the practice of coloring engravings and the employment of colorists, see Alison Adburgham, *Women In Print,* 204–7.
28 *The Lady's Monthly Museum,* Jan. 1813.
29 *La Belle Assemblee,* March 1806.
30 *[New Series of] The British Lady's Magazine,* June 1817.
31 Edward Copeland, *Women Writing About Money: Women's Fiction in England,*

'desire, emotion, sensuality, and fantasy as legitimate and motivating aspects of identity'.[32]

Third, the women's magazines extend the practice of earlier epistolary periodicals by being interactive – 'communication and correspondence are' as *La Belle Assemblee* declares, 'ardently invited'.[33] The early women's magazines in fact relied on their readers, not only as customers but as significant contributors. *The British Lady's Magazine* solicits articles, stories, information 'from the more elaborate effort, to the simple ideas, suggestions, or enquiries of individuals on points of interest':

> The original and essential characteristic of a Magazine undoubtedly consists in its openness to spontaneous and versatile communication on any subject connected with general information . . . these may be invited and rendered useful by the selection of such a medium as we have been describing, which, by establishing a beneficial connexion between the great body of subscribers, will tend to the interest and entertainment of all.[34]

Going beyond the practice of publishing readers' questions with editorial answers that was popularized early in the history of the periodical press,[35] the women's magazines established themselves from the start as multi-authored, polyvocal texts. 'These early magazines, then, positioned readers as members of a reading/writing community rather than simply as consumers . . . the magazine was a communal space in which

---

1790–1820 (Cambridge: Cambridge University Press, 1995): 'her trip through the magazine becoming itself a kind of shopping expedition with no expectation to buy, window-shopping of the most guileless sort among the ideas and images of the *Lady's*' (117).

[32] Kathy Peiss, 'Going Public: Women in Nineteenth-Century Cultural History', *American Literary History* 3 (Winter 1991): 817–28; 825. For a discussion of early depictions of the female shopper and the interiorization of shopping in the eighteenth century, see Elizabeth Kowaleski-Wallace, *Consuming Subjects: Women, Shopping, and Business in the Eighteenth Century* (New York: Columbia University Press, 1997). Kowaleski-Wallace cites Mica Nava's pertinent observation that 'Consumerism is far more than just economic activity: it is also about dreams and consolation, communication and confrontation, image and identity' ['Consumerism and Its Contradictions', *Cultural Studies* I (1987): 204–10; 209].

[33] *La Belle Assemblee*.

[34] *The British Lady's Magazine*, Jan. 1815.

[35] See Kathyrn Shevelow, *Women and Print Culture*, esp. 37–49.

the fair sex felt welcome.'[36] Such an account of the 'beneficial connexion' or 'communal space' established through the printed pages of
the magazines may be speculative or even a touch sentimental, but the
fact that the magazines provided a forum for multiple readers – metro-
politan and provincial, the lady of the house and her domestic servant[37]
– to express, imagine, imitate, or even masquerade through writing, begins to look like the commerce among women – 'woman after woman,
without sequence or number' – that Irigaray envisions in 'Commodities
among Themselves'. In Irigaray's fantasy of the exchange between
women that could take place outside of a strictly masculine proprietary
economy, there is 'pleasure without possession'. For the reader of the
early women's magazine, whose transactions were located within the
evolving economy of 'men and things', and by many accounts increasingly regulated there,[38] pleasure may have come from the opportunity to
take the means of production (temporarily) into her own hands;
pleasure may have come from performing two functional modes – of production and consumption – as one, a performance that might enable an
oppositional, or at least a different mode of being, a different economy.
For the reader writing in the women's magazine, perhaps, 'use and exchange would be indistinguishable' and 'the greatest value would be at
the same time the least kept in reserve'.

If commercial society is born in the eighteenth century and, as Colin
Campbell has argued, Romanticism is born with it as the expression of
the individualist spirit of modern consumerism, then the readers of early
women's magazines help chart the conflicted progress of that labor,
shaping through their desire the world that is still with us. Those magazines model for us an account of the function of consumption as 'an active form of relationship' – an instrument of self-identification or
pleasure as well as of social consolidation. To read the magazines this
way is also to see in objects the stuff out of which individuals imagine
their own possibilities and their places in the cultural context – a personal consciousness that has its inevitable, if not always fully realized,

---

[36] Margaret Beetham, A Magazine of Her Own?: Domesticity and Desire in the
Woman's Magazine, 1800–1914 (London: Routledge, 1996), 20.
[37] I discuss the slippage of class boundaries and locations in the magazines in
'Classifying Romanticism: The Milliner Girl and the Magazines', Sexual Politics
and the Romantic Author (Cambridge: Cambridge University Press, 1998).
[38] See Kathryn Shevelow, Women and Print Culture, esp. 174–90, on the
women's magazine as regulatory syllabus.

public dimension. To read the magazines this way is to imagine a response to this culture's dazzling proliferation of wares and words that recognizes the political implications of such abundance and sees in it the possibility for making a material difference.[39]

[39] Early consumers indeed recognized in consumption the possibility for political action, especially for women whose political agency was otherwise limited. An example would be the boycott of sugar and rum which was part of the popular campaign against the slave trade in the early 1790s. See Clare Midgley, *Women Against Slavery: The British Campaigns, 1780–1870* (London: Routledge, 1992), 35–40; and Charlotte Sussman, 'Women and the Politics of Sugar, 1792', *Representations* 48 (Fall 1994): 48–69.

Letitia Landon: Public Fantasy and the Private Sphere

EMMA FRANCIS

IN THE ONLY SUBSTANTIAL feminist consideration of Letitia Landon to be published before 1992, Germaine Greer argues that the mythology which was constructed around the poet by her contemporaneous critics represents 'an acute and spectacular case of what might be called the "Woman of Genius syndrome" ' (Greer 1982, 19). This pernicious ailment exhibited itself in such symptoms as 'an impecunious father, female relatives who sought to exploit the child's gift, an apparently happy and sunny child's conviction that she was rejected and unloved and the usual haphazard education afforded the gifted female children of impoverished middle class families' (Greer 1982, 19). As Landon reached adulthood, Greer argues, this incipient melodrama was grafted onto an hysterical, feminised Romanticism and a certain erotic suggestiveness, which Landon's culture desired and demanded of her, but which ultimately provided the grounds for her severe censure and sacrifice. Greer's description adds up to a picture of a woman whose aesthetic was fatally compromised by the commercial and cultural pressures upon her. Landon fell victim to her attempt to engage seriously with accounts of femininity and of feminine aesthetic identity imposed upon her by cynical publishers who, in all probability, knew the 'pathology' for what it was – a crude but lucrative stereotype which they exploited to the full. Greer continues her diagnosis of Landon's failings, identifying specifically her eagerness to take up a place within the public sphere as the cause of her artistic downfall.

> If only L.E.L. had been discouraged from publishing, she might have accomplished more and suffered less. Her poems might have languished in tiny hand-sewn books hidden away in drawers, but they would have borne the mark of no pressure but her own eagerness to set down the fantasy, instead of the dreary imprint of poetry by the foot. (Greer 1982, 23)

Greer's essay, confidently entitled 'The Tulsa Center for the Study of Women's Literature: what we are doing and why we are doing it', was the flagship article of the first issue of a new feminist journal. As its title suggests, its purpose was to introduce the work of the research centre, the major projects of recovering the work of women writers eclipsed by the traditional canon and of developing a broader legitimation for the study of women's writing per se. In this context Landon seems an odd and rather defeatist choice for an explanatory case-study. It is not Greer's argument that Landon's work is of sufficient excellence to merit serious study or revaluation in its own right; she is not offered as an example of the kind of glittering prize properly funded and properly focussed feminist criticism will uncover. Landon is set up merely as a cautionary tale of the perils of the 'Woman of Genius syndrome' – '[i]f we could understand its pathology correctly we might know what therapies to adopt in the less advanced stages of the disease' (Greer 1982, 19) – she is a worst-case scenario of the results of capitulation to commercialism and to patriarchy. Greer advocates research on Landon in order to reveal the precise nature of her exploitation, what she sees as the tacky reality of Landon's sexual, social and professional vulnerability, which lurks behind the gloss of publicity, an understanding of which, Greer argues, might make her giddy behaviour and the lamentable quality of her work more intelligible.

It is perhaps little wonder that after the indictment of this article, published in 1982, feminist criticism maintained ten years of virtually unbroken silence on Landon.[1] Since 1992 Landon has re-emerged with the publication of several important studies, as part of the long delayed feminist assessment of the full scope of nineteenth-century women's poetry. However, the terms of her depiction, and the kinds of anxiety and disapproval she produces in a feminist context, seem to have changed very little. She figures in these readings as an important precursor to Christina Rossetti and Elizabeth Barrett Browning (a link which Greer also made, and elaborates on in her longer study *Slipshod Sybils*, published in 1995), but is seen as largely failing to establish a legitimate aesthetic in her own right.

Whereas Greer's earlier article was focussed primarily around Landon's failure to negotiate her own exposure, her anomalous position within the 'public sphere', the critics writing a decade later elaborate on the other side of the coin, what they see as Landon's capitulation to the concept of the gendered separation of spheres and her endorsement of conservative ideologies of femininity, its location within the 'private sphere'. In Angela Leighton's study *Victorian Women Poets: Writing*

[1]   The feminist critical silence was broken briefly by two studies – Hickok 1984 which concentrates on Landon's accounts of femininity, and Rosenblum 1986, which includes a brief discussion of Landon's influence on Christina Rossetti.

Against the Heart, Landon bears a large share of the responsibility for cultivating what Leighton sees as the invidious myth that the nineteenth-century woman poet composed in an effortless process of 'improvising heart inspiration' (Leighton 1992, 63). She sees Landon's aesthetic of sensibility and sensuality as politically flaccid, a continuous emotional ooze which cannot contain itself sufficiently to ossify into a basis for analysis or action. Leighton locates a dissident cynicism in texts produced toward the end of her career, as, she argues, Landon came to recognise the contradictions implicit in the demands upon her and the void this had created in her poetic identity, but holds up her early work as the 'heart' which subsequent poets had to 'write against', as they sought to delineate a more politically valid poetics.

In her essay of 1992, 'Letitia Landon and the Victorian improvisatrice: the construction of L.E.L.' (flagship of her later book of 1995 *Letitia Landon: The Woman Behind L.E.L.*), Glennis Stephenson elaborates on the conditions determined by the predominantly male controlled publishing industry, with which Landon negotiated. Stephenson claims that 'her image as "poetess" was to a large extent imposed upon her, and, consequently, has a potentially limiting rather than liberating effect', because the 'poetess' was expected to embody the conservative image of femininity integral to the development of theories of the 'separate spheres' (Stephenson 1992, 1). She argues that Landon played a perilous game with the conventions of femininity, attempting to negotiate a simultaneous submission to and subversion of them, a gamble, Stephenson believes, she ultimately lost.

Stephenson's and Leighton's main worry about Landon, just like Greer's, is what they see as her willingness to stake her poetics on her body and sexuality, on the spectacle of vulnerable, seductive and suffering femininity which she consistently reiterated within her texts and attached to her own public image. Both critics argue that this display was ultimately recuperated by a culture which sought to confine women within the plenitude of their bodies and emotions – within private sensibility – as a way of situating them outside of the political and of legitimate aesthetic and intellectual identity. Their argument adds up to the neat equation that Landon capitulated utterly to the process of the exclusion of women from successful intervention into the 'public sphere' by her endorsement of the values of the 'private sphere'.

Because Landon and her contemporary Felicia Hemans were the first British female poets to achieve large scale commercial success and massive public exposure and because they were both writing across the transition between the late Romantic and early Victorian periods, at a time when discourses of sexual division were at a crucial point of rearticulation, this issue of the relation between the 'public' and the 'private' was vastly over-determined both in their writing and in its reception.[2] It is the purpose of this essay to explore what Landon's work has to say about the way in which this relation and its political imperatives were configured at this time.

This question is important because of the way in which the distinction between the 'public' and 'private' spheres has become so central to literary critics' frames of reference in discussions of the later eighteenth and nineteenth centuries. I would argue, and will seek to demonstrate through an examination of Landon's poetry and the cultural fantasies to which it responded, that the meanings which have coagulated around these terms within feminism have sometimes been misleading, giving rise to the kind of imperious dismissal of the work of women who chose to negotiate with rather than simply repudiate dominant accounts of femininity, which we have just seen in the critical assessments of Landon discussed above, and blinding feminist criticism to some of the complexities (both political and aesthetic) of this negotiation. I am interested in the specific issue of the role that images of the 'private' have within the public articulation of the poetry – the extent to which the 'private' is in fact a publicly tradeable commodity – and in what I see as

---

[2] During the course of this essay I sometimes describe the literary period within which Landon is located as the 'late Romantic' period. However, at points where it is appropriate I also describe it as the 'early Victorian' period, or simply, the 'nineteenth century'. This oscillation is necessary because women's poetry disrupts the conventional critical demarcation between Romanticism and Victorianism, which critics have based upon the sharp contrast between the politics, aesthetics and poetic language of the male second generation Romantic and early Victorian poets (see Bristow 1987, 1–26). The distinction is far less sharp in women's poetry. One reason for this is simple; whereas Keats, Shelley and Byron died in 1821, 1822 and 1824 respectively, the two most important female Romantic poets, Landon and Hemans, lived and published well over a decade longer, dying in 1835 and 1838 respectively, and thus writing right across the chronological divide. They also have points of entry into both Romantic and Victorian cultural politics which are very different from those of the male poets. They carry a characteristically Romantic confidence into the 1830s, but, as I argue in this essay, elaborate a defence of their poetry which draws upon discourses of the social provenance and purchase of femininity which became hegemonic in the Victorian period. Both 'Romanticism' and 'Victorianism' have very different articulations in the work of female and male poets; we need to dislocate the classification in order to ask what the work of women poets might do to our understanding of them.

the dialectical relationship between the two terms.[3] Therefore, the first part of my essay is directed to the consideration of configurations of the 'private' construction of femininity which we find in Landon's work, its precise dimensions and referents, which, as I will show, are slightly different from those which govern the work of other poets and writers of the period. The second section offers some preliminary notes towards a critical reconsideration of the way in which 'private sphere' and its

---

[3] The invocation of the terms of a debate about the 'separate spheres' of women and men has been a feature of feminist criticism of nineteenth-century women's writing since at least Virginia Woolf onwards. Woolf's account of women's literary history was informed by the thesis that from the early modern period women have been excluded from literature as one of the forms of public and political engagement. Woolf argues that this exclusion became even more profound in the Victorian period and expends considerable rhetoric energy on her description of the way in order to construct a coherent literary or poetic identity women writers need to repudiate the disabling prescriptions of Victorian patriarchy. (See Woolf 1929.) Despite the strenuous critique of various other aspects of Woolf's theory made by the Anglo-American feminist critics who took up her terms from the late 1970s, this element has remained largely unchallenged.

More recently feminist literary critics have been drawn to the work of Jurgen Habermas, whose texts, including the major study *The Structural Transformation of the Public Sphere: An Inquiry Into a Category of Bourgeois Society*, have argued that a split between the 'public' and the 'private' is axiomatic to modernity. Habermas, unlike the feminist critics, argues that the split is liberatory. The public sphere provides a space in which subjects come together to participate in discourses governed by reason, from which individual emotion and exclusive self-interest are excluded. In Habermas the separation of the 'public' from the 'private' is more or less the precondition of the emergence of democracy and its precursors. Feminist philosophers and social theorists have objected to Habermas' thesis on the grounds that it is gender-blind. It fails to take account of the fact that within patriarchy the separation inevitably results in the lines of demarcation being drawn up not just between different roles or experiences of individual subjects, but between categories of subjects themselves, namely women and men. Whereas in modern Western culture men move between and have roles within both 'private' and 'public' spheres, women have been wholly identified with the discourses of the 'private' sphere and have thus been excluded from full participation in the 'public' sphere, severely limiting the liberatory potential of the split (see Meehan 1995). I do not choose to route my discussion through Habermas' terms first, because I am interested in a feature of the history of feminist literary theory and criticism which predates the invocation of his work and second, because my argument operates at a slightly different level. I am interested in the dynamics of the imbrication and implication of the two categories in each other operating in the cultural fantasies of a specific period, rather than in the rules of their demarcation and how it determined the emergence of modern political systems.

relation to the 'public sphere' have been contextualised by feminist literary criticism and of resources we might draw upon in order to construct a fresh and more historically sensitive account of its politics.

It is indeed the case that the terms in which Landon described her poetry's cultural mission are explicitly articulated into some aspects of the late eighteenth- and early nineteenth-century discourse which came to be known as 'woman's mission'.[4] In the Preface to her fifth published volume of poetry, The Venetian Bracelet (1829), she made a declaration which became something of a touchstone for her contemporaneous critics.

> Believing as I do in the great and excellent influence of poetry, may I hazard the expression of what I have myself sometimes trusted to do? A highly cultivated state of society must ever have for concomitant evils, that selfishness, the result of indolent indulgence; and that heartlessness attendant on refinement, which too often hardens while it polishes. Aware that to elevate I must first soften, and that if I wished to purify I must first touch, I have ever endeavoured to bring forward grief, disappointment, the fallen leaf, the faded flower, the broken heart, and the early grave . . . [As to] my frequent choice of Love as my source of song, I can only say, that for a woman, whose influence and whose sphere must be in the affections, what subject can be more fitting than one which it is her peculiar province to refine, spiritualise, and exalt?   (Landon 1844, IV:v–vii)

Isobel Armstrong has argued that this manifesto envisages 'a politics of the affective state' in which Landon claims that women's poetry can ameliorate 'what would now be called the phallocentric hardness and imaginative deficiencies of an overcivilised culture' (Armstrong 1993, 328). Its terms resonated through the accounts of Landon written by her early Victorian critics, who looked to her work to support a variety of political and moral imperatives. For example, William Jerdan, Landon's lifelong friend, who launched her literary career by printing her poems in his journal The Literary Gazette, in the 1820s, incorporated elements of the formula into his appreciative posthumous assessment of her career, contained in the third volume of his autobiography, which was dedicated to his long association with Landon:

---

[4]   See, for example, Ellis 1838, 1842, 1843a and 1843b, Lamb 1844 and Lewis 1858.

so long as love and passion animate the breast of youth, so long as tenderness and pathos affect the mind of man, so long as glowing imagery and natural truth have power over the intellect and heart, so long will the poetry of L.E.L. exert a voice to delight, touch, refine, and exalt the universal soul.   (Jerdan 1852, 170).

Sarah Sheppard, in *L.E.L., Characteristics of Her Genius and Her Writings*, her critical and biographical study published in 1841, shortly after the poet's death, redeploys Landon's metaphorics in her claim that society is not over- but under-civilised. She advocates Landon's poetry as a remedy for the 'coarseness' and 'vulgarity' of a society governed by rampant material interest.

It is a moral impossibility for genuine poetic feeling to coexist with coarseness of mind and vulgarity of habits: whatever be the station in life, once admit the Spirit of Poetry, and you may admit an influence which will soften, refine and exalt ... Every production that tends in this age of selfishness and expediency to expand the heart, to dignify the character, to raise the hopes of society to a better order of things than the wearying round of heartless ceremonies, of bustling love of gain, of disgusting self-indulgence; such productions must have a moral value far beyond the consideration of their mere marketable price.   (Sheppard 1841, 70)

The articulation of Landon's poetry into the social and moral mission of femininity happened on terms rather different from those which were deployed around Felicia Hemans. Many of Hemans' critics argued for a neat elision of the domestic and the poetic in her work and life. Hemans exercised a judicious circumspection over her public image, living with her mother and children in rural North Wales for most of her career and keeping her distance from the critics, which permitted the elements of her domestic life which detracted from the ideal, such as her separation from her husband, to be discreetly veiled. Hemans' publicity and criticism focussed on the moral benefits which would be conferred on the readers of her poetry, because of their redolence of the continent domestic location in which they were composed. Paradoxically, for her Victorian critics it is precisely the domestic and familial seclusion in which they are written which creates a charge on Hemans' poems powerful enough to resonate at the furthest colonial outposts. For example, in her work of substantial scholarship *The Literary Women of England* (1861), which argues for Hemans as the ideal type of the woman poet, Jane Williams invokes this bizarre dialectic in her comments upon the domestic setting of the poems' production, and, in particular, on the elevating influence of Hemans' mother upon them. She argues that Hemans' poems can be credited with giving rise to

> the performance of 10,000 good deeds in remote countries by people awakened to spiritual energy through the simple agency of a book, or a single poem . . . the writings of Mrs. Hemans met with immediate and extensive popularity alike in the most distant alienated colonial settlements and in the old home of the British race.
>
> (Williams 1861, 437 and 493)

The fact that Hemans' poems often appeal to the maternal affections reinforced the narrative of domestic propriety which her critics located her within.

Landon's unmarried state and high-profile life in the thick of literary London meant that she could not be absorbed into this narrative. It was abundantly clear that she was not a matronly 'angel in the house' but a social butterfly, flitting between the bedsit and the literary soirée.[5] After apparently quarrelling with her mother she removed herself from the protection and propriety of her family and worked and organised her social life for most of her adulthood in a series of rented rooms. The moral potency attributed to Landon's poetry was described in terms which are more sexual than domestic or familial. The emphasis she and her critics place in the passages above on her work's ability to 'delight' 'soften' and 'touch' as well as 'refine' and 'elevate' indicates the importance of seduction within and in the marketing of her poetry. Hemans and her critics traded on her sexual *unavailability*, her secure positioning as adored and protected daughter and adoring and self-sacrificing mother. Landon and her critics traded on her sexual *availability*. In the Preface to *The Venetian Bracelet*, Landon presents her poetry as a kind of pedagogy of heterosexual romance, as a model of the value of loving in 'actual life' as well as in literature, in a way which is 'intense' 'true' 'pure' and 'deep', which rejects both vacuousness and cynicism. Yet her claim to be able to anatomise this superior form of love rests not upon experience, but upon inexperience. Switching from high-minded solemnity to mischievous comedy, the preface continues:

---

[5]   There are numerous nineteenth-century accounts of the events of Landon's life and death, a body of writing whose intense and contradictory fantasmatic investments pose a number of problems. A clear-sighted synthesis of the often conflicting accounts is provided in Leighton 1992, 45–57.

With regard to the frequent application of my works to myself, considering that I sometimes pourtrayed (sic.) love unrequited, then betrayed and again destroyed by death – may I hint the conclusions are not quite logically drawn, as assuredly the same mind cannot have suffered such varied modes of misery. However, if I must have an unhappy passion, I can only console myself with my own perfect unconsciousness of so great a misfortune.   (Landon 1844, IV:vii–viii)

Landon stakes her poetics on sexuality but simultaneously flaunts her own innocence of the passions she depicts, the fact that her own initiation into them has yet to take place. Her attraction for her early nineteenth-century readers lay at least partly in the way in which she arouses but then holds off sexuality, her strategy of hyperinvestment in and eroticisation of her own virginity.

This process of the simultaneous arousal and deferral of sexuality is also a consistent feature of her poetry. Particularly in her earlier work, she frequently depicts her heroines in a manner heavily coded with sexual arousal – there is a good deal of flushing of cheek, throbbing of pulse and tumbling loose of hair – but scarcely ever permits them consummation. Many of the poems of Landon's early and mid-career are extended narratives, often running to several hundred pages, but the structure of the plot is always secondary to the lengthy digressions on the state of her heroines' emotional states. Typical is this passage from the early stages of 'The Venetian Bracelet', where the narrator limbers up by displaying her own emotional and perceptive credentials, in line with Landon's manifesto set out in the preface to the volume.

> But now, whenever I am mix'd too much
> With worldly natures till I feel as such; –
> (For these are as the waves that turn to stone,
> Till feelings keep their outward show alone) –
> When wearied by the vain, chill'd by the cold,
> Impatient of society's set mould –
> The many meannesses, the petty cares,
> The long avoidance of a thousand snares,
> The lip that must be chain'd, the eye so taught
> To image all but its own actual thought; –
> (Deceit is this world's passport: who would dare,
> However pure the breast, to lay it bare?) –
> When worn, my nature struggling with my fate,
> Checking my love, but, oh, still more my hate; –
> (Why should I love? flinging down pearl and gem
> To those who scorn, at least care not for them:

Why should I hate? as blades in scabbards melt,
I have no power to make my hatred felt;
Or, should I say, my sorrow: – I have borne
So much unkindness, felt so lone, so lorn,
I could but weep, and tears may not redress,
They only fill the cup of bitterness) –
Wearied of this, upon what eager wings
My spirit turns to thee, and bird-like flings
Its best, its breath, its spring, and song o'er thee,
My lute's enchanted world, fair Italie.

(Landon 1844, IV:4–6)

This detailed anatomy of sensibility, which forces itself inside the main clause, drastically elongating the sentence, is the essence of Landon's poetics. The narrative structure of her poems is always attenuated in precisely this way in order to create space inside it for extensive depictions of the state of the heart. Her poems generate a huge sexual tension which is never fully released. Both Landon herself, as she appears in her publicity, and her aesthetic are, as Glennis Stephenson puts it, a tease (Stephenson 1992, 13).

A group of poems in her final posthumously published collection, *Subjects for Pictures*, shows the darker, less titillating and more tragic side of this aesthetic. These poems figure women paralysed by progressive melancholia. Their distress is the result of desertion by or bereavement of men – brothers, husbands or lovers. Each poem relates a story effaced by the classical or historical texts, they delineate the fate of the women left behind after the departure of the heroes who carry the focus of the narrative with them. They inscribe an emotional history marginalised by a narrative which prioritises the affairs of men and leaves women condemned to bear the full emotional burden of relationships for which men will take no responsibility. For example, 'Calypso Watching the Ocean' is an addendum to an episode in *The Odyssey*. Homer's text opens with Odysseus sitting on the shore of Calypso's island where he has been washed up on his way home after the Trojan wars. He is grieving because the nymph will not let him leave her and return to his family and principality in Greece. Landon's poem retains the preoccupation with stasis, confinement and misery but inverts the subject positions and depicts Calypso on the shore gazing out to sea many years after Odysseus' departure, still in love with him. As an immortal she cannot even look forward to a release from her grief via death. The poem ends by asserting that Calypso's stasis, her incarceration within a frustrated desire and a consuming grief, is the fate of any woman who buys into this politics of femininity, who gives herself over to the rule of the 'heart'.

> She is but the type of all,
> Mortal or celestial,
>   Who allow the heart,
> In its passion and its power,
> On some dark and fated hour,
>   To assert its part.
> Fate attends the steps of Love, –
> Both brought misery from above
>   To the lone and lovely island
> Mid the far off southern seas.   (Blanchard 1841, 207)

Another poem in the sequence, 'Ariadne Watching the Sea After the Departure of Theseus', also occupies a narrative space adjacent to a classical story. Greek legend records that Minos, King of Crete, demanded of the Athenians a tribute of seven youths and seven maidens every eighth year, to be fed to the Minotaur in the labyrinth at Knossos. When he reaches the age of the young people who will be sacrificed, Theseus, son of the Athenian king, decides to defend his compatriots by going himself to Crete as part of the tribute and confront the monster. With the help of Ariadne, daughter of the Cretan king and sister of the Minotaur, who has fallen in love with him, Theseus successfully slays the monster. He takes Ariadne back to Greece with him. Landon's poem takes up the narrative the day after their marriage. Theseus has departed over the sea to new adventures, leaving Ariadne stranded on a foreign shore. She has sacrificed her family and her home for the love of a husband who has deserted her. It is difficult not to find in this poem an allegory of Landon's own unfortunate marriage (which had just begun when she was drafting the poem) to the dubious George Maclean, who removed her to the Gold Coast immediately after their wedding and then, according to an account written by Landon, grossly neglected her, leaving her to her own devices and the management of their native domestics from early morning until evening.[6] Just like the study of Calypso,

---

6   In *A Book of Memories of Great Men and Women of the Age, From Personal Acquaintance*, Samuel Carter Hall reproduces a letter sent to his wife in which Landon complains that Maclean leaves her alone from seven in the morning until seven at night, refuses to allow her to have one of the many empty rooms in his house for her personal use and 'expects me to cook, clean, wash, and iron, in

this poem ends with the warning that Ariadne's grim predicament is the fate of any woman who capitulates to her emotions.

> There the Cretan maiden stands,
> Wringing her despairing hands,
> Lonely on the lonely sands –
>   'Tis a woman's lot:
> Only let her heart be won,
> And her summer hour is done –
>   Soon she is forgot;
> Sad she strays by life's bleak shore,
> Loving but beloved no more!   (Blanchard 1841, 232)

In these poems the positioning of the women beside the sea is an important focus of the allegory. The movement and vastness of the waves stand for both the freedom of the men to whom they are emotionally ransomed, and the women's unsatisfied sexual desire. The flowing water forms a sharp contrast with the stasis Calypso and Ariadne are caught within. These poems argue that for women love is synonymous with, is a female form of melancholia. As soon as she falls in love, woman's psychic and emotional chronology is frozen for ever, she cannot escape from love by the work of mourning.

This group of poems takes up a place within a tradition of female dramatic monologues of grief and protest which begins with Ovid's *Heroides*. In a manner which is typical of her relation to antique and historic texts and myths in other parts of her work, Landon takes up some of the terms of the original – Ovid writes a monologue from Ariadne to Theseus – but also develops her own interventions, exploring even more instances of female exploitation and abandonment within the mythologies of Western and Eastern civilisation. Other poems in the series, 'The Zegri Lady's Vigil,' 'The Moorish Maiden's Vigil', study the experiences of women in another culture which fascinated Landon – Islam. But whatever the setting, the script is always the same. These late texts explore the untold story of the role women are compelled to take up on the margins of political space, left to clean up after and bear the emotional fall-out of the events recorded by history and myth. They seem to offer themselves as the terminal point of Landon's poetics, acknowledging the political bankruptcy of the private sphere but at a loss

short, to do the work of a servant'. Landon adds the cryptic report that '[h]e says he will never cease correcting me until he has broken my spirit' (Hall 1871, 278).

for new directions to take out of it. Landon's aesthetic seems locked into its own immanence, just as Calypso and Ariadne are locked within a disabling, destructive and untenable desire.

The question which Landon's texts confront us with in the late 1990s is essentially the same as that which troubled Germaine Greer in the early 1980s: how do we want to understand the politics of femininity? What do we do with a woman who chose to negotiate with rather than repudiate dominant accounts of femininity of her period? What do we do with a woman whose claim to a place in the 'public sphere' relied on her endorsement of the discourses of the 'private sphere'? What seems to me to be most interesting about the history of Landon's recuperation by feminist criticism is the way in which it shows up the gaps in our critical and political assumptions and languages – demonstrated particularly baldly in the ten years of bemused silence between Greer's pioneering reading and the commencement of sustained work. Rather than being a suitable illustration for the definition of the feminist critical project, of what we are doing and why we are doing it, as Germaine Greer tried to deploy her, Landon is a disruptive force, who undermines and problematises many of the assumptions about gender, genre, language and political space axiomatic to feminist criticism. She forces an inversion of the terms of Greer's statement and turns it into a question: what *are we* doing with a writer like Landon, and why *are we* doing it? I would argue that the limitation of the critical responses, which veer between headshaking over her capitulation and hand-wringing over her exploitation, points to an impasse in feminist criticism's understanding of the relationship between the 'public' and 'private' spheres in the late eighteenth and early nineteenth centuries, which I want to pursue in the remainder of this paper. Landon certainly deploys a conformist account of femininity but she does so within a context which foregrounds it as an idea, as a representation. Her texts exhibit a knowingness about the structure and dynamics of representation, about the way it can be manipulated and negotiated in order to create distance from the claustrophobia of femininity, to hold femininity up for scrutiny at the same time as inhabiting it. Understanding these strategies allows us not only to reassess Landon, but also to think again about the politics of the 'private sphere', the dynamics of its relation to the 'public sphere' in the early nineteenth century.

It seems to me to be crucial to grasp that Landon's occupation of the conventions of femininity is simultaneous with her interrogation of them. I suggest that we begin to take seriously the representation of femininity as a strategy for scrutinising the cultural fantasies projected onto it. Isobel Armstrong has written of the importance of the dramatic monologue form and of masks within Landon's poetry (Armstrong 1993, 325–6). Feminist critics are perhaps more habituated to the notion that femininity might need to *be* concealed or masked by women writers, for example, by the use of a male or gender indeterminate pseudonym, than that a woman writer might *deploy* a feminine mask – and this is what Landon's female speakers are, dramatic portraits, not autobiography – in order to display and flaunt femininity.

Another important technique Landon deploys in this scrutiny is her complex account of specularisation. Visibility is vastly overdetermined in her work. She complicates representational space by insisting perpetually, in the midst of texts which revel in the seductive power of written language, on the visual. She is obsessed, in particular, with colour. In this passage from 'The Venetian Bracelet', for example, the heroine (cocooned in luxurious domestic space) is described in almost obscenely overdetermined technicolour.

> . . . . each silken blind
> Waved to and fro upon the scented wind,
> Now closing till the twilight-haunted room
> Was in an atmosphere of purple gloom,
> First scarcely letting steal one crimson ray,
> Then flung all open to the glowing day.
> Pictures were hung above; how more than fair!
> The changing light made almost life seem there.
> A faint rose-colour wander'd o'er the cheek,
> Seem'd the chance beams from each dark eye to break;
> And you could deem each braided auburn wave
> Moved, as its gold the glancing sun-light gave.
> And fitting mistress had the charmed scene;
> Leant, like a beautiful and eastern queen,
> Upon a purple couch – how soft and warm
> Clung the rich colour to her ivory arm!
>   (Landon 1844, IV:15–16)

In their titles and projects, Landon also cultivates the association of her texts with the dimension of visibility. For example the studies of Calypso and Ariadne are contained in a series called *Subjects for Pictures*. Each text presents itself as a poetic depiction of a postulated visual text. This has the effect of locating the reiterated image of static, suffering femininity these lyrics present, *precisely as an image*. To think of it located within a picture implies a material dimension in which it can be approached or walked away from, viewed from different perspectives. The femininity these poems depict may be locked into its own immanence, but the text negotiates a position within representational space which foregrounds the gap between the production of the image and its reception. Landon produced several series of poems situated in this way in her full length published collections, some are studies of real pictures (not reproduced in Landon's text) such as the *Poetical Sketches of Modern Pictures* or the *Poetical Portraits*, in which, as in *Subjects for Pictures*, the visual texts are not real but are constructed by the poetic texts.[7] By foregrounding the dimension of visibility, Landon's texts are not just falling prey to the process whereby femininity collapses back on itself into the status of specularised object, rather they are drawing attention to and interrogating the process of specularisation itself, of the way in which femininity is constructed and subjected to fantasmatic investment.

Landon also makes clear that this process is not wholly determined by men, her women are not just subjects for pictures, they are sometimes painters themselves. In Landon's poetry women occupy positions on both sides of visual space, they are looked at, but they also look. For example, 'The Improvisatrice', title poem of Landon's volume of 1824 and the first of Landon's many reworkings of Germaine de Staël's 1802 novel about the female poet-genius, *Corinne, Or Italy* (about which I will say more later), contains a complicated trope of the production of painting. Although the memorial portrait of the improvisatrice which hangs in her lover's hall has been commissioned by him, the improvisatrice herself is, like Corinne, also a painter, who depicts her own subjectivity within a painting. Landon places much greater emphasis upon her heroine's talents as a painter than de Staël. The improvisatrice opens her monologue by describing herself as 'a daughter of that land,/ Where the poet's lip and the painter's hand/ Are almost divine, – where the earth and sky,/ Are picture both and poetry' (Landon 1844, I:1). Italy is a guarantee of her identity as a painter to as great an extent as it is of her poetic identity. In fact, the poem describes her ability as a painter before it describes her performances of poetry. In the first few pages of the text, the improvisatrice recounts her thrill at visiting a gallery in which her paintings are hung. Their subjects are poets, she depicts Petrarch and Sappho. This complication of representational space, by beginning a poem with descriptions of pictures which study the creation of poetry, is complicated even further when the improvisatrice allows Sappho (and

---

7   The 'Poetical Sketches of Modern Pictures' are contained in Landon 1844, II: 157–301 and the 'Poetical Portraits' in Landon 1844, IV: 175–196.

perhaps significantly, not Petrarch) to ooze over the boundary of the canvas into her own performance of poetry. The improvisatrice recounts Sappho's last song, which she is singing in her portrait. This exchange between painting and poetry, their flow in and out of one another, is indicative of the way in which in Landon's work, poetry is implicated with visibility as much as it is with femininity.

Later in the text, the improvisatrice returns to painting. After her desertion by her lover she pours her frustration into her depiction of Ariadne (as we have already seen, a figure who fascinated Landon) in the hope that after her death, he will see the picture and in it 'find my grief; – think – see – feel all/ I felt, in this memorial!' (Landon 1844, I:89). The portrait commissioned by her lover depicts her as a composed beauty, at ease with both her poetic gift and her femininity, it erases the history of the pain he has inflicted on her. But in her painting of Ariadne, the improvisatrice produces her own representation of her fate, which insists on telling the truth of her suffering.

> I drew her on a rocky shore: –
> Her black hair loose, and sprinkled o'er
> With white sea-foam; her arms were bare,
> Flung upwards in their last despair.
> Her naked feet the pebbles prest;
> The tempest-wind sang in her vest;
> A wild stare in her glassy eyes;
> White lips, as parched by their hot sighs;
> And cheek more pallid than the spray
> Which, cold and colourless, on it lay;
> Just such a statue as should be
>   Placed ever, Love! beside thy shrine;
> Warning thy victims of what ills –
>   What burning tears, false god! are thine.
>   (Landon 1844: I:89)

No doubt Landon's work for the annuals and albums heightened her awareness of the possibilities of the space created by the dialogue between visual and written texts, although it is important to highlight the fact that 'The Improvisatrice', which predated her extensive involvement with them, was one of Landon's most intense preoccupations with the dialogue.[8]

As I mentioned above, the poem is the first of Landon's many

8   Landon contributed to many of the albums on an occasional basis and edited

engagements with Germaine de Staël's *Corinne, Or Italy*. It is well worth examining this crucial novel in the context of these debates about the interrelation of the 'public' and 'private' spheres. The impact of *Corinne* on British women's poetry in the nineteenth century is a topic whose surface has hardly been scratched. It is sometimes difficult for the late twentieth-century reader, for whom Corinne, English-Italian hybrid and improvising poet-genius, has been comparatively inaccessible, to catch the countless echoes of de Staël's novel which resonate across nineteenth-century British women's poetry.[9] Angela Leighton usefully points to her presence in the work of the poets with which she is concerned at several points in her study. Leighton argues that Corinne was linked in the nineteenth-century female poetic imagination with Sappho, another archetype revitalised in the nineteenth century, as a composite image of 'the ideal of creative but suffering femininity'. Leighton highlights the tragedy, romance and hysteria of the symbol they form, arguing that 'on the one hand, lovelorn and suicidal they seem to stand for a woman's writing which is always on the brink of self-denial in the face of male rejection. On the other hand, triumphalist and obsessively self-expressive, they represent a flow of poetic inspiration which thrives on a covert, transmittable enthusiasm between women' (Leighton 1992, 3–4).

Landon, as Leighton suggests, does cultivate an association with the enthusiastic, tragic and deathly elements of the myth, but just as important is the way in which Corinne stands in her work and that of other late-Romantic and early Victorian female poets and their critics, for the complex relation between the 'public' and the 'private' which the poetry negotiated. In addition to the image of suffering, self-obsession and self-expenditure which Leighton points to, which organised itself chiefly around Corinne's descent into death due to her desertion by her lover Oswald, other scenes, much earlier in the novel, are worked through repeatedly by Landon and other poets, those of Corinne's

and wrote all the poetic copy for one, *Fisher's Drawing Room Scrapbook*, for an eight year period, 1832–40.
9   In her doctoral thesis, 'The Intimacy Which is Knowledge: Female Friendship in the Novels of Women Writers' (1988), Gill Frith has explored some aspects of the legacy of *Corinne* for nineteenth-century British women's fiction, in particular the way in which the figure of the half-sister, modelled on Corinne's relationship with Lucile was obsessively reworked by British novelists. An important account of the significance of the novel for women's poetry is Cora Kaplan's introduction to her 1978 edition of *Aurora Leigh, and Other Poems*.

public improvisations of poetry, in particular her improvisation at the Capitol in Rome.

Here the two aspects of Corinne's identity, her two articulations as both national 'public' heroine and as 'private' affective subject are brought together. Her improvisation on this occasion, on the subject of *'The Glory and Bliss of Italy!'* addressed to her 'fellow citizens', is her greatest public triumph (de Staël 1987, 26) and de Staël's prose dwells in great detail on the homage paid to her by the people of Rome and by its structures of civic power. It is also the first time she is seen by Oswald, who is attracted to her not in spite of her genius and the public homage it receives, but because of them. He is 'electrified' by the spectacle of her procession, which he acknowledges to himself he would find repellent were it taking place in England for an Englishwoman, but finds utterly compelling in Italy with Corinne at its head (de Staël 1987, 22). Unlike the situation at the end of the text, in which Corinne has lost Oswald because he is unable to cope with her role as national poet, this scene envisages the possibility of the compatibility or at least co-existence of emotional fulfilment and the display of genius, of Corinne's 'private' and 'public' identities.

At last four white horses drawing Corinne's chariot made their way into the midst of the throng. Corinne sat on the chariot built in the ancient style, and white-clad girls walked alongside. Wherever she passed, perfumes were lavishly flung into the air. Everyone came forward to see her from their windows which were decorated with potted plants and scarlet hangings. Everyone shouted: *Long live Corinne! Long live genius! Long live beauty!* There was universal emotion. . . . She was dressed like Domenichino's Sybil, an Indian turban wound round her head, intertwined with hair of the most beautiful black. She wore a white tunic with blue drapery fastened beneath her breast. While colorful, her dress did not so diverge from accepted practice as to seem affected. Her bearing as she rode was noble and modest: she was visibly pleased to be admired, but her joy was suffused with a timidity that seemed to beg indulgence for her triumph. Her expression, her eyes, her smile spoke in her favor, and one look made Lord Nelvil her friend even before any stronger feeling brought him into subjection. Her arms were ravishingly beautiful; her tall full figure, reminiscent of Greek statuary, vigorously conveyed youth and happiness. In her expression there was something inspired. Her way of greeting people, of thanking them for their applause, revealed a kind of naturalness in her that enhanced the splendour of her extraordinary position. She seemed at once a priestess of Apollo making her way towards the Temple of the Sun, and a woman perfectly

simple in the ordinary relationships of life. Indeed in her every gesture there was a charm that aroused interest and curiosity, astonish-
ment and affection. (de Staël 1987, 21)

The text makes clear that Corinne is a symbol not only of exemplary
womanhood, but also of civic and national pride. After her entry, as
Corinne prepares herself for her improvisation, Prince Castel-Forte,
Rome's most respected citizen, makes a speech extolling her virtues, in
which he declares:

> Corinne is the common bond shared by her friends; she is the im-
> pulse, the interest of our life; we depend on her goodness; we are
> proud of her genius. To foreigners we say: 'Gaze on her, for she is the
> image of our beautiful Italy; she is what we would be except for the ig-
> norance, envy, discord and indolence to which our fate has con-
> demned us.' It gives us pleasure to behold in her an admirable product
> of our climate and our arts, an offspring of the past, a prophet of the
> future.
>
> (de Staël 1987, 25)

At the Capitol Corinne, in fact, commands two kinds of attention, two
kinds of gaze, two kinds of feeling. She is both 'priestess' and 'simple . . .
woman', both 'noble' and 'timid', both 'extraordinary' and 'ordinary'.
Before her improvisation, she sits through a series of poems written in
her honour by the poets of Rome and during the time the recitation
takes, Oswald falls in love with her. As he watches her kneel before
Rome's civic dignitaries on her way to take up her seat beside the sena-
tor, he finds himself moved to tears. Prince Castel-Forte and her other
spectators read in Corinne Italy's best self, Oswald responds to what he
thinks of as her private self: 'it seemed to him that in the very midst of all
the splendour and all her success, Corinne's eyes pleaded for the protection of a friend, a protection no woman can ever do without, however
superior she may be' (de Staël 1987, 22). In one sense the novel is the
story of Oswald's attempt to prioritise Corinne's 'private' over her 'public' self. But we should not lose sight of the fact that his attraction to
her is governed by both, and his abandonment of her in favour of her
half-sister Lucile, who has only a private identification, results in his im-
poverishment and suffering as well as Corinne's. It is Corinne's simultaneous negotiation of both 'public' and 'private' gazes, gazes which
construct her as both a 'public' and a 'private' figure, which was so reso-
nant for Landon and other nineteenth-century women poets and their
critics, who were attempting to negotiate a similar political complexity.

Landon's work is politically uneven, but it seems to me that this oscillation opens up a scene of investigation at the heart of a restricted aesthetic space. Landon sticks to her brief, to produce the spectacle of suffering heterosexual femininity, but negotiates with it in a way which stages a crisis on its limits. It is tempting to grasp these moments of fracture and to lose sight of the fact that Landon is a poet who worked out her aesthetic firmly within the boundaries of her cultural permission. Feminist literary criticism does not have a language to represent this as anything other than false consciousness. Nevertheless, if we are to understand Landon it is vital that we find a way to hold together her radical and conservative aspects.

The account which is more or less hegemonic in feminist criticism, that of all genres women's poetry has always fallen under the most severe restriction from patriarchal culture, is misleading. From the late-Romantic period women's poetry was required at least as much as it was restricted. Between the 1820s and 1860s it was legitimated in a large body of critical and theoretical writing on the grounds that it provided a public display of private virtue and emotion.[10] The great insight of Landon's texts, worked through her obsession with Corinne and her explorations of colour, visibility and the mechanics of the gaze, is that the femininity in which such a huge cultural investment is made is not private at all. Landon reveals the extent to which the concept of the private construction of femininity is a fantasy, that femininity only comes into being because of its public significance, that the 'private sphere' itself is a publicly constructed fantasy. The greatest challenge which Landon's poetry poses to feminist criticism is that of the need to rethink the politics of the 'separate spheres'.

As we set about this, feminist literary critics would do well to take note of new directions in feminist historical and historiographical research, dealing with the question of the effect of the development of 'domestic ideology' on the lives and opportunities open to women in the late eighteenth and early nineteenth centuries. Amanda Vickery's recent historiographical review 'Golden Age to Separate Spheres? A Review of the Categories of English Women's History' is a landmark essay which is already sending shock waves through historical studies, and asks questions which seem to me to be especially pertinent to the study

---

[10] Some significant works in the genres of criticism and theorisation of British women's poetry are Dyce 1825, Stodart 1842, Elwood 1843, Bethune 1848, Rowton 1848, Moir 1851, Coppee 1860, Williams 1861, Robertson 1883, Adams 1884 and Sharp 1887.

of Landon. Vickery develops two main and interlinked theses. First, she argues that sexual division has been central to human culture in all historical periods, and the thesis accepted by feminist historians, that the division between masculinity and femininity was greatly intensified from the late eighteenth century, is misleading. Vickery argues that there never was a 'golden age', which from their reading of Friedrich Engels' essay 'The Origin of the Family, Private Property and the State' (1884) many feminist historians locate in a period prior to the widespread development of industrial capitalism. Conversely, she contends that the 'unquestioned belief that the transition to industrialised modernity robbed women of freedom, status and authentic function [which] underlies most modern women's history' misrepresents the nature of the complex changes in the layout of political space which came about in the period (Vickery 1993a, 401).

Second, Vickery calls for a reassessment of the investment which feminism has made in the concept of the 'separate spheres' in the late eighteenth and nineteenth centuries. The narrative which has structured women's history in which 'capitalist man needed a hostage in the home', and as 'near prisoner in the home, [woman] led a sheltered life drained of economic purpose and public responsibility . . . immured in the private sphere and [unable to] escape till feminism released her' fails to account for the effects of the rise of counter-revolutionary consciousness (whose effects on women's writing are discussed in detail by Gary Kelly elsewhere in this volume) and the campaigns for the moral renewal of the nation which sprang from it in the 1790s (Vickery 1993a, 387). Vickery argues that 'the extent to which shifts in public morality actually stripped women of power remains obscure', and suggests that, in fact, the economic and cultural changes of this period did not result simply in middle-class women's increased incarceration in the home and consequently decreased access to public and political influence, but in fact, in the creation of wider spheres of public articulation:

> the conservative backlash of the 1790s offered opportunities for greater female participation in the new public life of loyalist parades, petitions and patriotic subscriptions. Reactionary politics offered these 'angels of the state' a higher public profile, not a gilded cage.
> (Vickery 1993b, 6)

I concur with Vickery's argument that the terms 'public sphere' and 'private sphere', although current in the late-Romantic and early Victorian periods, are problematic, which is why I place them within scare-quotes. In feminist literary criticism as well as in women's history they have come to signify a complete separation of women from the cluster of discourses and spheres of legitimation including literature, art and the political. The phenomenon of Landon, of the high level of awareness her texts demonstrate of the fact that the private emotions and virtues, supposedly superintended by femininity, as well as femininity itself are public fantasies, challenges us to rethink some of the most sacred edicts of feminist theory.

Works Cited

Adams, W.H. 1884. *Celebrated English Women of the Victorian Era*, London: F.V. White.

Armstrong, I. 1993. *Victorian Poetry: Poetry, Poetics and Politics*, London: Routledge.

Bethune, G.W. 1848. *The British Female Poets*, Philadelphia: Lindsay and Blakiston.

Blanchard, S.L. 1841. *Life and Literary Remains of L.E.L.*, London: Henry Colburn.

Bristow, J. ed. 1987. *The Victorian Poet: Poetics and Persona*, London: Croom Helm.

Coppee, H. 1860. *A Gallery of Distinguished English and American Female Poets*, Philadelphia: E.H. Butler and Co.

de Staël, G. 1987. *Corinne, Or Italy*, trans. A. Goldberger, New Brunswick and London: Rutgers University Press.

Dyce, A. 1825. *Specimens of British Poetesses*, London: T. Rodd.

Ellis, S. 1838. *The Women of England*, London: Fisher.

Ellis, S. 1842. *The Daughters of England*, London: Fisher.

Ellis, S. 1843a. *The Wives of England*, London: Fisher.

Ellis, S. 1843b. *The Mothers of England*, London: Fisher.

Elwood, A. 1843. *Memoirs of the Literary Ladies of England from the Commencement of the Last Century*, London: Henry Colburn.

Engels, F. 1986. *The Origin of the Family, Private Property and the State*, ed. M. Barrett, trans. A. West, London: Penguin.

Frith, G. 1988. 'The Intimacy Which is Knowledge: Female Friendship in the Novels of Women Writers', unpublished Ph.D. thesis, University of Warwick.

Greer, G. 1982. 'The Tulsa Center for the Study of Women's Literature: what we are doing and why we are doing it', *Tulsa Studies in Women's Literature*, 1:1, 1–25.

Greer, G. 1995. *Slipshod Sybils: Recognition, Rejection and the Woman Poet*, London: Viking.

Hemans, F. 1928. *Records of Woman, With Other Poems*, London: T. Cadell and Edinburgh: William Blackwood.

Hickok, K. 1984. *Representations of Women: Nineteenth-Century British Women's Poetry*, Westport: Connecticut: Greenwood Press.

Habermas, J. 1989. *The Structural Transformation of the Public Sphere: An Inquiry Into a Category of Bourgeois Society*, trans. T. Burger, Cambridge, MA: MIT Press.

Hall, S.C. 1871. *A Book of Memories of Great Men and Women of the Age, From Personal Acquaintance*, London: Virtue.

Jerdan, W. 1852. *Autobiography of William Jerdan*, Vol. 3, London: Hall.

Kaplan, C. ed. 1978. *Aurora Leigh, and Other Poems*, London: The Women's Press.

Lamb, A.R. 1844. *Can Woman Regenerate Society?*, London: John W. Parker.

Landon, L.E. 1844. *The Poetical Works of Letitia Elizabeth Landon in Four Volumes, A New Edition*, London: Longman, Brown, Green and Longman.

Leighton, A. 1992. *Victorian Women Poets: Writing Against the Heart*, Hemel Hempstead: Harvester Wheatsheaf.

Meehan, M. ed. 1995. *Feminists Read Habermas: Gendering the Subject of Discourse*, New York and London: Routledge.

Moir, D. 1851. *Sketches of the Poetical Literature of the past Half-Century*, Vol. 6, Edinburgh and London: William Blackwood and Sons.

Ovid. 1977. *Heroides and Amores*, trans. G. Showerman, second edition revised by G.P. Gould, London: William Heinemann.

Robertson, E. 1883. *English Poetesses*, London: Cassell.

Rosenblum, D. 1986. *Christina Rossetti: The Poetry of Endurance*, Carbondale and Edwardsville: Southern Illinois University Press.

Rowton, F. 1848. *The Female Poets of Great Britain*, London: Longman, Brown, Green and Longman.

Sharp, E. 1887. *Women's Voices*, London: Walter Scott.

Sheppard, S. 1841. *L.E.L., Characteristics of Her Genius and Her Writings*, London: Longman.

Stephenson, G. 1992. 'Letitia Landon and the Victorian improvisatrice: the construction of L.E.L.', *Victorian Poetry*, 30:1, 1–17.

Stephenson, G. 1995. *Letitia Landon: The Woman Behind L.E.L.*, Manchester: Manchester University Press.

Stodart, M.A. 1842. *Female Writers: Thoughts on Their Proper Sphere and Their Powers of Usefulness*, London: R.B. Seeley and W. Burnside.

Vickery, A. 1993a. 'Golden age to separate spheres? A review of the categories and chronology of English women's history', *Historical Journal*, 36:2, 383–414.

Vickery, A. 1993b. 'Shaking the separate spheres', *Times Literary Supplement*, 12.3.96.

Williams, J. 1861. *The Literary Women of England*, London: Saunders and Otley.

Woolf, V. 1929. *A Room of One's Own*, London: Hogarth.

Emily Dickinson and
the Romantic Comparative

DARIA DONNELLY

'Curiouser and curiouser!' cried Alice (she was so much surprised,
that for a moment she quite forgot how to speak good English).
                                    Alice's Adventures in Wonderland

THE PERVASIVE INFLUENCE of the English Romantic tradition on Emily
Dickinson was first charted by Michael Yetman (1973, 129–47), who argued for three major areas of likeness: a preoccupation with the relationship between mind and world, an intuitional basis for poetic perception,
and a religious skepticism based on the sense that the only consciousness accessible to the poet is her own. Each of these elements is driven to
extremity in Dickinson, so that the relationship of inner and outer is
tense and even antithetic, perception is not only sudden but traumatic,
and religious skepticism is registered as desolation. My purpose here is to
describe Dickinson's Romantic extremity and argue for it as a resistance,
frequently gendered, to certain strains within Romanticism itself, by focusing attention on her comparatives, and setting them within the context of a Romantic shift in the comparative as a signifying grammar.

Richard Wilbur astutely characterized Emily Dickinson as 'a Lin-
neaus to the phenomenon of her own consciousness, describing and dis-
tinguishing the states and motions of her soul' (1960, 35). Like the
botanist, Dickinson accomplished much of this description and classification by means of the grammatical comparative, a form which is widespread in her poetry, and which, surprisingly for a poet so hyperbolic,
outnumbers her superlatives two to one.[1] The ubiquity of her comparatives would barely register if not for their characteristic strangeness.
Since it is in their oddity that Dickinson's comparatives strain against
both Romanticism and empiricism, a catalogue of how they are strange
will orient us.

I am grateful to Professors Mary Campbell, Anne Janowitz, and Christopher
Ricks for their conversation and generous readings of drafts, and to the late Dr
Celia Millward who got me started. I refer to Dickinson's poems (P) and letters
(L) by the numbers assigned them in the Johnson editions.

[1] By my count, one quarter of her poems contain one or more comparatives:
more than 500 comparatives in all.

Dickinson's comparatives are sometimes arresting because they are so metaphysically extravagant ('My Eye is fuller than my vase –' P 202) or because the 'er' morpheme of inflected comparatives creates such an aurally lush effect (e.g., 'The fairer – for the farness –' P 719 and: 'My tenderer Experiment/ Toward Men –' P 902). More often, a reader stumbles over them because they are solecisms. Dickinson violated standard use by forming inflected comparisons from words of three or more syllables: 'contenteder' (P 639; 762), 'audibler (P 643; 1068v), 'admirabler' (P 827), 'terribler' (P 244; 879; 1277), 'odiouser' (P 1388), 'durabler' (P 1192), 'culpabler' (P 1274). The comparatives that she made from disyllabics – 'gallanter' (P 126); 'consciouser' (P 762); 'ancienter' (P 1241); 'graphicer' (P 1422) among others – would probably have sounded as bizarre to contemporaneous ears as those she formed from trisyllabics, since her recommended school grammar, William Harvey Wells's *The Elements of English Grammar*, being surprisingly more conservative than our present day ones on this matter, argued that all disyllabics (with the exception of words ending in y or e) take the periphrastic form.[2]

Dickinson's defiance of conventions governing the formation of comparatives is not the final determinant of their strangeness. A Dickinson comparative as impeccably grammatical as 'sorer' sounds odd because its service as a modifier, both adjectival and adverbial, for the particular words to which Dickinson attaches it, is so unexpected and original: 'It's sorer to believe!' (P 149); 'What sorer – puzzled me –' (P 600); 'Wouldn't Dungeons sorer grate' (P 728); 'There Marauds a sorer Robber' (P 1296). Much of the tension and energy in Dickinson's comparatives stems from this yoking together by violence of a comparative with its modified noun or verb.

The most extreme examples of Dickinson's unusual combinations of modifier and modified occur when she attaches a comparative to a term that rejects comparison, e.g., 'an Ampler Zero' (P 422); 'In further

---

[2] C.M. Millward reports that in PDE morphology, common disyllabic adjectives can take either the periphrastic or inflected form of comparative (1989, 271–72). According to Quirk et al. (1985, 462) disyllabic adjectives that *most readily* take the inflected form are those ending in an unstressed vowel. This would make Dickinson's 'dapperer' as impeccable in principle as it sounds to the ear. Pace Wells, Dickinson's contemporaries did form inflected comparatives from disyllabics (e.g., Emerson's lines in 'The Sphinx': 'Profounder, profounder,/ Man's spirit must dive') although my impression, from reading in the period, is that the oddity of Dickinson's disyllabic comparatives are without parallel among her contemporaries.

Infinite –' (P 522); 'Through less Infinity –' (P 573). In like manner, and in explicit defiance of Wells, she forms comparatives from 'infinite,' a word that does not admit comparison: 'Born infiniter – now –' (P 625); 'With infinite Affection –/ And infiniter Care –' (P 790). These inflected infinites point to another means by which Dickinson estranges comparatives, namely, by using syntax to intensify or reduce grammatical solecism: the adverbial comparative, 'Born infiniter', sounds much stranger than 'infiniter care' because in the latter case we have been prepared for the comparative adjective by its positive form, and thus scarcely register the violation of standard use. Even where normal grammar prevails, poetic sentences that contain both a positive and a comparative can be shaped by a poet to maximize oddity, as for example, in Melville's poem 'The Conflict of Convictions', where the force of the positive makes the subsequent comparative appear bizarrely equivocal: 'So deep must the stones be hurled/ Whereon the throes of ages rear/ The final empire and the happier world.' Dickinson's poetry posits not only suggestive syntactic but even meaningful lexical asymmetry between positives, comparatives, and superlatives as for example in the invocation of the term itself in poem 800: 'The quality conceive/ Of Paradise superlative –/ Through their Comparative.'

Dickinson's eager recourse to linguistic and syntactic deformations has been interpreted as one outcome of the value she places upon compression and also as the result of her desire to maintain hymn meter. In *Emily Dickinson's Grammar*, Christanne Miller gives several sentences to the comparative, and, drawing on Dickinson's propensity to repress one term of the comparison, argues for them as minor examples of referential deletion in a poetics of compression (1987, 29). Mutlu Konuk Blasing, while not referring explicitly to comparatives, argues that Dickinson's fidelity to a syllabic economy puts pressure on her word choice, and draws attention to the 'historical and linguistic processes of articulation and composition' that are both embodied and extended by those choices (1987, 180).[3]

In decoding a stanza such as 'I felt my life with both my hands/ To see

---

[3]   Blasing (1987, 180) argues: 'Dickinson's choice of words, pressurized by the demands of syllabic economy, calls attention to etymology, spelling, and the agglutinative process by which syllables and morphemes add up to words. In exposing the historical and linguistic processes of articulation and composition, she reveals the creative word to be the created word that goes on reproducing, either legitimately by etymology, whose connections are historically sanctioned, or illegitimately by literal accidents, whose connections are capricious though irrepressible.'

if it was there –/ I held my spirit to the Glass,/ To prove it possibler –'
(P 351), Miller's work alerts us to the labor involved in recovering the
terms of comparison (more possible than what), an effort which is re-
doubled by the referentially slippery 'it' and the supercharged meaning
of 'spirit' (as that which, in the Christian view, survives death and also
that breath which evidences the presence of organic life), especially
given the impeccable parallelism of the syntax. As we read through the
stanza, Dickinson's comparative puts us in the position of actively comparing between interpretive choices (my life is more possible than I
thought; my spirit is more possible than my life).

Blasing's work, on the other hand, draws our attention to the ways in
which 'possibler' redounds in the poem: the 'er' morpheme creates a
breathy final syllable, and a pun with 'blur', both of which make concrete the absurdly empirical act of testing for the presence of life by holding a mirror to one's own mouth. More significantly, this extension of
inflection beyond the normative use assures that this stanza is the only
perfect realization of hymn meter in the poem, which then underscores
where the meter is odd, as in the fifth stanza, where a nine syllable line
that results from the article 'the' before 'Heaven' finally identifies the
speaker as a religious skeptic. Within the context of individual poems then,
Dickinson's comparatives are one element in a poetics designed to fore-
ground the createdness (as opposed to naturalness) of language, and to
emphasize the reader's role in wresting meaning from an opaque creation.[4]

---

[4] Dickinson's comparatives are most successful when their deformations in-
carnate an argument, be it theological and poetic. They are irritating when they
obfuscate a sentiment that is unworthy of the reading effort, as this poem, sent
to her sister-in-law, Sue Dickinson (P 819):

> All I may, if small,
> Do it not display
> Larger for the Totalness –
> 'Tis Economy
> To bestow a World
> And withhold a Star –
> Utmost, is Munificence –
> Less, tho' larger, poor.

The message: 'my small offering is superior to the larger ones you have re-
ceived/will receive because mine is the utmost I can give'. Present here is a conventional ironic reversal in the repetition of the comparative 'larger'. There is
also a more promising play between positive, comparative, and superlative types
of words (small; larger; utmost) that animates her powerful lyrics on theodicy.
But the total effect is a disappointing, but not unusual, asymmetry between medium and message. Partly because she did not publish and therefore was under
no constraints to sort the good from the bad, and partly because poems that are

When her comparatives are considered collectively, they emerge as a central means by which Dickinson contended with Romantic ideas about cosmology and teleology, particularly as those ideas were embodied in what I will call 'the Romantic comparative'. Dickinson's comparatives are odd not only because of the pressure that her fidelity to compression or to syllabic economy places on her linguistic choices, and because of her self-delighted tendency to rebellion, but also because she is trying to place her use of them in relationship to a recent and not fully realized shift in the comparative as a signifying grammar. British Romantic poets, whose works Dickinson avidly read in her household anthologies,[5] transformed the comparative by emphasizing the temporal (horizontal) dimension inherent in it, embedding even its (vertical) service as a register of quality and intensity within linear time. Just as in Lovejoy's account, the Romantic temporalizing of the Great Chain of Being began as a slight shift in dialectical emphasis that subsequently wrought profound changes in Western theology and literature (1939, 288–314; esp. 296), so too the Romantic temporalizing of the comparative, again a change of emphasis rather than an innovation, both reflected and promoted the increasingly horizontal understandings of relativism, naturalism, and progressivism that were emerging throughout the period in which Dickinson (1830–86) was writing.

When Dickinson attended the theologically conservative Mt Holyoke Female Seminary in 1847–48, she encountered both the pre-Romantic comparative and the transitionally Romantic one. Her rhetoric course was designed around a close reading of Pope's *Essay on Man*, a poem in which comparatives demonstrate 'the strong connexions, nice dependencies, gradations just' of the Great Chain of Being. In Pope's apotheosis of the Chain of Being, natural and social phenomena are arrayed in a vertical hierarchy where 'whatever is, is right': thus, 'oaks are made taller and stronger than the weeds they shade' and 'some are and must be greater than the rest,/ More rich, more wise: but who infers from

occasional and spontaneous were saved by her appreciative correspondents, we now have equal access to the poems that are mediocre and those that are great. In fact, the poems that are undermined by a compulsive use of the comparative (seven in P 639; five in P 422) testify to its prominent role in her mode of thinking.

5   Charles A. Dana, *The Household Book of Poetry*, 6th edn (1860); Rufus W. Griswold, ed., *The Sacred Poets of England and America* (1849) and the two volume Robert Chambers, ed., *Cyclopedia of English Literature* (1847) present a generous selection of British Romantics including all the poems I cite in this essay.

hence/ That such are happier, shocks all common sense'. In like manner, Dickinson's pre-Darwinian textbooks in natural history use comparative classification to show that a benevolent and superlative God has created an immutable and perfect hierarchy of living objects.[6]

A more organic and temporalized comparative can be found in her other rhetoric text, Samuel Philips Newman's *A Practical System of Rhetoric*, which recommends the comparative as a sign of 'refinement of the intellectual powers': 'Taste, as judgment, calls into exercise various intellectual faculties; comparisons are to be instituted, inferences to be made, conclusions to be drawn; and the more perfectly this work is performed, the higher is the order of taste possessed.'[7] While Newman conceptualizes refinement as progress upward toward a stable Superlative, he argues that taste develops within a temporal framework in which social and personal progress is presumed: 'This difference in feeling with which the same object is regarded at different periods, is found connected with different advances that have been made in knowledge, and in the cultivation and refinement of intellectual powers' (1847, 60).

In the *Preface to Lyrical Ballads*, Wordsworth argues that the poet is a master of time, creating poems within a temporal process of contemplation which refines 'the spontaneous overflow of emotion' into art: 'Emphatically may it be said of the poet, as Shakespeare hath said of man, that "he looks before and after".' In emphasizing temporality, Romantics underscored not only the organic connections between life-forms, but also the volatile character of both the human mind and the natural world, the relationship of which Romantics were so interested in exploring. Romantic poets emphasized the consonance between flux in the world and in the mind, so that abrupt and capricious shifts in nature found in the greater Romantic lyric are often benevolent passing

---

6   Dickinson's textbook of natural history, William Smellie's *The Philosophy of Natural History* (1841), instructed her to be satisfied with the static hierarchy of the Great Chain: 'let man therefore be contented with the powers and spheres of action assigned him. There is an exact adaptation of his powers, capacities, and desires, both bodily and intellectual, to the scene in which he is destined to move. His station in the scale of nature is fixed by wisdom. Let him study the world of nature, and find in the contemplation of all that is beautiful and curious and wonderful in them, proofs of the existence and attributes of his Creator' (307).

7   Newman 1847, 63. According to Jack L. Capps (1966, 190) Dickinson used the 50th edition (which he dates circa 1834). Lacking that edition, I looked at several editions prior and posterior to that date, and discovered that they are only reprintings.

spurs to introspection or to a shift in human mood (e.g., Coleridge's 'The
Æolian Harp', 'And now, its strings/ Boldlier swept, the long sequacious
notes/ over delicious surges sink and rise', or William Cullen Bryant's
'The Prairies', 'All at once/ A fresher wind sweeps by, and breaks my
dream,/ And I am in the wilderness alone'). M.H. Abrams modulates
this consonance by arguing that the central feature of the greater Romantic lyric is a sustained interweaving of mind and world which most
frequently occurs when a speaker registers palpable changes in the self
by means of objects in nature, which are to different degrees stable
('Lines Composed Above Tintern Abbey'; 'Elegiac Stanzas'; 'Frost at
Midnight'; 'Dejection: An Ode'; 'Mont Blanc').[8] Romantic poets distinguish themselves, one from the next, by the way each contextualizes
his or her own volatility (as maturation, mutability, progress, violent
abruption, as having an endpoint, or not having an endpoint). Wordsworth and Coleridge, for example, focus on the maturation of consciousness, itself a compensation for the diminishments of biological
ageing; Shelley registers more violent and less enduring changes in perception.

But for American poets, under the guidance of Emerson, American
Romanticism's pre-eminent thinker, volatility has a less personal inflection, and seems most consequential in its impact on theology, epistemology, and politics. That may be why American representations of flux
are so charged with ecstasy and despair. In 'Circles', a first series essay
which is regarded as having deeply influenced Dickinson (Diehl 1981,
165), Emerson's abundant use of comparatives ('lower', 'longer', 'better',
'faster', 'nimbler', 'finer', 'larger') underscores his argument that 'Permanence is but a word of degrees. Every thing is medial.'[9] That everything

8   Abrams 1970, 201. Abrams falls into comparative vocabulary in describing
the unfolding of these lyrics of double consciousness: 'In "Frost at Midnight" . . .
the images in the initial description are already suffused with an unstated significance, which, in Coleridges's terms, is merely "elicited" and expanded by
the subsequent reflection, which in turn "superinduces" a *richer* meaning upon
the scene to which it reverts' (223). This fits with Emerson's view in 'Circles'
that revelation is not simply progressive but that each new discovery reorganizes
and reveals the connections between ideas which before seemed antagonistic:
progressive revelation tends always to unity.
9   In her study of Emerson's 'romantic style', Julie Ellison observes that Emerson's early encounter with the German Romantic higher criticism, a comparative approach to the Bible, inaugurates his rejection of church religion and his
life as an essayist. This new and controversial tool for biblical interpretation
proceeded by comparing conflicting biblical accounts (synoptic gospels), dis-

(virtue, love, truth, works of art) is vulnerable to change and re-evaluation, did not strike Emerson as a threat to personal or social stability. In 'Circles', Emerson is positively rapturous about volatility: 'No love can be bound by oath or covenant to secure it against a higher love. No truth so sublime but it may be trivial tomorrow in the light of new thoughts'; 'In the thought of to-morrow there is a power to upheave all thy creed, all the creeds, all the literatures of the nations, and marshal thee to a heaven which no epic dream has yet depicted.'

Emerson's tone here is mild in comparison to his disciple Whitman, who in *Song of Myself* (1855) uses comparatives to rhapsodize progressive revelation even as he severs it from any recognizable framework in which that revelation would produce a lasting insight.[10]

> I open my scuttle at night and see the far-sprinkled systems,
> And all I see, multiplied as high as I can cipher, edge but
>   the rim of farther systems.
>
> Wider and wider they spread, expanding and always
>   expanding,
> Outward and outward and forever outward.
>
> My sun has his sun, and round him obediently wheels,
> He joins with his partners a group of superior circuit,
> And greater sets follow, making specks of the greatest
>   inside them.
>
> There is no stoppage, and never can be stoppage;
>
>   (Section 45)

closing relationships between biblical narratives with other mythologies, and comparing Christian versions of history with other historical sources. It put into question biblical unity and traditional understanding of the Bible as univocal divine revelation. (Ellison 184, 6–8; 44).

[10] Comparatives can be found throughout *Song of Myself*: see section 3, 6, 14, 15, 20, 21, 24, 26, 29, 30, 32, 44, 45, 47, 48 and can be divided into three principle types: those which assert the perfect balance of world as it is (these tend to be formed by negation): 'I do not call one greater and one smaller,/ That which fills its period and place is equal to any'; second, those which assert the completeness of self, which requires no supplement: 'The scent of these arm-pits is aroma finer than prayer'; and those which assert continual journey forward as in section 45. In contrast to Dickinson, only one time does Whitman appear to be pressed into a comparative by the demands of the structure of his poem (section 6): 'This grass is very dark to be from the white heads of old mothers,/ Darker than the colorless beards of old men,/ Dark to come under the faint red roofs of mouths.'

Whitman exceeds Emerson in the inconclusiveness and relativism of his comparatives: not only does Whitman refuse to regard any judgment or perception as final, he decisively rejects Emersonian retrospection, the belief that, 'each new step in thought reconciles twenty seemingly discordant facts, as expressions of one law' ('Circles'), in favor of continual self-transcendence ('My feet strike an apex of the apices of the stairs,/ On every step bunches of ages, and larger bunches between the steps,/ All below duly traveled – and still I mount and mount' (Section 44)).

Whitman's extension of the liberating quality of impermanence, implicit in Emersonian comparatives, underscores the quarrels that Dickinson, Emerson's other great disciple, had with the latter's cheerful view of volatility. For Dickinson, temporality is appalling because it is fatal to organic being. Benevolence seems to her a quality as absent in Nature as it is in Deity. She is a skeptical Emersonian at best. Karl Keller has argued that Dickinson experienced Emerson 'as push, as stimulus, as prophet motivator, as prime mover, as provocateur', but also concluded that 'if it is possible to conceive of Emily Dickinson's poetry as a single unified production from a single unified sensibility . . . it provides an argument *against* much of Emerson' (1979, 164–165). Dickinson follows him in forgoing the vertical and communal consolations of faith, and in focusing on the (sometimes simply capricious) fluctuations of self and of nature. Emerson's public withdrawal from the Unitarian ministry (1838) supported her decision, made against considerable evangelical pressure from her peers and teachers, not to make a profession of faith that would allow her to take communion in the Congregational Church. But her poetry, her very syntax and grammar, registers the bewilderments attendant on the loss of a coherent nature presided over by God. She used her Calvinism to defeat her Romanticism and vice versa.

Dickinson's representation of her necessarily thwarted efforts to make sense of death departs sharply from the Romantics. She repudiates the compensatory economies of maturation and retrospection as strongly as Whitman but by other means: where he ceaselessly goes forward, she doubles back, circling death over and over again, claiming that the 'Wilderness of Size' experienced in the wake of 'Death's bold Exhibition' yields 'preciser' inferences of 'what we are' (P 856). Like Alice in Wonderland, Dickinson uses deformed comparatives as markers of incremental change in a journey without forward motion, weirdly registering her arrest by means of a grammar of progress.

For the remainder of this essay I will flesh out these speculative statements about Dickinson's vexed Romanticism in two ways: first, by

showing how Dickinson's comparatives talk back to the Romantic organization of volatility, especially as it is articulated by Emerson, whose
work she avidly read throughout her life, and also by Wordsworth,
whose organic and heterogeneous principles of poetic classification are
credited as having inspired her fascicle arrangements (Cameron 1992,
49–50), and whose familiar comparative-charged 'Tintern Abbey' embodied Newman's sense that the cultivation and refinement of intellectual powers unseats stable vision. Secondly, I will dwell on the
inconclusiveness inherent in the grammatical comparative and examine how Dickinson's comparatives assert taste or judgment, and to what
extent they do so in a manner different to that of the Romantics. The
gradual collapse of the Chain of Being's stable hierarchies following the
new emphasis on temporality presents challenges to the poet's authority
to speak. From where does that authority come? How is it maintained? Is
it undercut by privileging the comparative over the superlative? What
particular challenges does the woman poet confront in asserting her
authority to express taste?

Talking Back to Romanticism

Dickinson's strenuous and strained use of the comparatives constitutes a
conversation with Romantic ideas of mutability and progress. Like the
Romantics, Dickinson is centrally interested in the volatility of nature
and the human mind and uses comparatives to describe it. But her sense
that flux is essentially tragic distinguishes Dickinson from both Emerson
and Wordsworth and makes her highly resistant to ameliorative com-
pensations of wisdom and maturation that each offers for the impover-
ishing effects of aging and mortality. Her quarrel with their efforts to
convert loss into gain is waged implicitly by her lack of attention to
maturation as a poetic subject, her representational focus on witnessing
and imagining the scene of death, and her positing that comparative
change in herself occurs primarily in relationship to changes in other
people. These arguments become explicit in poems which reproduce
and resist Emerson's and Wordsworth's views.

The most distinctive aspect of Dickinson's representation of
volatility is her consistent focus on the violent abruptions that result
from mortality,[11] abruptions which so daze the poetic speaker that her

[11] See especially Diehl 1981, passim and Paglia 1990, 623–73. Their accounts
require qualification: despite Dickinson's reputation as a poet who projects her-

command of quotidian language is jeopardized. David Porter has observed that a majority of Dickinson poems are written from the perspective of surviving trauma or loss or death itself (1981, 9–24). In her poetics of 'the aftermath', Dickinson, the 'pale Reporter, from the awful doors/ Before the Seal' (P 160), focuses our attention on the effort to narrate indescribable experiences, rather than on the difference between before and after, an alteration that might be registered comparatively. Her comparatives do not connect a former to present self (as do Wordsworth's) because, for her, change so radically deprives the mind of its familiars. The absence of evolution in her poetic style and concerns over a period of forty years' writing which so astonishes Porter (1981, 139) finds its parallel in her almost total disregard of personal evolution as a poetic subject.

While Dickinson virtually never represents herself maturing (in an opus of more than 1,700 poems 483; 563; 652; 968 stand as exceptions), she is concerned with diminution, by degrees, of feeling over time. This combination of attitudes vexes her relationship to Wordsworth, whose 'Lines Composed a Few Miles Above Tintern Abbey' considers the changes wrought by time by means of an extended comparison of a present self to the particular incarnation of self that visited the ruin five years earlier. Wordsworth's abundant comparatives ('more deep', 'purer', 'coarser', 'remoter', 'warmer', 'deeper', 'holier') argue strenuously for personal progress in vision and understanding, doing so against an undercurrent of anxiety that the speaker's affective life has diminished over time. In poem 652, 'A Prison gets to be a Friend', Dickinson argues against that flow of comparatives.

Although it is sometimes read as a reprisal of Byron's 'Prisoner of Chillon' (Capps 1966, 79), poem 652 strikes me as a compressed and wry rewriting of 'Tintern Abbey'.[12] Wordsworth's wistful invocation of 'the coarser pleasures of my boyish days', 'that had no need of a remoter charm,/ By thought supplied' is both echoed and commented upon by

self onto nature or who is overwhelmingly concerned with violent breaks, there is a whole class of comparatives which show Dickinson as wonderfully attentive to predictable changes in nature, for example this description of summer's end, 'The Dusk drew earlier in –/ The Morning foreign shone –' (J 1540). In addition to such seasonal changes, she charts, by means of comparatives, the daily drama of sunrise and sunset, the movement of birds, the outburst of a storm (see poems 12; 140; 152; 232; 335; 574; 624; 634; 748; 794; 938; 941; 1045).

[12] Dickinson was disposed to this kind of rewriting: she once sent a four line poem to her mentor Thomas Wentworth Higginson in response to his rambling civil war elegy, 'Decoration'. He recognized it as a revision of his poem, and 'far

her 'As plashing in the Pools –/ When Memory was a Boy –/ But a Demurer Circuit –/ A Geometric Joy –'. The first two lines of the stanza reproduce Wordsworth's argument of boyish pleasure, and the 'Demurer Circuit' of the third line evokes the 'remoter thought' of his present self. The fourth line seems to me to refer, by means of the suggestion of 'metre' in the term 'geometric' and the compressed allusion in the term 'joy', to Keats's 'A thing of beauty is a joy for ever',[13] to Wordsworth's conversion of diminution ('a Demurer Circuit') into a thing of beauty, a poem.

Dickinson unsettles Wordsworth in several ways. She uses the equivalence that her syntax creates between 'Demurer Circuit' and 'Geometric Joy' to expose what his comparatives mask, namely, that his nagging sense of loss has produced the poem's central argument for gain. Secondly, she uses comparatives with a distinctly downward arc ('demurer' and 'passiver') to argue that the losses attendant on the passage of time are so incontrovertible that they are most honestly registered by comparatives of decline: 'The narrow Round – the Stint –/ The slow exchange of Hope –/ For something passiver – Content'. She judges Wordsworth's effort to repress loss, as embodied in his intensifying comparatives, as an unwarranted evasion of the prison house of being. At the end of the poem, she rejects his Romantic retrospection in favor of what she judges as a dubious and only slightly less deluding promise of future redemption, arguing against comparing past and present selves mainly because she thinks it can only make the present seem more perilously mutable, more proximate to death: 'the Liberty we knew/ Avoided – like a Dream –'. At least the consolation promised by Eternity, however suspect its reality, does not intensify anxiety about where one stands in the inexorable march toward death, as poem 802 argues: 'Time feels so vast that were it not/ For an Eternity –/ I fear me this Circumference/ Engross my finity –'. (Notice in line two, that as in poem 351, skepticism about the religious character of Eternity is suggested by an article.)

On the very rare occasions that Dickinson thinks about time as a theatre in which her own attachments and interests change, rather than a torturer who wrests away those she loves, she sounds like a benign version of Emerson (is a benigner possible?), without the outlaw energy of 'Self Reliance' and 'Circles' or the stoical despair of 'Experience': 'I smile

finer'. Throughout her letters she rewrites poetic lines and responds to poems she is reading with her own poems.
[13] See also P 1639 (circa 1885): 'A Letter is a joy of Earth –/ It is denied the Gods –.'

upon the Aims/ That felt so ample – Yesterday –/ Today's – have vaster claims –' (P 563). Such serenity suggests that Dickinson experiences this quotidian volatility in the self as a rare reprieve from change that is external, unsought, and violent. But it equally reflects what Joanne Feit Diehl claims sets her apart from Emerson and the Romantics: that she does not attempt to repress antithetical nature nor moralize experience; rather her poems 'present a spectrum of reaction to the amorality of nature'.[14]

That 'spectrum', as well as Dickinson's view of time as a depleting force, accounts for the surprising nature of the comparatives by which she describes the process of mourning. Given her major occupation with the trauma of mortality, their report of reparative progress is arresting, even as they register the blunting aftershocks of death: 'It ceased to hurt me, though so slow/ I could not feel the Anguish go –/ . . . Nor what consoled it, I could trace –/ Except, whereas 'twas Wilderness –/ It's better – almost Peace –' (P 584) or 'We see – Comparatively –/ The Thing so towering high/ We could not grasp its segment/ Unaided – Yesterday –// This Morning's finer Verdict –/ Makes scarcely worth the Toil' (P 534). 'Almost' and 'scarcely' are slight dissonances in the bewilderments and shallow calm of a grief diminished. There is similar dissonance in poem 1540, where Dickinson so trusts the subtlety and naturalness of mourning that she uses it to describe seasonal mutability, even as she disturbs the calm by positing that this diminution of attachment necessarily requires disloyalty to the dead: 'As imperceptibly as Grief/ The Summer lapsed away –/ Too imperceptible at last/ To seem like Perfidy –'.

More frequently, Dickinson overtly undercuts the force of dependable alterations in feeling by projecting ameliorative comparatives into a scene where they are clutched at as consolations rather then affectively experienced:

> It don't sound so terrible – quite – as it did –
> I run it over – 'Dead, Brain, 'Dead'.
> Put it in Latin – left of my school –
> Seems it don't shriek so – under rule.
>
> . . .
>
> I suppose it will interrupt me some
> Till I get accustomed – but then the Tomb

---

[14] Diehl 1981, 161 and 165. This is at odds with Diehl's earlier assertion that, in contrast to Wordsworth, Dickinson demands from the natural world a coherence and morality which will definitely reveal the character of its creator (36).

> Like other new Things – shows largest – then –
> And smaller, by Habit –
>
> It's shrewder then
> Put the Thought in advance – a Year –
> How like 'a fit' – then –
> Murder – wear! (P 426)

Dickinson's ameliorative comparatives are more frequently speculative than effective, promising to limit pain by imaging a state or temporality in which present feeling would be different: for example, 'It might be lonelier, without the Loneliness –' (P 405); 'If one wake at Midnight – better –/ Dreaming of the Dawn –' (P 450); 'I tried to think a lonelier Thing/ Than any I had seen –' (P 532); 'Tis good – the looking back on Grief –/ To re-endure the Day –/ . . . And though the Wo you have To-day/ Be larger – As the Sea/ Exceeds its Unremembered Drop –/ They're Water – equally –' (P 660).

The reparative design of these comparatives bears a strong resemblance to the way Emerson's comparatives check present sorrow (itself caused by the very impermanence he celebrates) by heralding its future transformation, as in this portion of the poem 'To Rhea':

> But I, from my beatitude,
> Albeit scorned as none was scorned,
> Adorn her as was none adorned.
> I make this maiden an ensample
> To Nature, through her kingdoms ample,
> Whereby to model newer races,
> Statelier forms and fairer faces;
> To carry man to new degrees
> Of power and of comeliness.
> These presents be the hostages
> Which I pawn for my release.
> See to thyself, O Universe!
> Thou art better, and not worse.

In contrast to the reparative comparatives written by Dickinson, who first read this poem as a young woman on the particular recommendation of the boy who gave her Emerson's 1846 *Poems*, his comparatives are absurdly grandiose in their promised effects. But like Dickinson's, the wishful nature of the ameliorative progress they describe writes defeat onto hope.

The second series essay, 'Experience', in which Emerson grapples with his young son's death and the 'evanescence' of world and mind which that loss underscores, helps us to sort Emerson from Dickinson because here comparative change is neither felt nor available as a consolatory resource. A series of thwarted comparatives registers the devastating underside of his assertion that everything is medial:

> In the death of my son, now more than two years ago, I seemed to have lost a beautiful estate, – no more. I cannot get it nearer to me. If tomorrow I should be informed of the bankruptcy of my principal debtors, the loss of my property would be a great inconvenience to me, perhaps, for many years; but it would leave me as it found me, – neither better nor worse. So it is with this calamity . . . I grieve that grief can teach me nothing, nor carry me one step into real nature.

Emerson's earlier enthusiasm about volatility is challenged by the lack of vigor in his closest attachments and the lack of progress in understanding his grief, both of which are registered by negated comparatives. The stolidness of his own grief constitutes a major defeat for his cosmic optimism, the belief that there is 'a force always at work to make the best better and the worst good'.[15]

The pain that accompanies the volatile quality of our organic, mental and affective lives becomes too terrible for Emerson to face, and he blinks at the end of his essay, when he domesticates the problem of evanescence:

> We dress our garden, eat our dinners, discuss the household with our wives, and these things make no impression, are forgotten next week; but, in the solitude to which every man is always returning, he has a sanity and revelations which in his passage into new worlds he will carry with him.

Where he trivializes the momentousness of domestic life, to evade the fact that it is within that sphere that the most devastating instance of evanescence lived and died, Dickinson considers the problem of pain from a wholly domestic perch.

Being a woman matters to her consideration of volatility because this identity imposed certain constraints and roles which Dickinson internalized (and, further, parodically embraced),[16] constraints which

---

15 From 'Speech' [Free Religious Association], *Miscellanies* quoted in Kateb 1995, 78.
16 Gertrude Hughes argues that Dickinson embraces the cult of true womanhood with 'parodic fidelity' and thus subverts it (1986, 18). I do not think her

Dickinson used to sharpen her own thinking about and representation of volatility. In contrast to the activity and fresh air that animate Wordsworth's charting of changes in himself by looking at a stolid ruin, and Emerson's consideration of the nature of change by shifting from example to example of volatility over the course of an essay, there is a decidedly domestic inflection in Dickinson's frequent positing that world and mind change in relation to other persons. Because the poems in which she changes by acts of the will, putting on personae with great panache, are so much more appealing[17] there has been a general critical silence about how frequently her poetic speakers change in response to new absences caused by death ('where I have lost, I softer tread –' P 104 see also 217; 296; 313; 786), or to the love given by another, as in poem 493, 'The World – stands – solemner – to me –/ Since I was wed – to Him –', and poem 506, 'He touched me, so I live to know . . . /I'm different from before,/ As if I breathed superior air – . . ./ My Gipsy face – transfigured now – To tenderer Renown –.' If these speakers tend to merely passive receptivity, at least they know that they are social creatures. More balanced are those poems in which Dickinson's speakers bend themselves, by an act of the will, to the new poverty caused by death: 'Severer Service of myself/ I – hastened to demand/ To fill the awful Vacuum/ Your life had left behind –' (P 786). Without mobility, by choice and chance, and thoroughly instructed in the value of domestic care, Dickinson sits with the problem of pain and death much longer than the male Romantics.

Dickinson's sometimes disturbing preoccupation with the physical dimension of pain is the result of her desire to block the pain from having meaning; to not fold it into a personal (Romantic) or theological (Calvinist) narrative, to keep it a stolid fact that will serve no larger purpose. Dickinson is a connoisseuse of pain, using comparatives to provide acute descriptions of sensation, variations of sensation, as well as to gauge and compare pain: for example, 'I've seen a Dying Eye/ Run round

---

only or even primary attitude toward constraint is subversive, but certainly parody (hard to distinguish from phobia) is present alongside acceptance, rebellion, and frustration. Some examples of gender inflected constraints are fidelity to family which Dickinson exaggerated by refusing to 'cross my Father's ground to any House or town', and which she more painfully lived out by remaining loyal to her adulterous brother at the cost of her most important friendship, and middle-class female decorum, which she exaggerated by refusing to address her own envelopes so that her handwriting would not be seen by an unknown public, and had internalized in her complex decision not to publish her poems.

17 Consider, for example, the relative loss of female power between poem 290 and 659.

and round a Room . . . Then Cloudier become –' (P 547); 'It is simple, to
ache in the Bone, or the Rind –/ But Gimblets – among the nerve –/
Mangle daintier – terribler –' (P 244); 'This thirst would blister – easier –
now' (P 296); 'For some – an Ampler Zero –/ A Frost more needle keen/
Is necessary, to reduce/ The Ethiop within' (P 422).

Some of Dickinson's readers feel that her attraction to pain compro-
mises her resistance to making it meaningful.[18] Dickinson continually
returns to the scene of death not only because it confirms her radical
skepticism but also because it is such a comparatively intense experience ('A Cheek is always redder/ Just where the Hectic stings!' P 165);
because it provides, by comparative contrast, a relief from the pain she is
in, or more typically, proof of her exceptionalism ('I measure every Grief
I meet/ With narrow, probing, Eyes –/ I wonder if It weighs like Mine –/
Or has an Easier size' P 561); because it unsettles the orderly diminution
of feeling in mourning ('Enlightened to a larger pain' P 561). What I
find most disturbing in Dickinson's comparative descriptions of pain is
that they explore only distinction, not likeness. Her representations of
pain are never the ground of connection, or empathy. This seems consistent with the American disposition to regard death as an event that primarily presents theological and epistemological problems. She is so
committed to thwarting the received consolations for loss that the new
ground for human connection that she is creating through her descriptive accuracy (see 'Comparative Judgment' below) is blunted.

The vampirism and isolationism evidenced by Dickinson's representation of pain tend to overshadow the important way that it is talking
back to Emerson and his disposition to reconcile what he calls 'stupe-
ndous antagonisms' of being. The movement of 'Circles' is always toward unity: new insights serve not as aimless vastating progress but as
perches from which the connection between seemingly incompatible
ideas can retrospectively be understood. For Emerson, multiplicity
tends to harmonious unity when the thinker and poet 'looks before and
after'. Dickinson objects both to his optimism and to the way that distinctions, antagonisms, pain, suffering, feelings, bad hierarchies are sub-
merged and denied by his idea of accreting experience as necessarily
tending toward unification.

Poem 695 invokes Emerson's idea of progressive revelation but strips
it of a positive or even organizing value:

---

[18] A position most fully articulated by Camille Paglia who calls her the Ma-
dame de Sade of Amherst (1990, 623–73).

As if the Sea should part
And show a further Sea –
And that – a further – and the Three
But a presumption be –

Of Periods of Seas –
Unvisited of Shores –
Themselves the Verge of Seas to be –
Eternity – is Those –

This poem, which bears likeness to the Whitman lines cited above, thwarts Emerson's Neoplatonist view of revelation by disallowing its reflexiveness, and by placing it on a continuum with the Biblical revelation ('As if the Sea should part') that they both have overthrown as mystification. In the final line, Dickinson proffers 'Eternity' as the perfect rhyme to close off and domesticate those proliferating and vastating seas, but then yanks it away in favor of the distance enforcing deictic 'those'.

Like George Kateb, one of Emerson's most astute disciples today (1995, 61–95), Dickinson cannot abide Emerson's concept of the 'All', the ghost of a Unitarian God,[19] a post-Christian principle of unification that, as she argues in poem 284, threatens to silence her *as a woman*, particularly her ability to make distinctions (that is, to feel precisely and not deny or bend feeling reflexively):

The Drop, that wrestles in the Sea –
Forgets her own locality –
As I – toward Thee –

She knows herself an incense small –
Yet *small* – she sighs – if *All* – is *All* –
How *larger* – be?
The Ocean – smiles – at her Conceit –
But *she*, forgetting Amphitrite –
Pleads – 'Me'?

The speaker of this antagonistic love poem expresses anxiety that, if allowed, her desire ('toward Thee') will disempower her and submerge her identity (see also P 246). In its course, the poem posits a steady decrease in female power by the downward arc of its verbs ('wrestles', 'sighs',

---

19 The Calvinist God at least has the benefit of being a patriarch, with all the attendant family drama.

'pleads') and the movement from subject, 'I', to object, 'me'. The argument or 'conceit' (a wonderfully charged term) that Dickinson launches in the second stanza is most apposite to our engagement with the comparative, because here she uses the form to consider the problem of both Romantic cosmology and the Enlightenment Chain of Being. Because it is a sideways leap from 'small', the comparative 'larger' draws attention to the illicit mingling of social and empirical difference found in both. The reason the speaker is diminishing (getting smaller so to speak) is because socially determined hierarchies of value (not verifiable by empirical comparison) infect both the Great Chain of Being and the All. Why, for example, in Smellie's representation of the former, are Africans and Mongolians credited with less intellectual and moral capacity than Caucasians (1841, 31)? Why does Emerson represent the women's sphere in 'Experience' as a lesser ground for doing philosophy? The poem's comparatives (its expressed larger and impressed smaller) support Dickinson's argument here that her power is best maintained by renunciation, wrestling against the seductive pull of comprehensive cosmologies, and by writing their contradictions into grammar.

The lines 'Yet *small* – she sighs – if *All* – is *All*/ How *larger* – be' invite another interpretation, one that appears to contradict but actually extends the problem of making qualitative judgments that the reading above considers. Dickinson wants to be able to make comparative distinctions and judgments, so of course she throws off Emerson's All. Given her estrangement from cosmology, what licenses her judgments and keeps them from incommunicable solipsism?

Comparative Judgment

For Dickinson, the comparative is a grammatical sign of mental agility, because inconclusiveness is inscribed in the form. According to Dickinson's own dictionary,[20] the comparative is 'not positive or absolute'. For a skeptic, and poet who is said to have designed a poetics of 'choosing not to choose' (Cameron 1992, 21–29), that definition is suggestive. Comparatives have the power to shift both positives and superlatives, as Carlyle's sentence under the *OED* heading 'superlative' makes clear: 'So many highest superlatives achieved by man are followed by a new higher; and dwindle into comparatives and positives!' Carlyle's locution evidences the progressive emphases that Romantics gave the form, as

---

20 Webster's *American Dictionary of the English Language* (1844).

well as the unsettling capacity of the comparative, the social, theological and aesthetic instability that attends an endless usurpation of the superlative by the comparative, by ignoring that usurping instance ('a new higher') and imagining 'comparatives' only as a form into which superlatives dwindle.

Dickinson embraces the comparative because its inconclusive nature keeps the world open to description. While poem 657 is usually read as a straightforward declaration of the superiority of poetry to prose, I think that 'Prose' stands in for positive statements that are not modulated, as so many of her definitions are, by comparatives. This lack of modulation, she argues, limits perception. The ubiquity of comparatives in the first stanza recommends them as central to the more comprehensive poetic 'Occupation' of 'spreading wide my narrow Hands/ To gather Paradise –':

> I dwell in Possibility –
> A fairer House than Prose –
> More numerous of Windows –
> Superior – for Doors –

Dickinson checks the inconclusive force of comparatives by inscribing them into positive definitions ('Suspense – is Hostiler than Death –' P 705; 'Dreams – are well – but Waking's better,/ If One wake at Morn –/ If One wake at Midnight – better –/ Dreaming – of the Dawn –' P 450; 'Eternity – is Those –' P 695; 'Possibility [is] a fairer House than Prose –' P 657).[21]

In like manner, Dickinson shifts the vertical axis of comparatives by embedding them in metaphors. Comparison is a poetic privilege closely related to the privilege of poets to make metaphor: 'Shall I compare thee to a summer's day?/ Thou art more lovely and more temperate.' Shakespeare's yoking of beloved and summer's day has the impulse of metaphor which, if followed, would directly consider and compare aspects of day and beloved, rather than the quality of those aspects. In poem 657, the force of the metaphor Dickinson draws between 'House' and 'Possibility' is kept minimal by the comparatives, but the metaphor itself reduces the banality of asserting that multiplicity ('more numerous') is an aspect of possibility.

---

21 This tendency to inscribe comparatives into definitions goes a long way toward reducing and addressing the self-aggrandizement (and critical slovenliness) which Christopher Ricks sees in Pater's compulsive use of the comparative 'finer' (1984, 393).

Similarly, although Dickinson argues for the superior accuracy of comparative insights as against those established by a superlative God, the reason they are judged superior is because they remain locked in a struggle with a point of view underwritten by God.[22] In the poem 'Two were immortal twice' (P 800), the asymmetry between the capitalized 'Comparative' and 'superlative' underscores the poem's argument for the superiority of consciousness granted by comparative thinking to the consolation underwritten by a superlative Paradise:

> Two – were immortal twice –
> The privilege of few –
> Eternity – obtained – in Time –
> Reversed Divinity –
>
> That our ignoble Eyes
> The quality conceive
> Of Paradise superlative –
> Through their Comparative.

The poem is a commentary on Christ's raising of Lazarus and Jairus's daughter, which overturns the theological message of those redemptions, even as it appears to reproduce it. If Eternity has the consolatory value that Christianity argues, then God hurling them out of that temporality, to make a dramatic religious point about its availability, rather undercuts his benevolence (an argument allowed by the ambiguous syntax of line 3 and 4). Lazarus and Jairus's daughter are without parallel, because they are able to compare, from concrete experience, time posterior and anterior to death. Comparisons proliferate as we are solicited to compare this version of the story to the Biblical one, and their perspective on their temporary version of redemption (they will have to die again) to God's.

The ascent of the comparative as the grammar of accuracy begs the question of where poets derive their authority to speak, especially when they regard permanence as 'a word of degrees'. That authority is

---

[22] In *Natural Theology*, William Paley explicitly argues for a theologized use of the superlative: ' "Omnipotence", "omniscience", "infinite" power, "infinite" knowledge, are superlatives, expressing our conception of these attributes in the strongest and most elevated terms with language supplies. We ascribe power to the Deity under the name of "omnipotence", the strict and correct conclusion being, that a power which could create such a world as this is, must be, beyond all comparison, greater than any which we observe in other visible agents, greater also than any we can want . . .' (1851, 247).

itself asserted by comparison, in Wordsworth's case, to the average person, whose representative he pledges to be. Wordsworth's self-commissioning, in the *Preface to Lyrical Ballads*, is achieved by comparatives:

> He is a man speaking to men: a man, it is true, endued with *more* lively sensibility, *more* enthusiasm and tenderness, who has a *greater* knowledge of human nature, and a *more* comprehensive soul . . . who rejoices *more* than other men in the spirit of life that is in him . . . affected *more* than other men by absent things . . . has acquired a *greater* readiness and power in expressing what he thinks and feels.

In the essay 'The Poet', Emerson, more radically committed to the leveling effects of comparative thinking, critiques Wordsworth's view of the superiority of the poet even as he iterates it, by explicitly setting the poet's superior capabilities within an array of important national labor; it is his emphasis on the commonwealth, and the contractual aspect of poetic commissioning, that Whitman advances in his 1855 *Preface to Leaves of Grass*: 'the proof of the poet is that his country absorbs him as affectionately as he has absorbed it'.

By contrast to their self-commissioning in relationship to the rural folk, or peers, or fellow citizens whom the poets honor but whose sensibilities they find in need of more articulate representation, Dickinson authorizes her poetry by comparison to divine creation (P 307; 308; 569). In poem 308, Dickinson reports a ludicrous competition to create a sunset which she imagines occurring between herself and Day; she does quite well, dashing off at least two sunset poems while day is doing its thing; Day's sunset may be 'ampler' but Dickinson favors her own as 'more convenient/ To Carry in the Hand –'.[23] In 569, which argues for their primacy, poets are shown as creating Heaven of equal beauty to the possible one that God has crafted, but superior in its inclusiveness. Dickinson takes to an extreme the Romantic secularizing of the Muse, by asserting her comparative superiority to God, and seeing her poetic commissioning as necessarily involving competition in which the poet bests God: 'Audacity of Bliss, said Jacob to the Angel "I will not let thee go except I bless thee" – Pugilist and Poet, Jacob was correct –' (L 1042).

What are the gender implications of Dickinson's steady and deformed use of the comparative? That the comparative reflects an

---

23 In this vein, her favorite Wordsworth line is from 'Elegiac Stanzas': 'The light that never was, on sea or land'.

unwillingness to commit to absolute statements radiates not only within a theological context as rebellion, but within a social context as potentially assenting to the constraints on female 'analytic aggression', constraints which Julie Ellison argues present female writers with specific challenges as they negotiate the Romantic conflict between that aggressiveness and receptivity (1990, 217ff). Dickinson is complex in this regard: her propensity to conscript comparatives into definitions, and her continual announcement that her self-reliance is superior to faith, both suggest that she is not shy about her authority to weigh and judge, especially as it is circumscribed within the domestic realm (she doesn't publish poems in print; rather she encloses them in letters and organizes them into private portfolios). Although there are rare poems in which the comparative is a marker of anxiety and unworthiness (P 235; 237; 238), most often they appear as signs of exacting acuity and power to describe. In poem 199, the register of the loss of female power in marriage is the speaker's concluding refusal to compare: 'But why compare?/ I'm "Wife"! Stop there!'

In like manner, the deformed quality of Dickinson's comparatives radiates not only in a theological context as bewilderment and/or the distortions attendant on continuing to assert the value of hymn meter from a skeptical perspective, but also in a social context in which defying the rules of grammar is a defiance of decorum. Their oddity writes pain and bewilderment into her renunciation of both social and theological conformity. Their deformation also indicts the jovial subjectivity and overreaching claims of authority in Romantic comparatives like those in 'To Rhea' or Keats's line 'Heard melodies are sweet, but those unheard/ Are sweeter; therefore, ye soft pipes, play on' ('Ode on a Grecian Urn'), where the announcement of a comparative judgment is followed by a command. Dickinson's comparative judgments make nothing happen.

Dickinson's use of the comparative to describe the world and her relationship to it, from the perspective of committed inconclusiveness, is as indebted to Linnaeus as it is to the Romantics. Even when Dickinson's speakers are dead, as in 'I felt my life' (P 351), they want to use the instruments of empirical science to verify their judgments. The empirical impulse of Dickinson's comparatives makes her poems hospitable to readers, who themselves must bring tools of the scientific method to the dense materialism of her art. At the same time, Dickinson's Romanticism in extremis, her pushing the temporalized comparative toward a secularized Eternity, makes her as hostile to the ameliorative impulses of Romanticism as she is to the consolation of faith.

Works Cited

Abrams, M.H., 'Structure and Style in the Greater Romantic Lyric', in *From Sensibility to Romanticism*, ed. Frederick Hilles and Harold Bloom (Oxford: Oxford UP, 1965), reprinted in *Romanticism and Consciousness*, ed. Harold Bloom, NY: W.W. Norton, 1970, 201–29.

Blasing, Mutlu Konuk, *American Poetry: The Rhetoric of Its Forms*, New Haven: Yale UP, 1987.

Cameron, Sharon, *Choosing Not Choosing*, Chicago: The University of Chicago Press, 1992.

Capps, Jack L., *Emily Dickinson's Reading*, Cambridge: Harvard UP, 1966.

Diehl, Joanne Feit, *Dickinson and Romantic Imagination*, Princeton: Princeton UP, 1981.

Ellison, Julie, *Delicate Subjects: Romanticism, Gender, and the Ethics of Understanding*, Cornell UP, 1990.

——, *Emerson's Romantic Style*, Princeton: Princeton UP, 1984.

Hughes, Gertrude, 'Subverting the Cult of Domesticity: Emily Dickinson's Critique of Women's Work', *Legacy* 3 (Spring 1986): 17–28.

Johnson, Thomas, ed. *The Poems of Emily Dickinson*, 3 vols, Cambridge, MA: Belknap Press of Harvard UP, 1955.

Johnson, Thomas and Theordora Ward, eds. *The Letters of Emily Dickinson*, 3 vols, Cambridge, MA: Belknap Press of Harvard UP, 1958.

Kateb, George, *Emerson and Self Reliance*, Thousand Oaks, CA: Sage, 1995.

Keller, Karl, *The Only Kangaroo Among the Beauty: Emily Dickinson and America*, Baltimore: The Johns Hopkins UP, 1979.

Lovejoy, Arthur O., *The Great Chain of Being*, Cambridge: Harvard UP, 1939.

Miller, Christanne, *Emily Dickinson: A Poet's Grammar*, Cambridge: Harvard UP, 1987.

Millward, C.M., *A Biography of the English Language*, NY: Holt, Rinehart Winston, 1989.

Newman, Samuel Philips, *A Practical System of Rhetoric*, NY: Mark H. Newman & Co, 1847.

Paglia, Camille, *Sexual Personae*, New Haven: Yale UP, 1990.

Paley, William, *Natural Theology*, Boston: Gould and Lincoln, 1851.

Porter, David, *Dickinson: The Modern Idiom*, Cambridge: Harvard UP, 1981.

Quirk, Randolph, Sidney Greenbaum, Geoffrey Leech, Jan Svartick, *A Comprehensive Grammar of the English Language*, London: Longman, 1985.

Ricks, Christopher, *The Force of Poetry*, Oxford: Clarendon Press, 1984.

Smellie, William, *The Philosophy of Natural History*, Boston: Simpkins, 1841.

Wilbur, Richard, 'Sumptuous Destitution', 35–46 in Archibald MacLeish, Louise Bogan, Richard Wilbur, *Emily Dickinson: Three Views*, Amherst: Amherst College Press, 1960.

Yetman, Michael, 'Emily Dickinson and the English Romantic Tradition', *Texas Studies in Literature and Language* 15 (Spring 1973), 129–47.

'Precious Allusions':
Female Muses and Authorising Writing

BRIDGET BENNETT

I delight in a palpable imaginable *visitable* past – in the nearer dis-
tances and the clearer mysteries, the marks and signs of a world we
may reach over to as by making a long arm we grasp an object at the
other end of our own table. The table is the one, the common ex-
panse, and where we lean, so stretching, we find it firm and continuous. That, to my imagination, is the past fragrant of all, or of almost
all, the poetry of the thing outlived and lost and gone, and yet in
which the precious element of closeness, telling so of connexions but
tasting so of differences, remains appreciable.   (James 1934, 164.)

Our libraries are crammed with the lives of distinguished men, and
yet how rare it is to get a glimpse of the real man as he was in life. It is
like unrolling an Egyptian mummy, wrapped in countless cerecloths
and containing nothing but dry bones. In my brief records, first issued
in 1858 and now issued with very large augmentations, I have en-
deavoured to portray men as men, as they were in their every-day
lives. In public life men say and do the same things, and are as difficult to distinguish one from the other as sheep. Their writings are
open to all the world; individual censure or praise should go for
nothing.   (Trelawny 1887, vi)

HOW MIGHT THE inheritance of Romanticism be envisaged in the closing decades of the nineteenth century and in what terms might it be alluded to? These are two of the questions which this essay will address as
it examines the response of two writers and correspondents, Henry
James and Edith Wharton, as they looked back over the nineteenth century and set themselves up within a distinctive modern literary tradition
which originated in the late eighteen and early nineteenth centuries. In
a striking passage from his preface to 'The Aspern Papers' (1888) Henry
James indulges in a fantasy about the relation between an 'imaginable'
past and the lived present. He considers the way in which the past may
be brought into the present by an act or gesture of appropriation, of own-
ership, and in this way ascribes an active role to the figure who might
make this imaginatively possible, in this instance himself as a writer of
fiction. By envisaging the past, present and future as potentially a single
and continuous terrain he sets up a domestic and material metaphor

which he uses to bring the past and present into being and to read them against each other. The past is represented both as constantly evolving and as reachable; further, the idea of reaching over to the past 'at the other end of our own table' has intensely personal connotations. For by making the past '*visitable*', 'palpable', one might bring it into meaning in relation to one's own life, might find a form of self-identification. It is certainly in that double context that E.J. Trelawny, looking backwards into his own life, contemplates the friendships with Byron and Shelley which he will commemorate in a memoir. At his writing table Trelawny reaches over, in one of the ways envisaged by James, and makes the past palpable, bringing it back to life. He creates a memoir of incidents and conversations which he hopes will flesh out the 'dry bones' of reality and act as an antidote to competing, but (he believes) duller, accounts of the poets which might be found in libraries. He intimates that it might be possible to re-animate the past, as James wishes, to bring it back to life – or rather to bring it into life – to render it '*visitable*' in James' phrase. Trelawny's avowed ambition, 'to portray men as men, as they were in their every-day lives', might be read as a grand democratising gesture. Yet memoirs sell, they appeal to the sensibilities of the market rather than a more discriminating audience: Trelawny's memorialising might equally be read as a great entrepreneurial piece of writing which recognises and aims to appease the huge public appetite for gossip.

The activities of such a memoir writer were to prove problematic for James, for the figure most likely to provide a model of opening up the past is the biographer, journalist, or a writer of memoirs – like Trelawny – and the figure whose past is likely to be opened up for such imaginable communications is that of the writer or other public figure – like James. Though these roles are not completely fixed, the differentiation broadly holds.[1] As I will show later, James became acutely aware of the difficulty of maintaining his two conflicting positions: his fascination with the sexual intrigues of other writers – his desire for knowledge – and conflicting impulse to maintain his own privacy. This conflict produced an intriguing and paradoxical debate in his writings and private correspondence about the necessity and desirability for privacy on the one hand

---

1   In notes for an article of reminiscences called 'Mr and Mrs James T. Fields' which eventually appeared in the *Atlantic Monthly* of July 1915, James begins to debate the way in which he might construct his memories and occupy the role of memoir writer as follows: 'What was to follow made for itself other connections, many of which had already begun; but what I think of in particular as a veracious historian, or at any rate as a beguiled memoriser, or say memorialist . . . ' (Edel and Powers 1987, 536).

and the desire for knowledge of the intrigues of others and a thrill with
gossip on the other. These were allied to issues about the problematical
nature and status of biography in the late nineteenth and early twentieth centuries.[2] A striking fictional example of James' engagement with
each of these debates can be seen in 'The Aspern Papers' in which conflicting desires to know the contents of the elusive papers, letters of the
dead poet Jeffrey Aspern, and to keep them hidden, splinter the text
and create a vital suspense. Trelawny quotes Byron as complaining
that ' "My private and confidential letters are better known than any of
my published works" ' (Trelawny 1887, 95). It was this confusion between public and private which, for James, was one of the inheritances
of a Romantic past. It is that inheritance and its personal consequences
which he probes in his correspondence and fiction as I will show. As
Marilyn Butler has persuasively argued, journals and journalists had an
enormous influence in the early nineteenth century as 'initiators of a
culture to which we might agree to give the word "Romantic", which . . .
emerged as the world was robbed by death or physical decline of the
main writers we call the "English Romantics" '. At the same time, as
middle-class journals such as *New Monthly*, *Blackwood's*, and the *London
Magazine* were 'shaping Post-Romantic culture' by the 1820s, she argues
that the executors and editors of Byron and Shelley 'had to resort to re-
interpreting, censoring and burning the documentary record in order to
bring them into line with the more decorous and much less political
norms of later generations' (Butler 1993, 142–43). It was this Romantic
documentary record and the way in which it might be preserved or destroyed which became the subject of speculation throughout the nineteenth century.

As the drama of 'The Aspern Papers' demonstrates, James became intrigued by the instability of the past and the way in which it might be
made available to the interested through correspondence, diaries or
memoirs. He was concerned about the extent to which the subject or
author of letters and diaries might be denied an editorial or controlling
voice, might not be able to shape the way she or he was presented to the
world and might indeed be vulnerable to the 'shaping' of others,
whether hostile or not. From early on in his writing career he was highly
conscious that the writer was always subject to exposure through the
revelations of diaries or memoirs, publishing of correspondence or

---

[2]   For details of this, and of the relation between correspondence and biography, see Brake 1994, chs 9–10.

circulation of gossip. To some extent he envisaged this as an inevitability, and one not entirely without advantage. In a review of *The Journal of Eugénie de Guérin* in 1865, for example, he wrote that ' "genius is not a private fact: sooner or later, in the nature of things, it becomes common property" ' (Strouse 1981, 275).[3] Yet the notion of ' "common property" ' articulated here in a manner which suggests relative unconcern is one which would not remain constant as James became more celebrated himself and as he saw the consequence for figures of 'genius' (such as Oscar Wilde) of exposure and publicity within their own lifetime, and as he witnessed the vicissitudes of the reputation of Byron throughout the nineteenth century, a writer who intrigued him and one who repeatedly emerges throughout his writings. In one sense he welcomes and celebrates the notion of the communality of 'genius' since it confirms his belief that 'genius' (by implication his) will ultimately be recognised. Yet transformations within the periodical press after 1865 (the development of 'new' journalism with its reliance on interviews and photographs and its fascination with celebrity) and developments in the methodology and popularity of biography, allied to James' own increasing fame, contested the whole notion of genius and made him increasingly uncomfortable with it, as I will argue later. Writing on George Sand in what Laurel Brake calls 'the post-Wilde' *Yellow Book* in January 1897, James 'foresees a future in which the "pale forewarned victim" of biography will be a match for "the cunning of the inquirer", "with every track covered, every paper burnt and every letter unanswered" ' (Brake 1994, 210). George Sand would, like Byron, provide a model of author as celebrity which James returned to avidly, as I will show. Like James she realised that her correspondence was not likely to remain private, as Kathryn Crecelius has demonstrated (Crecelius 1989, 258).[4] Sand

---

3   James reviewed her correspondence in the same journal, the *Nation*, the following year.
4   Crecelius writers that 'even before she became famous, her friends shared and passed round her letters. . . . Once she was a published author and known as such, Sand clearly recognized that her letters might become public property and might even be used against her. She frequently cautions her correspondents against allowing her letters to fall into the wrong hands. Such an incident did in fact occur in 1845, when a letter she sent to Bettina von Arnim was opened in transit and served as the basis of articles in the *Gazette de Leipzig* and the *Revue de Paris*.' The invocation, by James, of George Sand as an example of female writing genius, and the way in which he discussed her with Edith Wharton, is significant here. In *Gender and Genius: Towards a Feminist Aesthetics* (1989) Christine Battersby has argued that Sand occupies an anomalous position for nineteenth-

occupied a crucial position in the history of the relation between the
Romantics and the Victorians. Her scandalous affairs and notorious
cross-dressing kept her within the public eye: in this respect she was the
inheritor of a tradition of public performance which Byron had occupied earlier. Yet it was not just her risqué reputation which makes her
significant within my argument. Patricia Thomson has argued that
Sand occupies a particular, mediatory role as a writer owing to her treatment of sexuality within her writing. She sees her as being part of a continuum which includes Richardson, Scott, and notably, Byron, and
being influential in the development of later nineteenth-century British writers (Thomson 1977, p. 9). For James then, Sand is a figure who
reaches across the table in a literary sense, mediating between past and
present writing and writers alike.

The notion of a battle of wits between victim and victimised is one
which James had articulated nine years before his 1897 piece on Sand in
his portrayal of the relationship between the potential memoirist in
'The Aspern Papers' and the formidable Juliana Bordereau, the ancient
one-time lover and muse of Jeffrey Aspern. Sand, Byron and the desti-
nation of letters were all subjects which interested Edith Wharton as
well as Henry James and their letters as well as their fiction became territory within which they could engage in allusions to these interests. The
long friendship and epistolary relationship between Edith Wharton and
Henry James seemed, initially, doomed never to happen at all. James was
already a fêted author when, in 1885 and again in 1890, the two sepa-
rately attended dinner parties at which the other was present. In her
autobiography A Backward Glance (1934) Wharton recounted that, on
the occasion of her first anticipated meeting with James, she had been
very careful when dressing in an attempt to catch James' attention,

> I could hardly believe that such a privilege could befall me, and I
> could think of only one way of deserving it – to put on my newest
> Doucet dress, and try to look my prettiest! . . . These were the princi-
> ples in which I had been brought up, and it would have never oc-

century critics who worked within a framework of male genius inherited from
Romantic ideology. Her argument, which has been widely influential, is that
Romanticism has relied upon a 'logic of exclusion' which has marginalised
women's creative roles and envisaged the project of Romanticism as being one
which has been the product of a hegemony of male poets (Battersby 1989, 6).
Much recent criticism has re-read cultural history and re-inserted women's creativity as central to the period, and these developments in feminist scholarship
are sufficiently established now not to have to be rehearsed here.

curred to me that I had anything but my youth, and my pretty frock, to commend me to a man whose shoe-strings I thought myself unworthy to unloose.   (Wharton 1934, 172)

This strategy was both misguided and unsuccessful, and five years later when, keen to tell James of her enthusiasm for *Daisy Miller* (1878), she wore a spectacular new hat ('*a beautiful new hat*' as she emphasises) to attract his attention, it failed again. As she remarked he 'noticed neither the hat nor its wearer – and the second of our meetings fell as flat as the first'. James later acknowledged that he had no recollection of Wharton at all (Wharton 1934, 169–73). Foiled twice in the performative she resorted to the epistolary, writing to James in 1895 with her good wishes for the forthcoming première of *Guy Domville*. James was evidently touched by this and gradually a friendship started to be formed. Four years after that she began to send him her work, starting with *The Greater Inclination* (1899), a collection of essays which included 'The Muse's Tragedy' and 'The Pelican' both of which centre on the problematic position for women who engage with writing. Their exchange of work was cemented when, on 17 August 1902, James sent her 'A rather long-winded (but I hope not hopelessly heavy) novel of mine', *The Wings of the Dove* (1902) (Powers 1990, 33).

Throughout the rest of James' life the two would correspond regularly. Initially Wharton addressed James, 20 years her senior, as 'Cher Maître' which suggests her early awe of the older man, but eventually their terms of address became far more intimate. However, this initial mode of address suggests a significant feature of the way in which the two writers were respectively envisaged: early reviewers of Wharton's work often compared her with James in ways not always advantageous to her, and this soon began to trouble her, especially since she was not sympathetic towards his later work.[5] In June 1904 she wrote that 'I have never before been discouraged by criticism, . . . but the continued cry that I am an echo of Mr. James (whose books of the last ten years I can't read, much as I delight in the man) . . . makes me feel rather hopeless' (Powers 1990, 5). Later it would be James himself who felt somewhat hopeless at Wharton's success and Wharton who would break out of such attributions of influence as she became a successful writer, and the dynamics of their friendship began to shift. Though it is true that her early work shares similarities with James' writing, I would argue that she

---

5   Of *The Wings of the Dove* she wrote to her publishers Scribner's 'Don't ask me what I think of *The Wings of the Dove*' (Powers 1990, 5).

extends the range of James' preoccupations in key, gendered ways, and while establishing a critical relationship with his writing based on a keen admiration for him she also occupies territory being mapped out by other women writers of the period as they tried to investigate what George Egerton called the 'terra incognita' of women's lives and emotions. This essay will look specifically at one of James' early tales, 'The Aspern Papers', and will examine his interest in a Romantic inheritance and the way in which that past, and the reputation of a male poet clearly modelled on Byronic lines, might be held in the hands of women who are keepers and makers of reputations, and who mediate between a personal, private, history and a public one. Further, I will look at Wharton's written response to this, in one of her early stories, 'The Muse's Tragedy', as well as her epistolary relationship with James, and the crucial significance which women's letters and their readers have in her writings. I will show that though these two pieces of short fiction share many themes, Wharton was keen to show women not just as keepers of the reputations of men but as active creators, often writing creators of their own reputations too.

Reaching over the table: 'The Aspern Papers' and 'The Muse's Tragedy'

James' account of his initial imagining of what would become 'The Aspern Papers' is given in some detail in his notebooks in which he routinely worked through ideas for possible future writing. This, now famous, account of the relation between incident and creative act – the way in which anecdote might be reworked as fiction – provides a way of contesting a Romantic notion of authorship as of singular creative act and re-reading creativity as a form of collaboration, even collectivity in which women play crucial roles.[6] For James' private notebooks, now publicly available, show how his painstaking recording of anecdotes told to him, or incidents observed or undertaken, might become the basis for writing. His notebooks, with their careful, rehearsed and detailed plans, demonstrate the process of authorship in all its complexity and difficulty. Furthermore the anecdote James notes down on 12 January 1887 invokes the relation of codes of censorship and silencing to the way in which literature might be brought into life, and by attesting to

6   For a wonderful account of Byron's anxiety about the relation between women, literary culture, and authorship, see Hofkosh 1988, 93–114.

the centrality of correspondence and gossip to authorship it challenges notions of what might be appropriate subjects for writing. Finally, albeit elliptically and even reluctantly, it reinstates women within the equation of writing and creativity though in largely negative terms, and only to the extent that they might reveal masculine 'genius'. James' account is as follows:

> Hamilton (V.L.'s <Vernon Lee> brother) told me a curious thing of Capt. [Edward] Silsbee – the Boston art-critic and Shelley-worshipper; that is of a curious adventure of his. Miss Claremont, <Clairmont> Byron's *ci-devant* mistress (the mother of Allegra) was living, until lately, here in Florence, at a great age, 80 or thereabouts, and with her lived her niece, a younger Miss Claremont – of about 50. Silsbee knew that they had interesting papers – letters of Shelley's and Byron's – he had known it for a long time and cherished the idea of getting hold of them. To this end he laid the plan of going to lodge with the Misses Claremont – hoping that the old lady in view of her great age and failing condition would die while he was there, so that he might put his hands upon the documents, which she hugged close in life. He carried out this scheme – and things *se passèrent* as he had expected. The old woman *did* die – and then he approached the younger one – the old maid of 50 – on the subject of his desires. Her answer was – 'I will give you all the letters if you marry me!' H. says that Silsbee *court encore*.

The description of the anecdote is remarkably close to what would eventually become 'The Aspern Papers'. Already, as he writes the anecdote in his notebook, he is beginning to turn it into fiction. It is a 'curious thing' which is, for the protagonist, a 'curious adventure': as he sketches out the anecdote it assumes the proportions of a story rather than a longer piece of fiction. Certain key words – 'interesting'; 'cherished'; 'worshipper' – will become the basis of central narrative issues: the contents of the letters, always at stake, are never revealed in the tale, the language used to denote the narrator's shifting relation to the letters is crucial. In order to fictionalise this anecdote further James changes the name of the women involved to Bordereau, and he Americanises it by renaming the poet Jeffrey Aspern and making him, and the women, Americans, though the women have been away from America for so long that their nationality has become indeterminate. He continues his note in the following way:

> The Countess Gamba came in while I was there: her husband is a nephew of the Guiccioli – and it was *à propos* of their having a lot of

Byron's letters of which they are rather illiberal and dangerous guardians, that H. told me the above. They won't show them or publish any of them – and the Countess was very angry once on H.'s representing to her that it was her duty – especially to the English public! – to let them at least be seen. *Elle se fiche bien* of the English public. She says the letter – addressed in Italian to the Guiccioli – are discreditable to Byron; and H. elicited from her that she had *burned* one of them.   (Edel and Powers 1987, 33–34)

The emphasis he places on '*burned*' will be picked up on in 'The Aspern Papers' for though in the anecdote about Silsbee the fate of the letters themselves is not revealed burning will occupy a crucial and dramatic role in the final paragraphs of 'The Aspern Papers', as it does in the notebook.[7]

As this entry shows, James was fascinated by the way in which discreditable papers might still incriminate reputations years after the death of the protagonists. In this context Byron repeatedly crops up for James both before and after he wrote 'The Aspern Papers'. In 1895 he was invited to listen to another discreditable story concerning Byron and lost or hidden papers. Once again he collects the details of the incident in his notebook. On 5 February he went to dinner at the house of the second Earl of Lovelace, Byron's grandson. He writes that he was shown 'some of their extremely interesting Byron papers; especially some of those bearing on the absolutely indubitable history of his relation to Mrs. Leigh, the sole *real* love, as he emphatically declares, of his life' (Edel and Powers 1987, 110). James says little or nothing about the way in which he considered the papers in his notebook, but he does expound at some length about 'the possible little drama residing in the existence of a peculiar intense and interesting affection between a brother and a sister'. In December 1909 he was again called in to examine a collection of Byron's letters, together with the popular novelist John Buchan who was married to the niece of Lady Lovelace. An early biographer of John Buchan, Janet Adam Smith, casts doubt on Buchan's memory of the incident in certain key respects, but agrees that the two men did examine a body of letters together and does not refute Buchan's recollection of James' detached response. Buchan writes that he met James on two occasions, and having described the first goes on to the second:

---

[7]   James repeats details of this, though not in such an explicit manner, in his preface to the New York Edition. See James 1934, 159–79.

The other occasion was when an aunt of my wife's, who was the widow of Byron's grandson, asked Henry James and myself to examine her archives in order to reach some conclusion of the merits of the quarrel between Byron and his wife. She thought these particular papers might be destroyed by some successor and she wanted a statement of their contents deposited in the British Museum. So, during a summer week-end, Henry James and I waded through masses of ancient indecency, and duly wrote an opinion. The thing nearly made me sick, but my colleague never turned a hair. His only words for some special vileness were 'singular' – 'most curious' – 'nauseating, perhaps, but how quite inexpressibly significant'.

(Buchan 1984, 151–52)[8]

Unlike Buchan, James appears to take a detached view of the documentary record which he 'visits'. In an uncanny re-enactment of the narrative of 'The Aspern Papers' James takes on the position, though not the attitudes, of the narrator he had created. In 'The Aspern Papers' he demonstrates his profound preoccupation with the way in which the past might be rendered '*visitable*', might be opened up to a cultural tourist, and by the methods by which that visitable past might be protected against the importunities of the unscrupulous. Though the tale is about opening up the past – it is about the tantalising possibility of revelation – it is also about protecting it and rendering it hidden. Throughout 'The Aspern Papers' closed doors and shutters, locked doors, darkened rooms, shaded eyes, and fading splendours announce the way in which memories are being designated to closed places, to remain hidden and secret. Indeed as the tale closes the memories contained in the Aspern papers themselves remain unknown forever as the two women keepers of the letters refuse to open up their contents to the unscrupulous narrator who has entered into their lives and their home. After Juliana's death her niece burns the letters one night as she reveals to the narrator,

'I have done the great thing. I have destroyed the papers.'
'Destroyed them?' I faltered.
'Yes; what was I to keep them for? I burnt them last night, one by one, in the kitchen.'
'One by one?' I repeated, mechanically.
'It took a long time – there were so many.' The room seemed to go round me as she said this and a real darkness for a moment descended upon my eyes.   (James 1976, 105–06)

8   See also Smith 1985, 175–76.

The erasure of the documentary record through burning leads to the 'real darkness' momentarily felt by the narrator as the possibility of reaching over to the past is permanently destroyed. The tale meditates upon the relative functions of correspondence and memory, images and portraits, all the ephemera of the material and immaterial worlds. It poses, as its central theme, a fascination with biography and with what biography might offer to a study of literature, specifically with a Romantic past and the relation of that past to a world of realist narrative: contemporary critics and readers were quick to pick up on allusions to Byron and/or Shelley.[9] Further, it constructs an account of the way in which biography might be pieced together from sources which are always, by definition, dangerously (and flimsily) temporary and liable to destruction: glimpses and snatches of a long distant past, but one which might still be recreated. The notion of the way in which the past might be rendered visitable by way of remnants and fragments whose fragmentary and unstable nature makes them constantly subject to the mundane processes of everyday destruction adds a piquancy to the methods by which they might be understood and known. As pieces of a past which may have extraordinary associations they hold a special status. Yet their vulnerability also marks them as ordinary or at least subject to the mundane processes which affect us all. They are both unique and prosaic, hugely over-determined yet curiously irrelevant. Since the papers are destroyed at the end of the tale they remain permanently tantalising. Yet what if they were simply insignificant in their revelations? How might questions of significance be posed and quantified? It is the notion of cost, personal, moral, material, which is at issue for James.

As Philip Horne has argued in *Henry James and Revision*, questions of value (both moral and material) are central to 'The Aspern Papers', and the revisions to the tale which James completed in 1908 for the New York Edition 'frequently engage the relation between different ideas of value, of price and measure; a relation which is the dramatic substance of the story' (Horne 1990, 271). Horne goes on to argue that certain key words, 'extravagant', 'precious', 'measure', with their material and moral nuances act as keys to the central, paradoxical, preoccupation of the

---

9   See, for example, untitled review in the *Saturday Review* 66 (3 November 1888), 527; and 'Mr. James's *Aspern Papers*', *Critic* 14 (9 February 1889), 61–62: 'A correspondent has already called attention in these columns to the closeness with which Mr. James has followed out an early portion of Claire Clairmont's unfortunate early career in fashioning his tale.' Cited in Hayes 1996, 211 and 215.

tale, 'distrust of the excesses of biographical curiosity about writers' and 'his [James'] own biographical curiosity' (Horne 1990, 288). Certainly the vulgarity of excessive curiosity and of attempting to fix prices to the past are castigated here by James, as Horne clearly demonstrates, for the would-be memoirist is represented at some level as little more than an unscrupulous relic-hunter who initially will stop at nothing to get hold of the papers, yet ultimately stops short when he realise that the cost will be himself, through his marriage to Miss Tita. The tale is narrated, retrospectively, in the first person, unlike the narration of Edith Wharton's short story 'The Muse's Tragedy' which moves between the third person account of a Lewis Danyers' meeting with Mrs Anerton, the muse for 'Vincent Rendle's immortal sonnet cycle' as well as 'the Mrs. A. of *The Life and Letters*', a retrospective collection of Rendle's correspondence, a shift towards allowing the muse her own writing voice which James does not permit. It is this move towards the representation of the female voice, as well as the explicit reproduction of a key letter from Mrs Anerton which allows her to have the last word, which interests me here (Wharton 1990, 32). 'The Muse's Tragedy' emerges from 'The Aspern Papers' in ways which have been noted by other critics. Yet the point at which it diverges from James' tale is one connected with revelations made not within the letters of the dead poet, but the memories of his muse. Where James' tale is, in one sense, more conventional in that it concentrates on a documented love affair between Aspern and Juliana Bordereau, Wharton's re-writing of the poet-muse relationship transforms it into one which concerns itself with thwarted desire, frustration, silences and loss, gaps only filled by the revelations made by Mrs Anerton.

At the start of 'The Muse's Tragedy' Danyers reflects upon his first meeting with Mrs Anerton which has been partially predetermined by the intervention of the aptly named Mrs Memorall, a mutual friend. Mrs Memorall's name suggests the status she gradually assumes in Danyers' eyes, and the way in which women and books become almost synonymous in this short story. Initially he considers her in a hostile manner as 'the kind of woman who runs cheap excursions to celebrities' but gradually he sees her less in the manner of a cultural tourist and more in the manner of a book, 'like a volume of unindexed and discursive memoirs, through which he patiently plodded in the hope of finding embedded amid layers of dusty twaddle some precious allusion to the subject of his thought' (Wharton 1990, 33 and 35). As he realises that she may be of use to him he is willing to tolerate her, as his changing response suggests. By using the simile of a book Wharton subtly alludes to one of the key problems for woman in relation to writing men: she can be relegated to the status of fixed entity who is perceived only in relation to a man and what he writes. For the subject which initially interests Danyers is not, as might seem, Mrs Anerton, but the poet Vincent Rendle, whom Danyers thinks of as his 'divinity' (in a term which echoes the way in which the narrator of 'The Aspern Papers' considers Jeffrey Aspern and, tangentially – sometimes ironically – Juliana) and indeed Mrs Anerton becomes divine too, through her relation to Rendle. At first Mrs Anerton only exists for Danyers through Rendle's writing, and she first notices Danyers when Mrs Memorall sends her a copy of 'his first slim volume' on Rendle's poetry. The dead poet crucially mediates their relationship and is always present as a third party to it in its early stages. Metaphors of writing and of the way in which it can fix experience proliferate as Mrs Anerton describes her life with writing men. She worries that Danyers will turn her into 'a pretty little essay with a margin' and tells him that the experience of meeting her and their subsequent doomed relationship will 'be an episode, a mere "document", to you so soon!' (Wharton 1990, 46 and 45). Throughout the story letters play a similarly significant and loaded function. When Danyers goes off to visit Europe at the start of the story Mrs Memorall 'offered him letters to everybody, from the Archbishop of Canterbury to Louise Michel'. Yet she does not give him a letter of introduction to Mrs Anerton for 'Silvia objected to people who 'brought letters" ' (Wharton 1990, 36). What is significant here is not just the public status of such letters, but the shift in the way in which they are described in relation to Mrs Anerton. The movement from the name of her dead husband to the persona attributed to her by another dead man suggests a further preoccupation for Wharton in her treatment of the representation of poet and muse, the question of the attribution of status: which man will she be named after, when will she have any other meaning for the world? Though ultimately she emerges articulate from the stifling enclosures set up by these two men, in the process she gives up the prospect of any possibility of a lasting relationship with any other man.

On the day in which Danyers meets Mrs Anerton for the first time he sees her twice before she introduces herself to him. On the first occasion she is taking coffee alone, and on the second she is sitting alone surrounded by books and papers, writing. Although Mrs Memorall has already revealed that Mrs Anerton has been involved in editing Rendle's juvenilia it is not until later in the story that her crucial role as writer is revealed and it is this which, I would argue, is Wharton's most significant preoccupation in the story and the one which reveals her departure from the model of James. Wharton investigates the possibility that the woman muse might be, in some way, on a creative par with the artist whose work she inspires, indeed she even suggests that she might be a collaborator, a ghost-writer, an unrecognised additional voice subsumed within that of the male poet. In the brilliant, tragic and revealing letter which ends the story, Mrs Anerton reveals herself to be a careful and creative editor who saves scraps and fragments from Rendle's dustbin which she has brought to her each day before it is emptied. Letter-writing, the rescue of another's letters, the preparation and perhaps censorship of those letters prior to publication, and the reading of letters can all be seen here, as in other of Wharton's work such as *The House of Mirth* (1905), as central motifs which are in part about the way in which a woman writer at the turn of the century might try to position herself within a literary world, and the way in which she might be seminal to the construction of writing identities and reputations.[10] Whereas in 'The Aspern Papers' the revelations of the contents of the letters are kept from the reader and narrator as the letters are burned, in 'The Muse's Tragedy' the poet's letters are published with key sections omitted. Mrs Anerton hands Rendle's letters to her over to an editor only after she has copied them out for him. In the story's final surprising denouement when she denounces Rendle for having never loved her and sentencing her to a dull solitary life ('the dreariness of this enforced immortality!' she bitterly exclaims) she reveals that the truth behind their relationship was that there was no scandal to it: it was an intellectual comradeship on his side and a hopeless romantic attachment on hers. In the third section of the story, which is made up simply of the letter from Mrs Anerton which breaks off her relationship with Danyers, she explains the way in which she has shaped Rendle's public persona and created a sort of literary double bluff,

> But then, the letters? Ah, the letters! Well, I'll make a clean breast of it. You have noticed the breaks in the letters here and there, just as they seem to be on the point of growing a little – warmer? The critics, you may remember, praised the editor for his commendable delicacy and good taste (so rare in these days!) in omitting from the correspondence all personal allusions, all those *détails intimes* which should be kept sacred from the public gaze. They referred, of course, to the asterisks in the letters to Mrs. A. Those letters I myself

---

[10] For an extensive discussion of the role of letters in Wharton's work see Waid 1991.

prepared for publication; that is to say, I copied them out for the editor, and every now and then I put in a line of asterisks to make it appear that something had been left out. You understand? The asterisks were a sham – *there was nothing to leave out.*   (Wharton 1990, 42)

The Cultural Tourist as Visitant of the Past

A series of letters and postcards suggests further ways in which James and Wharton reached over the table to the past, and to each other, and gives insights into their epistolary relationship and their writing preoccupations, as well as their understanding of a notion of male Romantic genius and its inscription. In the early autumn of 1911 Wharton wrote to James inviting him to join herself and their mutual friend Walter Berry on a five week motoring holiday in northern Italy. James decided to remain in England, having had a restless and peripatetic year.[11] He replied on 27 September refusing her invitation in extravagant terms,

> Alas it is not possible – it is not even for a moment thinkable. I returned, practically, but last night to my long-abandoned home, where every earthly consideration, & desire of my heart, conspires now to fix me in some sort of recovered peace and stability; I cling to its very doorposts, for which I have yearned for long months, & the idea of going forth again on new & distant & expensive adventures fills me with – let me frankly say – absolute terror & dismay – the desire, the frantic impulse of scared childhood, to plunge my head under the bedclothes & burrow there, not to 'let it (i.e. Her!) [Wharton's car] get me!'   (Powers 1990, 192–93)

He compared his 'genius' to that of a brooding 'Hen, whom I differ from but by a syllable in designation'. Her 'beautiful genius', he claimed, was 'for great globe-adventures and putting girdles round the earth'. He had decided to ensconce himself in Lamb House for a period, and so his pun neatly implies the second, absent, syllable: the 'Hen' writes from Rye, begging Berry and Wharton plaintively 'Don't despise me for a spiritless worm.' His plan, while the two travelled to Italy, was to start work on his

11   His brother William had died in the United States in August 1910. James had accompanied the dying man on his return from Europe to the United States and remained there for much of 1911. On his return to England he had spent time in London and had visited Scotland. He had just returned from there when Wharton's letter reached him in Rye.

memoir of his brother William James, who had recently died. Yet William James was soon to be displaced. The anticipated memoir would eventually become the autobiography of Henry James which James began to make plans for and to hatch out while he stayed at home in England.

Wharton and Berry sent him regular and affectionate postcards, written in verse, to suggest the progress of their tour. From Bologna they sent him a witty card from Petrarch's place of death which suggested how his absence was felt. The picture on the card was a photograph of Petrarch's home at Arquà, which may have suggested the predominant rhyme of the short poem,

> Without the Worm the Beaks are growing starker,
> The more so in This Room; and if Petrarca
> Could live again he'd sing: 'We want the aura
> Of Henry more than all the lure of Laura!'
> (Powers 1990, 357).

The poem, in Berry's writing, though signed by both the travellers, sets James up in competition with Petrarch's muse Laura and continues the series of puns of which they were so fond. A second displacement takes place: the alluring Laura is displaced by the absent James. Petrarch is brought back to life, re-animated and re-written. A new narrative is imposed upon him by the versifying Americans, one in which his muse is transformed into an elderly American man whose 'aura' might challenge the sexual allure of the young woman. This second act of displacement is followed by a third which this time centres on Byron. Visiting Ravenna, Wharton and Berry made a special trip to Byron's home there and sent the following verse to James, on 13 October 1911,

> In such a place, in ties unholy,
> How could he live with La Guiccioli?
> Between Syarchate and Guiccioli
> Compelled to make a choice, oh which shall he
> Forsake forever? – No less grave
> Our problem by this sad sea wave:–
> Th'Italian accent's wilful truancy
> Is such a check upon our fluency!   (Powers 1990, 358).[12]

---

[12] Powers suggests that 'Syarchate' may be a slip for [Marianna] Segati, another of Byron's lovers while he was in Italy.

A further card of 15 October was sent from Florence and was followed by the final of the sequence, sent from Florence again on 17 October,

> Climbing hills & fording torrents
> Here we are at last in Florence,
> Or rather perching on the piano
> Nobile, at Settignano.
> Doing picture Galleries? No, sir!
> Motoring to Vallombrosa,
> Pienza, Siena, tutte quante,
> High above the Dome of Dante;
> Then (compelled by the busy lawyer),
> Back to France by a scorciatoia.   (Powers 1990, 359)

The series of postcards, witty, worldly and engaging, are clearly aimed at entertaining James and suggesting to him preoccupations which he had shared with Wharton for years and which had started to interest him before he had met her. Writing of Ravenna in 1874 James describes feeling as if he 'was breathing an air of prodigious records and relics' for, as he continues, 'Byron lived here and Dante died here, and the tomb of the one and the dwelling of the other are among the advertised appeals.' (Kaplan 1994, 366 and 370). Yet he found Ravenna dull, and Byron's house disappointing, though he recognised that Ravenna might have had other appeals than the architectural for Byron who 'had indeed a noble pastime – the various churches are adorned with monuments of ancestral Guicciolis'. Wharton and Berry's response to Byron's home suggests a similar disappointment, though their invocation of, and interest in, Byron's impossible sexual dilemma also recalls the interest of James and Wharton in the affairs of George Sand and also of Hortense Allart de Méritens. On 7 June 1905 he had started inventing a series of names with erotic connotations which he used for Wharton's car, such as the Vehicle of Passion and the Chariot of Fire. In this manner Wharton and James coded their fascination with the lives of Sand, Byron and others, making a private joke of their interest which sustained them for many years. James would enquire fondly of the state of Wharton's car, by one or another of its many names, and would look forward to their long journeys through the French countryside together. When mentioning the car in public their private passion was therefore coded, as was their fascination with literary lives – especially those of writers who flouted convention and were known as much for their lives and loves as for their writings. James' and Wharton's trips into the secret lives of writers are a regular feature of their private correspondence, an exchange which

ended with James' death. Their interest extended beyond literary pil-
grimages: they avidly read letters and biographies and advised each
other on new publications. On 8 November 1905 James writes to Wharton asking her if she has read the correspondence of George Sand and
her daughter'(have you read the luridly interesting little vol. *George
Sand & sa Fille* by the way?)' (Powers 1990, 55–56). Six months later, on
2 July 1906, he writes telling her that he has had 'a strange telepathic intuition' that Wharton has gone to Sand's house:

> A few days after you sloped away to France I said to myself suddenly:
> 'They're on their way to Nohant, d__n them! They're going there –
> they *are* there!' . . . There has been, you know, no *récit* (of the impres-
> sion of the place) of any sort of authority or value but George's own.
> How you must have *smelt* them all!'   (Powers 1990, 66)

In one of their own motor trips together in 1907 Wharton and James
visited George Sand's home together and excitedly discussed her affairs.
James was still thinking of them in 1912 when he wrote to Wharton
thanking her for the third volume of Wladimir Karénine's biography of
George Sand which he reviewed. Wharton had read the volume before
she sent it to James and marked sections in pencil for his special attention. James was delighted by the biography, not least because it recalled
this trip to Nohant. As he writes to Wharton on 13 March 1912,

> what a value it all gets from our memory of that wondrous day when
> we explored the very scene where they pigged so thrillingly together.
> What a crew, what moeurs, what habits, what conditions & relations
> every way – & what an altogether mighty & marvellous George! –
> not diminished by all the greasiness & smelliness in which she made
> herself (& so many other persons!) at home. Poor, gentlemanly, cru-
> cified Chop! – [Chopin] not naturally at home in grease – but having
> been originally *pulled* in – & floundering there at last to extinction!
>   (Powers 1990, 215)[13]

---

[13] On 5 February 1910 he writes to Wharton thanking her for a book of the letters of Alfred de Musset to Aimée d'Alton. The couple had an intense affair between 1837–38 and James thrilled to the details the letters offered of 'dirty
bedrooms' and illicit sex (Powers 1990, 147. Letter of 8 February 1910). The letters had been deposited in the Bibliothèque Nationale in 1880 by d'Alton and
she had been assisted in editing them by her former lover's brother, Paul, cur-
rently her husband. The stipulation was that they were not to be available to the
public for twenty years.

Sand's sexuality is portrayed as powerfully masculine here, while Chopin seems feminised, even emasculated ('crucified Chop!') in relation to her.[14] James's fears of being 'got' by Wharton and her enthralling though formidable car are echoed in the fate of 'poor . . . Chop'. George Sand's social and sexual energy (her capacity for work was also famous) alluded to throughout the letters of James and Wharton seems to emerge here, elliptically, as a source of profound anxiety for James. Sand, 'mighty and marvellous George', engulfs and smothers the sensitive and refined genius, Chopin, just as Wharton theatens to girdle the earth (in James' curious image) and, implicitly, James with it. The feminisation of male 'genius' in the nineteenth century, as exemplified by Chopin, suggests the emergence of the robust and energetic creative figures of women who would consolidate the progressive feminisation of the literary marketplace and investigate the possibilities of new voices for themselves, as Wharton had done in 'The Muse's Tragedy'.

The question of finding or sustaining a voice is crucial to the mediation of the James/Wharton letters. The correspondence of Wharton and James, with its prurient interest in the sexual intrigues of others, and its references to Wharton's disastrous marriage and her affairs, is marked by a persistent curiosity about, and regard with, the fragility of reputation, the possibilities of exposure and blackmail, and the ways in which correspondence moves uneasily between the public and the private. Yet it can only be known in a highly fragmentary way, chiefly through the words of James, since on two occasions (in November 1909 and October 1915) he burned large quantities of personal papers 'including most of Wharton's letters to him' at Lamb House (Powers 1990, 26). James was able in this manner to assert his power to destroy, to take control of his own documentary record, as he had already asserted his power to create through authorship. Yet paradoxically James's voice gradually fades out of his correspondence with Wharton: in Lyall Powers's edition of the letters James's final letter to Wharton on 22 September 1915 is dictated, for, as he tells her, he is 'very imperfectly inarticulate' while commending her 'magnificent time of life and force of activity' and asking her to

[14] Battersby argues that George Sand, like George Eliot, was associated with qualities more properly associated with masculinity: George Eliot's looks, and both women's sexual relationships as well as their writing ability, were read as signs of their masculinity. She further argues that Elizabeth Barrett Browning's 1844 sonnet 'To George Sand: A Recognition' (which opens with the lines 'True genius, but true woman') reflected Barrett Browning's desire to reinstate Sand's femininity (Battersby 1989, 22).

'push over to us for a few days and breathe upon us your heroic souffle' (Powers 1990, 354–55). As his voice diminishes and finally vanishes, the voices of Wharton and of Theodora Bosanquet, his amanuensis, take over, discussing James's health in the last days of his life, in a sense domesticating him and reinforcing his enforced silence. He becomes the subject of the writing of the two women but no longer has his own writing voice. Subsumed within the two women's newly-emerging correspondence, James gradually disappears. Yet even before his death a new subject enters the correspondence as Bosanquet's future working life, as writer and editor, is discussed. In the last letter which Wharton writes to her, on 1 March 1916, she makes a final mention of James which confirms his new silence and curiously condemns him to a feminised, passive position, one close to that of a silent but inspiring female muse: 'We who knew him well know how great he would have been if he had never written a line' (Powers 1990, 391).

Works Cited

Battersby, C. 1989. *Gender and Genius: Towards a Feminist Aesthetics*, London: The Women's Press.

Brake, L. 1994. *Subjugated Knowledges: Journalism, Gender and Literature in the Nineteenth Century*, Basingstoke and London: Macmillan.

Buchan, J. 1984. *Memory-hold-the-door: The autobiography of John Buchan*, with a new introduction by David Daniell, London and Melbourne: J.M. Dent and Sons Ltd.

Butler, M. 1993. 'Culture's medium: the role of the review', in Curran 1993, 120–47.

Crecelius, K. 'Authorship and authority: George Sand's letters to her mother', in Goldsmith 1989, 257–72.

Curran, S. 1993. *The Cambridge Companion to British Romanticism*, Cambridge: CUP.

Edel, L. and Powers, L.H. 1987. *The Complete Notebooks of Henry James*, New York and Oxford: OUP.

Goldsmith, E.C. 1989. *Writing the Female Voice: Essays on Epistolary Literature*, London: Pinter Publishers.

Hayes, K.J. 1996. *Henry James: The Contemporary Reviews*, Cambridge: CUP.

Hofkosh, S. 1988. 'The writer's ravishment: women and the Romantic author – the example of Byron', in Mellor 1988, 93–114.

James, H. 1934. *The Art of the novel: critical prefaces*, with an introduction by R.P. Blackmur, New York and London: Charles Scribner's Sons.

James, H. 1976. *The Aspern Papers and Other Stories*, with an introduction by S. Gorley Putt, Middlesex, New York, Victoria, Ontario, Auckland: Penguin.

Kaplan, F., ed., 1994. *Travelling in Italy with Henry James*, London, Sydney and Auckland: Hodder and Stoughton.

Mellor, A. 1988. *Romanticism and Feminism*, Bloomington and Indianapolis: Indiana University Press.

Powers, L.H. 1990. *Henry James and Edith Wharton, Letters: 1900–1915*, New York: Charles Scribner's Sons.

Smith, J.A. 1985. *John Buchan: A Biography*, Oxford: OUP.

Strouse, J. 1981. *Alice James*, London: Harvill.

Thomson, P. 1977. *George Sand and the Victorians: Her Influence and Reputation in Nineteenth-Century England*, London and Basingstoke: Macmillan.

Trelawny, E.J. 1887. *Records of Shelley, Byron, & the Author*, London: Pickering and Chatto.

Waid, C. 1991. *Edith Wharton's Letters from the Underworld: Fictions of Women and Writing*, North Carolina: University of North Carolina Press.

Wharton, E. 1934. *A Backward Glance*, New York and London: D–Appleton–Century Company.

Wharton, E. 1990. *The Muse's Tragedy and Other Stories*, with an introduction by Candace Waid, London, New York, Victoria, Ontario, Auckland: Penguin.

The 'No-Trump Bid'
on Romanticism and Gender

IRA LIVINGSTON

THIS ESSAY REHEARSES, around the notion of performativity, some of the principles of what I'm calling the 'no-trump bid' on Romanticism and gender; that is, the attempt to let no single framework dominate scholarly and classroom practice in these areas, and instead, to work maximally between temporal and cultural frameworks, between disciplines, between identity categories, and between the universalizing zoom of theory and the extreme close-up of 'thick' historicist description. While this may be a familiar – even canonical – post-structuralist mandate, it is less honored in the organization of scholarly work and classroom syllabi – especially in Romanticism – where the apparatus of disciplinary production seems to shamble along, zombie-like and slow – but nightmarishly hard to outrun. Recent and rampant privatization and downsizing of universities, the mandate to 'do more with less'– the ongoing crises of late capitalism – may drive disciplinary change, but they have also produced retreats to supposedly 'safe' disciplinary positions (though we should know, by now, the fate of such strategies in horror shows).

So while I embrace, here, theories of performativity in studies of sex and gender (and of ritual practice), I have become somewhat more hesitant (a function of old age, perhaps) about the ways intellectual and political cachet are sometimes attributed to theoretical positions in proportion to their participation in new historical and epistemological configurations, their counter-intuitiveness, their power to problematize or subvert. The reconfiguring claim tends to regard change as liberatory in itself, thus forgetting – for example – that continual revolutionizing of the mode of production (including knowledge-production) is also itself a primary mode of bourgeois control. The counter-intuitivity claim identifies intuition or 'common sense' as an ideological product but thereby tends to cede the possibility of engaging resistant strains also at work there. The problematizing claim tends dramatically to underestimate the sophistication of ideological formations, often casting ideologies as built on simple oppositions – straw men – whose subversion can be accomplished by complicating them (often from some more-or-less unexamined pose of transcendence), thereby losing sight of the extent to which ideology itself operates precisely by problematizing. I will try to suggest alternatives to these claims as I go. But the main thrust here is to cast performativity as part of a project of 'recovering' what Western modernity has necessarily rendered incoherent or made difficult to recognize or articulate – but not banished. 'Recovery' is admittedly a prejudicial word: for many reasons, what is 'recovered' can never be what was lost. 'Performativity' or 'constructionism' do not emerge as such except in opposition to 'reductionism' and 'essentialism' and are products of several centuries of discursive ecology. But recovery is a moment – a partial if definitive moment – in leveraging this ecology. To choose a more trenchant example, 'homosexuality' and 'heterosexuality' are late nineteenth-century constructs, and it is important to show how neither existed before then, but in order to affirm counter-hegemonic or minority genderings and sexualities, it is equally important to find ways of talking about the histories of 'same-sex desires' (though one cannot, by such a phrase, quite wriggle out of anachronism), not in a way that romanticizes a retro-topia of sexual practices without identities, but in a way that affirms that the identitarian regime – oppressive and productive as it is – has NEVER FULLY COLONIZED desire. If it is premature to celebrate the return of the Hong Kong of sexuality and gender to the mainland of difference, perhaps it is at least less prejudicial to talk about recovery *from* rather than *of*.

In any case, humanities scholars (among others) have in recent years increasingly recognized the interdependence of identities (such as genders, genres, sexes, races, classes, nations) and have begun to engage these as emergent and internally heterogeneous constellations in ongoing ecologies rather than as epiphenomena to be reduced to first principles – or as first principles themselves, tacit or otherwise. But if every identity co-evolves into being and meaning as a provisional constellation in a vast and minutely textured, heterogeneous, dynamic, topologically complex and discontinuous network of material-semiotic relations, how can any scholarly inquiry establish its proper limits, much less assemble the requisite expertise and evidence? While such a question is often a pressing and practical one, this way of posing it may serve mainly to heroize broad-ranging and interdisciplinary studies – or to make them seem unworkable. Limits are never 'proper' or 'organic' – or rather, even an organism is a set of boundary negotiations, all edges. The scholarly ideal of thorough mastery and exhaustive coverage of a given domain (a 'purity' ideal) has lost some ground – one hopes – to the contradictory, no less impossible and necessary ideal of maximal mixture and interdisciplinary resonance ('hybridity'), but this can as accurately be cast as a priority adjustment as an epistemic rupture. The hybridity ideal suggests a kind of 'holographic' selection principle that favors projects and topics that seem maximally to reflect and refract their whole contexts and domains; or, better, a 'fractal' principle that seeks maximal linkage across various parts, dimensions or levels; the 'whole' no less than its 'parts' being construed as provisional products of these processes rather than as pre-existing them. The whole is part of the parts, and the totalization of a given domain (whether it be gender, Romanticism, or the humanities) does not subsume or 'trump' everything under its rubric, but is one strategy alongside or subsequent to the often more potent and primary strategy of linkage. This anti- or inter-disciplinary mandate – the 'no-trump' bid – follows the signature strategy – the sprawl – of modern and postmodern power/knowledge. Gender identities, for example, may operate mostly normatively to bind certain sets of features to certain bodies, but this policing function also *requires* that there be undecideabilities and slippages between and within bodies and genders and sexualities; otherwise a gender identity would be unproblematically whatever a certain kind of body does or is at any given time; gender would be simply 'whatever'. This is not particularly imaginable, but it serves to indicate the political usefulness of both de- and re-problematizing strategies.

When the 'discursive ecological' approach is used flatly to demonstrate literature's implication in dominant ideologies or science's implication in metaphor and narrative – that is, for its 'gotcha' effect – it can underwrite attachment to the idea of an 'innocent' or 'pure' science or literature – a kind of nostalgia for what never was; that is, a Romanticism. The implication and overdetermination of all formations is a place to start and an ongoing axiom in an argument, not the payoff, which had better be sought in the creative and counterhegemonic possibilities of their pluralities and contradictions.

Recognizing the sprawl and slipperiness of identities does not deny specificity and particularity; quite the reverse. Gender and sexuality studies, for example, have been compelling in demonstrating ways in which specific sexual practices cut across sexual identities, and – especially – the ways in which current 'umbrella' categories belie specificities, failing to keep slippery sex safe or gender (cut and) dry in the present much less in the past. In her exemplary study of *Female Masculinity* (1998, in press), Judith Halberstam dubs 'perverse presentism' the strategy that operates by 'questioning in the first instance what we think we already know' about gender and sexuality and then 'moving back towards the question of what we think we have found' in the past, rejecting (with Eve Sedgwick) the paradigm of 'paradigm shift' in the history of sexuality as primarily 'stabilizing what we think we know to-day'. The argument is perhaps even more trenchant in cross-cultural studies, where a leading and ongoing question might be 'who do we think we are?' In the broadest terms, the prerequisite and goal of historical, contemporary, and cross-cultural studies of gender and sexuality are the same: to democratize the linkages and disjunctions within and among bodies, genders, sexualities, practices and identities, cultures.

Heterogeneities and contradictions within and between the fields of gender and sexuality have driven theorizing (following practice) in what is now sometimes called 'queer theory'. Foucault rejected any idea of 'sex *in itself*', observing that 'the notion of "sex" made it possible to group together, in an artificial unity, anatomical elements, biological functions, conducts, sensations, and pleasures', making it possible for sexuality to function as 'as an especially dense transfer point for relations of power; between men and women, young people and old people, parents and offspring, teachers and students, priests and laity, an administration and a population' (1990; 152, 154, 103). Sexuality is not only Humpty-Dumpty in reverse, being assembled and ascending to some monolithic Berlin Wall, but rather the wall itself was also broken up and rhizomically entended into a resilient network (so renegotiations of this process always also involve de- and re-monolithizing and pluralizing). The *betweenness* of sexuality is an aspect of the betweenness of modern power: rather than inhering in persons and positions, its extension and circulation differentiates and connects persons and positions; identities are provisionally impacted relations. Likewise, Judith Butler questions whether the meaning of a sexuality can be reduced to 'the phantasy structure, the act, the orifice, the gender, the anatomy? And if the practice engages a complex interplay of all of those, which one of these erotic dimensions will come to stand for the sexuality that requires them all?' (1991, 17). Eve Sedgwick (1990, 22–7) makes a compelling case for sexual democracy simply by listing some of the multifarious and often incommensurable ways people describe their sexualities (e.g., as natural, learned, essential, aleatory, expedient, discrete, ubiquitous, etc.), while resisting the impulse to either reconcile these under a single paradigm or to judge among them.

Furthermore, gender and sexuality are not 'add-ons' but rather integral to the way we name Romanticism, Modernity and Postmodernity. Romanticism can only very partially be engaged as a period of literary history (literary history and periodization themselves being unavoidably Romantically inflected), so one is led to explore Romanticism as also an ongoing ideological formation or complex, a kind of Enlightenment feedback (and 'feed-forward'), or more broadly a kind of anti-Modernity, one that can function as accomodationist or as oppositional. Elsewhere I have developed Sayre and Löwy's more specific formula that defines Romanticism as 'opposition to capitalism in the name of pre-capitalist values' (Livingston 1997, 12–14; Sayre and Löwy 1990, 26), but in any case Romanticism seems to name a structuring or narrativiza-tion of time that ongoingly, often nostalgically but always retroactively, produces a 'pre-capitalism' or 'pre-modernity' – or more fundamentally, a pre-cultural 'nature'. The important point is that such difference (in some contexts a 'paradigm shift') does not inhere in history; it does not simply happen once (nothing that means anything happens once) but is continually reproduced and sometimes renegotiated in the process; i.e., it is performative, and thus no scholarship on the topic can be simply descriptive.

The Romantic 'ideologeme' (see Jameson 1981; 76, 87) is not only a device to schematize historical eras, but also functions to schematize gender, for example, by representing femininity as a kind of 'hypercivil-ization', either as a kind of valorization (as in Victorian cultural femi-nism) or as a kind of dismissal (i.e., of women as superficial or artificial creatures). On the other (and equally ambivalent) hand, the same trope can just as well represent femininity as a less mediated relation to nature and thus, often, as a kind of superceded stage of (masculine) develop-ment (e.g., as in Wordsworth's 'Tintern Abbey'). This latter turn of the trope often structures Western caricatures of other peoples (though Western Orientalism in particular, as we will see, also deploys the 'hyper-civilization' trope as well). The Romantic ideologeme is less a simple opposition and more a chiasmic 'difference engine'.

Romanticism as 'retroactivism' is an overdetermined and often de-finitive 'structure of feeling' in modernity, stretching at least from narra-tives like Aphra Behn's 1688 *Oroonoko* to the 1995 'Unabomber manifesto', *Industrial Society and Its Future*; I consider these along with other problematically Romantic (and anti-Romantic) texts in the sketch of a 'syllabus' that follows. Partial antidotes to retroactivism can be found in postmodern 'heterochrony' (e.g., see Martin 1994, 7–8; Liv-ingston 1997, 239, 242) or in Bruno Latour's assertion that *We Have Never Been Modern* (1993); Latour, like Donna Haraway in her anti-Romantic studies of science as 'lumpy' (i.e., hybrid) discourse (1991, 203–4) shows how temporal and disciplinary limits (e.g., among sci-ence, politics and humanities) must be re-negotiated together.

In *Oroonoko*, royalist Behn romanticizes African society as an image of a noble English past in which everyone knew his or her place and lying and misrepresentation were unthinkable. In Behn's novel it is not slavery as such that is wrong but violation of hierarchy: only the slavers who duplicitously kidnap and hold in slavery the anglicized African prince are identified as unethical, while slaves 'freely' sold by the Africans are represented as defeated people, suited for a servile existence (the idea of a 'free market' ignoring the role of European destabilization of African societies in producing its conditions). Difference *within* and difference *between* are made to be echoes of each other – with no original, as it were. Behn seems to suggest that the English violation of the hierarchical order of African society is merely symptomatic of the breakdown of hierarchy within English society. The many descriptions of the African lovers communicating by wordless glances – as well as the curiously emphatic insistence that Africans *blush* – serve further to associate African society with a direct and even pre-linguistic communication in which misrepresentation is almost impossible in the immediacy of full presence, a condition even more extreme in the novel's indigenous Surinamians. But, as the trope turns back onto itself, this problematic valorization is also what Behn claims for *the novel itself*, making a show of rejecting 'Fancy' and 'Invention' in favor of a guileless 'Eye-Witness' realism, which subsequently works as backhanded praise-by-blame of Behn's own humble 'Female Pen' (1995; 57, 88). By another nice twist, 'any thing that seems Romantick' (i.e., unrealistic) is attributed to the way 'these Countries do, in all things, so far differ from ours, that they produce unconceivable Wonders' (1995; 56). About a century later, Mary Wollstonecraft, in her *Vindication of the Rights of Woman*, will like Behn champion and claim Enlightenment plain speech against 'turgid bombast' and 'flowery diction', but unlike Behn, Wollstonecraft associates cunning, duplicity and superficiality with unnatural and obsolete monarchical and aristocratic power and in turn with the ways in which women – denied independence and education in Reason – attempt to 'tyrannize' over their husbands and lovers (1796; 7–8, 73); upward mobility is the solution rather than the problem. The twists and turns of the Romantic mastertrope do not exhaust these texts – far from it – but they do inform the generative contradictions around which the texts – in their narrative and argumentative structures no less than in their generic or discursive positionings – are spun.

Two centuries later still, America's doyen of mail-bombers and anti-technology terrorists, known as the Unabomber, begins his 1995 manifesto with the Romantic assertion that 'the Industrial Revolution and its consequences have been a disaster for the human race' (1995, 3). The text's main thrust is to fetishize the autonomy and self-sufficiency of 'primitive INDIVIDUALS and SMALL GROUPS' (1995, 68; emphasis in original) against the crushing weight of modern collective institutions and the 'oversocialization' of 'modern leftism' (1995, 10). This clearly Romantic individualism seems now to be held in common by various U.S. militia groups and by a whole range of mainstream neoconservatives. Its masculinism is of a piece with the Romantic/Victorian ideology that works to pathologize women as inadequately individuated and/or to beatify them as nurturing and other-directed. This version of the trope also has its contemporary incarnations in pop psychologies of language (e.g., *He Said, She Said*) that follow Carol Gilligan in schematizing men's speech and psychological orientation as self- and women's as other-directed. This schematization has had a long life in Romantic literary history as well, tending to cast variously 'femininized' novels as negotiating intricate constellations of relationships (though often partially subordinated to the masternarrative of *bildungsroman*) against a supposedly more masculine, univocal and predominantly lyrical poetry of the 'self' in its depths, its troubled autonomy and heroic vicissitudes.

Psychologically as well as ideologically and historically in Western modernity, gender itself is compellingly describable as a retroactively Romantic formation. Judith Butler works through and over Lacan, for whom woman is made to represent 'the vain but persistent promise of pre-individuated *jouissance*'; Freud, for whom the ego is a kind of Romantic ruin, 'a precipitate of abandoned object-cathexes'; and especially Foucault, for whom 'the desire which is conceived as both original and repressed is the effect of the subjugating law itself' (1990; 45, 58, 65). For Butler, 'because identifications substitute for object relations, and identifications are the consequence of loss, gender identification is a kind of melancholia in which the sex of the prohibited object is internalized as a prohibition', the lost object is objectified and gendered oppositionally only in retroaction, and 'the stricter and more stable the gender affinity, the less resolved the original loss' (1990, 63). Thus 'melancholic heterosexuality' is 'an anti-metaphorical activity' whereby 'incorporation *literalizes* the loss on or in the body and so appears as the facticity of the body' in the apparent self-evidence of anatomical difference, forgetting the 'imaginary and, with it, an imaginable homosexuality' (1990, 71). 'Disavowed homosexual love' – which only can be named as such via its disavowal – 'is preserved through the cultivation of an oppositionally defined gender identity' (1990, 69).

But gaining leverage on such a structure cannot be a matter of simple remembering or recovery. Butler critiques Freud's notion of 'primary bisexuality' for retroactively mistaking the product of gendering (oppositionally defined genders) for its raw material. Gayle Rubin, among others, is critiqued for relying too much on a retroactivist vision of 'an alternative sexual world, one which is attributed to a utopian stage in infantile development, a 'before' the law that promises to re-emerge 'after' the demise or dispersal of that law' (1990, 75). And finally, Butler interrogates Kristeva's associations of a pre-semiotic 'Symbolic' matrix with the maternal body, with poetic language, with psychosis and lesbianism, and with 'all manner of things 'primitive' and 'Oriental' (1990, 89): while seeming to valorize these things, Kristeva's theorizing continues to underwrite – to require – their continual subordination.

Butler's strategy is thus an anti-Romantic one, rejecting retroactive utopias 'before the law' but insisting – in several senses – on the law's ongoing productivity (or rather, precisely its counterproductivity) – and its positivity and plurality. A differently inflected version of this strategy informs Deleuze and Guattari's *Anti-Oedipus*, which questions the developmental narratives of capitalism and sexuality by insisting on an *absolute* plurality – a plurality that continually exceeds its opposition to unicity and binarity (and thus also differs from Freud's 'primary bisexuality' or 'polymorphous perversity'). Blake's *Book of Urizen*, like Mary Shelley's *Frankenstein*, also offers a compelling narrative of the ongoing counterproductivity of law and reason in *The Making of the Modern Body*. Granted, this salad of texts is too lightly tossed, but as such serves to mark both their homo- and heterogeneity (in their historical and discursive positions) as neither given nor closed.

Historian James Hevia's 1995 *Cherishing Men From Afar*, an account of the 1793 British embassy of George Lord Macartney to the Qing empire, offers a rather different take on performativity. Hevia refuses the Romantic/Orientalist trope by exploring the Macartney expedition as a meeting between two expansive empires rather than (as previous studies have often cast it) between a modern Britain and a stagnant, premodern China. Hevia focuses on how the Qing imperium deployed 'guest ritual' to produce 'interdomainal' relations, specifically in enacting the subordination and incorporation of other sovereignties (and sometimes other religions or epistemologies) into the Qing empire. Incorporation here involves nested 'macrocosm-microcosm relations' (23); the rituals could be said to manage the complex and 'fractal' or 'holarchic' interaction of difference *within* and difference *between*. This recognition avoids the familiar characterization of China as stuck in a rigid and monolithic hierarchy of hierarchies, a 'Great Chain of Being' being shaken and even leveled by a pluralizing modernity in the West.

In fact, Hevia shows that Chinese guest ritual was significantly negotiable both in the sense of being continually updated in the light of new precedents and conditions, and in the sense that it dynamically managed rather flexible and nuanced relations, for example in allowing both parties to the ritual to retain some sense of the other's dependence. In turning the tables, one might also point to how the Western legacy of a single and singularly intolerant or 'jealous' god and the rationality fashioned in its image has continued to deny incorporation and plurality even as it seems to reject hierarchies. In any case, the English misrecognition of Qing ritual – as monolithically static and rule-bound, as representing or misrepresenting relationships rather than as performing or producing them, as rhetorical or cultural forms distinct from the real business of trade – links the failures of the Macartney embassy to those of its subsequent Western chroniclers.

While never mentioning performativity as such, Hevia follows Catherine Bell (1992) in approaching ritual activities as 'themselves the very production and negotiation of power relations'; ritualization is 'a strategic mode of practice' which 'produces nuanced relations of power, relationships characterized by acceptance and resistance, negotiated appropriation, and redemptive reinterpretation of the hegemonic order' (cited in Hevia, 21). Hevia finds the dynamic – verbal – function of guest ritual reflected in its stated function of 'channeling', 'centering', or 'negotiating a mean between overabundance and scarcity' (123). Hevia's take on Qing ritual makes performativity less an 'import' into the study of history from poststructuralist theory, rather casting it as the very thing whose misrecognition is foundational for modern Western power/knowledge, and whose 'recovery' therefore has far-reaching interdisciplinary and intercultural implications.

Hevia describes Orientalist ideology as it

> feminizes China; much like female, as opposed to male, sensibilities, China is jealous, misguided, caught up in appearances, irrational, arbitrary, and whimsical. On the other hand, this imaginary China functions to produce bourgeois masculine identity as that which is equivalent to the good, the true, the real, the rational and the upright. Among other things, this suggests that the negation of China, particularly of the Chinese past, produces the 'West', with a living China simultaneously a negativity for constructing a superior English national identity and for demonstrating that England had now transcended all past global orders. (73–4)

Pushing these constructions a bit further points up the radical inadequacy of the model of 'feminization', which assumes (if only provisionally) instead of accounting for the priority of gender to other kinds of difference and the 'always-alreadiness' of the association of femininity with all that is subordinated. Instead, then, one is driven to consider how the fiction of a dominant Western ideology of masculinity might be engaged as a 'repressive de-sinicization'; partially but importantly the product an 'interdomainal' encounter that is always (then and now) in the making.

Hevia recounts the sometimes farcical attempts of the British to engage, impress, assuage and defy their imaginary China. One of the expedition's members characterized other European nations' gifts to the Qing emperor as mere 'toys and sing-songs'; Macartney called previous gifts 'more glittering than useful' and sought instead to impress Qianlong with items 'whose merit lay in their utility' (cited in Hevia, 77); these characterizations clearly link rationalist epistemology with familiar tropes of gender and cultural difference, mobilizing the same trope to characterize Britain against other European nations and West against East. Burke, too, set an ideally nuanced British society in which 'the different shades of life' are aesthetically 'harmonized' against a revolutionary France of 'naked' power relations (90); de Quincey expressed horror and fascination with an Orient of 'castes that have flowed apart, and refused to mix, through . . . immemorial tracts of time' (i.e., too thoroughgoing or absolute difference), or in which 'man is a weed' (i.e., indifferentiation [442]). De Quincey's account follows the ongoing Orientalist schema of Asian emperors' godlike power in too-stark contrast to their faceless and abject masses; even Chinese painting was faulted (in a 1755 journal article) for lacking 'gradation in tint' and thus misrepresenting 'the truth of things' (cited in Hevia 70). These vicissitudes of imaginary and different difference also drove 18th-century phases of British idealization and derogation of China's 'mandarinate'. But British hopes for success depended on an always-already anglicized image of the Emperor as above his people at least far enough to be potentally capable of recognizing the superiority of British rationality. The centerpiece of the English gifts to Qianlong was a large and elaborate planetarium, intended to demonstrate the superiority of Western science in representing the true workings of the universe. However, anxious that the scientific value of the planetarium might not be compelling enough in itself, the British had it extravagantly decorated, so that the final product presented to Qianlong turned out somewhat less an example of robust British rationality and more a piece of kitsch *chinoiserie* of the kind Britons had alternately fetishized and rejected. In any case, in his response to George III, Qianlong was famously cool, asserting that 'we have never valued ingenious articles, nor do we have the slightest need of your Country's manufactures' (238).

This coolness was at least partly a response to Macartney's impatience to cut the Gordian knot of ritual and 'get down to business', an impatience that worked counterproductively to magnify the impasse. The farce of the Macartney embassy would be repeated as tragedy in Britain's later, more violent missions to open up the Chinese market. The impatience that regards ritual as mere foreplay (or in the old Marxist version, as mere 'superstructure') might well be dubbed 'performativity anxiety'. Henry Abelove has compellingly recounted the 18th-century invention of sexual 'foreplay' (1992, 340) in contradistinction to what came to be called, for the first time in 1799 (according to the OED) 'sexual intercourse'. That 'intercourse' had referred first to trade and commerce – before being gradually generalized and then almost monopolized by sexuality – is itself a fitting vignette of the priority of transaction or betweenness – the 'intercourse among intercourses' – to any fiction of the internal coherence or 'givenness' of sexual or gender difference and relation in themselves. Abelove finds that foreplay and intercourse came to be differentiated as Sunday was differentiated from the work-week to follow (gradually squeezing out the more casual holidays of an earlier economy). The logic of capitalism and capitalist ideology as it organizes and produces resonances between and among scales of time and sexual acts is both and neither monolithic and plural, 'imaginary' or 'metaphorical' and 'real' – nor is it by virtue of this alone uniquely modern or unique among ideologies and epistemologies, nor necessarily distinct (in this) from counter-hegemonic strategies.

It was to Jorge Luis Borges's imagined 'Chinese encyclopedia', with its radically plural list of incommensurable creatures, that Foucault (in *The Order of Things*, xv) and later Londa Schiebinger (in her study of . . . *Gender in the Making of Modern Science*, 40) turned for a model (or antimodel) of 'different difference'. It was against an Asian and pre-modern Western *'ars erotica'* that Foucault characterized the emergence of a modern *'scientia sexualis'* – which he proceeded to demonstrate as a mish-mash of incommensurables masquerading as a scientific unity (we have never been modern). The turn to an imagined 'Other' for recovery (*from* what we may have thought we were, or of what we had forgotten that we disavowed) is fraught with turbulence. To the paradigm of the 'list of incommensurables' I would like to add another, in the form of an admittedly much-too-long and old joke that (appropriately, as it turns out) only awkwardly translates into writing. I don't know where the joke comes from, but it seems to push to a perverse conclusion Hevia's description of how Qing guest ritual allowed each party to come away with different interpretations of the encounter and relationship. It goes – as they say – something like this:

> A medieval pope orders his cardinal to expel the Jews from Italy. The cardinal suggests that the head Rabbi be given an impossibly difficult test of Catholic dogma, and that his failure be used as grounds for the expulsion. Seeing no other way, the Rabbi agrees to the test, and after three months of study appears at the appointed hour to be tested. The cardinal walks in and sits across the table from the Rabbi. After a moment's consideration, the cardinal gestures toward the door with his thumb. The Rabbi responds by jabbing the table in front of him with his finger. The cardinal wags a single finger in the air in front of the Rabbi, and the Rabbi responds by shaking three fingers in front of the cardinal. Finally, the cardinal reaches into his robe and pulls out an orange, which he places on the table. The Rabbi responds by taking out a matzoh and placing it on the table. Grudgingly, the cardinal acknowledges that the Rabbi has passed the test; the Jews will be allowed to stay.
>
> The cardinal goes back and explains to the pope what has happened, recounting the gestural dialogue: 'First I asserted that "God is elsewhere" ' – pointing with his thumb – 'but the Rabbi said, "no, God is here". Then I said that "God is one" – holding up a finger – to which he replied, "no, God is three". Then I said "the earth is round" ' – taking out the orange – 'and he replied, "no, the earth is flat" – so I had to admit he'd passed the test.'
>
> The Rabbi explains to his congregation what has happened: 'First he said "get the hell out of here" and I said' – jabbing the table with a finger – ' "hell no, we're staying right here". Then he said "fuck you", and I said' – wagging three fingers – ' "fuck you three times". Then he took out his lunch and I took out mine.'

The joke offers a view of a utopian 'redemptive reinterpretation of the hegemonic order'; of the performatively 'happy' and simultaneous failure of both oppressive differentiation and assimilation in cross-cultural contact; of the ongoing preservation of irreconcilable difference in fortuitous misrecognition, undecideability and the impossibility of a common meta-language; and of curious aporia between Christian metaphysics and Jewish politics. A lot to claim for a bad joke, but preferable to the bad joke of a 'dominant ideology', finally, and it does give theories of difference something to shoot for, more or less systematically.

Works Cited

Abelove, Henry. 1992. 'Some Speculations on the History of "Sexual Inter-course" During the "Long Eighteenth Century" in England'. *Nationalisms and Sexualities*, ed. Andrew Parker et al., 335–42. New York: Routledge.

Behn, Aphra. 1995. *Oroonoko; The Works of Aphra Behn*, V. 3, ed. Janet Todd. 54–119. Columbus, Ohio: Ohio State University Press.

Bell, Catherine. 1992. *Ritual Theory, Ritual Practice*. New York: Oxford University Press.

Burke, Edmund. 1973. *Reflections on the Revolution in France*. New York: Anchor Press/Doubleday.

Butler, Judith. 1990. *Gender Trouble*. New York: Routledge.

Butler, Judith. 1991. 'Imitation and Gender Insubordination'. *Inside/Out: Lesbian Theories, Gay Theories*, ed. Diana Fuss, 13–31. New York: Routledge.

De Quincey, Thomas. *Confessions of an English Opium-Eater* (1856 ed.). *The Collected Writings*, ed. David Masson, 207–449. London: A.C. Black, 1897.

'FC.' 1995. *The Unabomber Manifesto*. Berkeley: Jolly Roger Press.

Foucault, Michel. 1990. *The History of Sexuality: An Introduction*, Vol. One. New York: Vintage/Random House.

Foucault, Michel. 1973. *The Order of Things*. New York: Vintage/Random House.

Halberstam, Judith. 1998, in press. *Female Masculinity*. Durham, NC: Duke University Press.

Haraway, Donna. 1991. *Simians, Cyborgs, and Women*. New York: Routledge.

Hevia, James. 1995. *Cherishing Men From Afar: Qing Guest Ritual and the Macartney Embassy of 1793*. Durham, NC: Duke University Press.

Latour, Bruno. 1993. *We Have Never Been Modern*, tr. Catherine Porter. Cambridge, Mass.: Harvard University Press.

Livingston, Ira. 1997. *Arrow of Chaos: Romanticism and Postmodernity*. Minneapolis: University of Minnesota Press.

Martin, Emily. 1994. *Flexible Bodies*. Boston: Beacon Press.

Sayre, Robert, and Michael Löwy. 1990. 'Figures of Romantic Anticapitalism'. *Spirits of Fire: English Romantic Writers and Contemporary Historical Methods*, ed. G.A. Rosso and Daniel P. Watkins, 23–68. London: Associated University Presses.

Schiebinger, Londa. 1993. *Nature's Body: Gender In the Making of Modern Science*. Boston: Beacon Press.

Sedgwick, Eve Kosofsky. 1990. *Epistemology of the Closet*. Berkeley: University of California Press.

Wollstonecraft, Mary. 1796. *A Vindication of the Rights of Woman* (Third edn). London: Joseph Johnson.

Notes on Contributors

Bridget Bennett is a Lecturer in the Department of English and Comparative Literary Studies at the University of Warwick. She is the author of *The Damnation of Harold Frederic* (1997) and editor of a collection of short fiction, *Ripples of Dissent* (1996).

Daria Donnelly has taught at Brandeis University and Boston University. She is completing a study of memorial poetry in nineteenth-century America.

Mary A. Favret is Associate Professor of English at Indiana University. She is the author of *Romantic Correspondence: Women, Politics and the Fiction of Letters* (1993) and co-editor with Nicola Watson of *At the Limits of Romanticism: Essays on Cultural, Feminist, and Materialist Criticism* (1994). Her current work centers on violence in the Romantic era, especially in warfare and slavery.

Emma Francis is Lecturer in English and Feminist Theory in the Centre for the Study of Women and Gender, University of Warwick. She has recently completed her doctorate, 'Poetic Licence: British Women's Poetry and the Sexual Division of Poetics and Culture, 1824–1889'. She is the author of essays on Amy Levy and Emily Bronte.

Sonia Hofkosh is Associate Professor of English at Tufts University. She is the author of *Sexual Politics and the Romantic Author* (1998), and co-editor, with Alan Richardson, of *Romanticism, Race, and Imperial Culture* (1996).

Anne Janowitz is Reader in Romanticism in the Department of English and Comparative Literary Studies, University of Warwick, and Director of the Warwick Humanities Research Centre. She is the author of *England's Ruins* (1990) and *Lyric and Labour in the Romantic Tradition* (1998).

William Keach teaches English at Brown University and is working on a book about politics and language in British Romantic writing. He has edited *The Complete Poems of Coleridge* for the Penguin English Poets series.

Gary Kelly is Professor of English at University of Alberta. He is the author of *English Fiction of the Romantic Period* (1989), *Revolutionary Feminism: the Mind and Career of Mary Wollstonecraft* (1992), and *Women, Writing, and Revolution 1790–1827* (1993). He is General Editor of Longman's *History of Women's Writing in English* and of *Bluestocking Feminism*, texts of the early Bluestocking writers.

Ira Livingston teaches in the English Department at the State University of New York at Stony Brook and is the author of *Arrow of Chaos: Romanticism and Postmodernity* (1997), and co-editor, with Judith Halberstam, of *Posthuman Bodies* (1995).

Josephine McDonagh is Lecturer in Humanities in the Department of English at Birkbeck College, University of London. She is the author of *De Quincey's Disciplines* (1994) and *George Eliot* (1997).